W9-AOK-324

Your Swedish Roots

A Step by Step Handbook

Per Clemensson & Kjell Andersson

Copyright © 2004
Per Clemensson
Kjell Andersson
Genline AB

Published by
Ancestry, a division of MyFamily.com, Inc.
360 West 4800 North
Provo, UT 84604
All rights reserved.

Published through a cooperative venture between
MyFamily.com, Inc. and Genline AB.

Cover design: Robert Davis
Interior graphic design & production: NYMEDIA Nina Soneson, Stockholm
Maps & graphic illustrations: NYMEDIA Stig Lindberg, Stockholm

Cover images: *Appelblom* by Carl Larsson, © Christie's Images/CORBIS
Gustav Adolf Rapp house courtesy Kjell Andersson

Back cover image: Postcard courtesy Kjell Anderson
Translation of postcard text:
Tacksam för vad hemmef gaf - Thankful for what the home gave -
Hälsning jag till Sverige sänder - A greeting I send to Sweden -
Och utöfver vida haf - And over wide oceans -
Mötas vänligt våra händer - In friendship our hands meet

No part of this publication may be reproduced in any form without written permission
of the publisher, except by a reviewer, who may quote brief passages for a review.

All brand and product names are trademarks or registered trademarks
of their respective companies.

Published 2004
10 9 8 7 6 5 4 3 2 1

Printed in the United States of America.

Your Swedish Roots
A Step by Step Handbook

TABLE OF CONTENTS

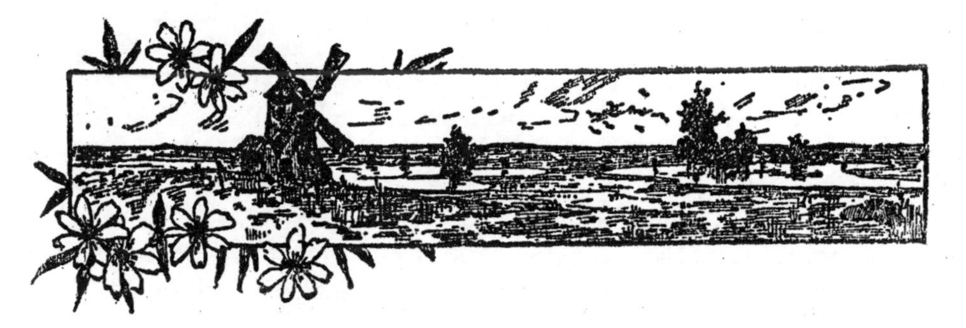

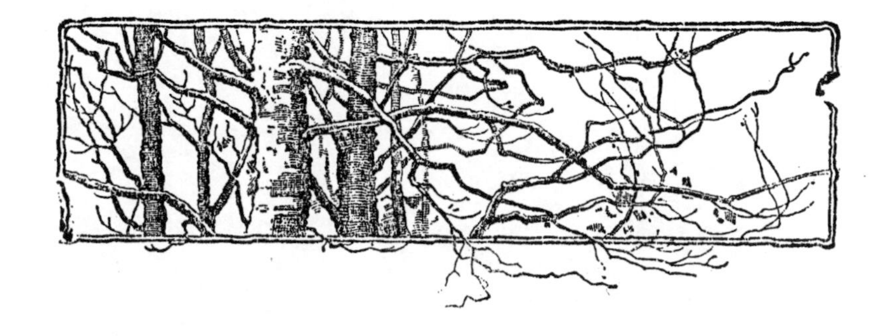

PREFACE

Today several million Swedish-Americans live in the United States. Up until now a comprehensive, step-by-step genealogical handbook in English for Swedish research has not been available. With this book we intend to fill this gap.

We have many years of experience as writers of genealogical handbooks. Our Swedish genealogical handbook (*Släktforska steg för steg*) is the leading comprehensive handbook on the Swedish market. Some years ago we wrote a handbook, also in Swedish, centered on research into the Swedish emigration to the United States, (*Emigrantforska steg för steg*).

The content of this book is based, in part, on these two previous books. But the research we describe here takes a different approach than the earlier books. A Swede who is researching emigration from Sweden to the United States wants to find relatives in America. An American who is researching immigration to the United States from Sweden is searching roots as well as living relatives in Sweden. Although these two groups have a common interest in the common sources, each uses the sources in a slightly different manner.

A Swedish-American researcher has many advantages, as well as some disadvantages. The Swedish sources and archives are very extensive and complete. Sweden has not been at war for close to 200 years. Very few archives have been destroyed by fire or other damage. The records are in good order and easy to find. The most commonly used church records are now even made available on the Internet, published by Genline, a private company. Internet access makes it possible to sit at home anywhere through-out the United States, Canada, or any other country, and do research into Swedish church records. Nevertheless, to be able to interpret these old documents, family historians must first know some basic facts. It is our purpose with this handbook to relay this foundational information.

The challenges facing family historians with Swedish ancestry are primarily the following: first, the research must be done in records written in Swedish. Second, the handwriting is sometimes difficult to read. To help researcher to overcome such obstacles we have put much emphasis on translating and interpreting individual documents in this book.

It is our hope that the book will give sufficient guidance and make it possible for the average family historian to understand and make use of the most common records in the Swedish archives.

Per Clemensson & Kjell Andersson

About the Authors

Per Clemensson has worked at the Regional Archive in Gothenburg as a senior archivist. He is a leading lecturer and writer in the genealogical field. The archive in Gothenburg is the main repository of emigrant records in Sweden, e.g., the ship's lists of the busy port of Gothenburg. Per Clemensson has taken a leading role in registering emigrants and making registers available to the public.

Kjell Andersson is a journalist and history major from the University of Stockholm. He and Per Clemensson have written a number of books on genealogy and local history research.

CHAPTER ONE

A Name on a Gravestone

In the Swedish cemetery in Portland, Connecticut, there stands a stone with the names *Adolph Rapp 1858 – 1935* and *Anna C. Carlson, his wife, 1855 – 1926*. This gravestone is the starting point for this book.

Many Swedish-Americans have only a vague idea about their Swedish ancestry. They know that Great-Grandpa and Great-Grandma came to America towards the end of the nineteenth century, but not much more. There may be some yellowing letters, written in Swedish, and some photos in a family album. And there is sometimes a gravestone like the one pictured above.

Unfortunately, Grandma, who could remember and tell the story, is gone, and so are many other older relatives. Younger relatives have vague stories and memories to tell.

More and more Americans want to know the answer to the question: where did my family come from? You might be one of them. You may have asked yourself the following questions:

Why did Great-Grandpa and Great-Grandma leave their home country? Where exactly did they come from? Is there still a farm or a cottage where the ancestors lived when they left the old country? You may even be wondering if you have living relatives in Sweden, distant cousins who bear some resemblance to you. How do you find them? You probably ask yourself, who your ancestors in Sweden were, and how far back in history you can trace your background?

Millions of Americans share a Swedish heritage. For most people, their Swedish ancestors appear within three to five generations. Many people are asking these same kinds of questions, just as you are. Often the information at hand is vague and scattered. But usually there is some starting point, like the gravestone.

In this book we will give you the tools you need to find your ancestors and living relatives using Swedish sources.

Welcome to Swedish Research

Swedish research can at times be frustrating and confusing. But it is more often rewarding. In many respects you are very fortunate to be able to work with Swedish sources. This is because…

1. Swedish historical records are of very good quality. The country has been at peace for nearly 200 years, and has not been invaded by foreign armies since the priests started keeping records of the people in their parishes. Church records, which are the primary source for you as a genealogist, are therefore very well kept. Very few are destroyed by fire, water, or neglect. In almost every parish you will find good population records beginning around 1700.

2. You can do research on the Internet. Church records are now being made available as high-quality digital pictures by Genline, a private Swedish company. Through this project you will have access to all the most important sources from all parts of Sweden (This project will be completed in 2005).

3. Swedish archives are well maintained and you can get good assistance from the archivists. For example, Swedish ship's lists have very good indexes that will help you find your emigrating relatives.

Challenges of Swedish Research

1. A major problem is, of course, the language. All documents in Sweden are in Swedish, and few fourth or fifth-generation Swedish-Americans have any knowledge of the language. The priests' handwriting can also be an obstacle, especially when you don't know the language and culture.

   To help you, in this book we will translate and explain everything we present. The examples we give are common cases. The church records at the end of the nineteenth century have a standardized layout with printed column heads.

2. Another major challenge is the naming practice in Sweden. There are scores of Anderssons and Johanssons, Carlssons and Nilssons, and it's not always easy to know if you've found the right person. But with good information about birth dates and other basic facts this obstacle can usually be overcome.

3. A third problem is distance. If you don't find your information on the Internet or on microfilm you may have to go to Sweden to complete your research. There are of course other options, like hiring a researcher in Sweden or turning to one of the research centers in Sweden. Another possibility is to correspond with Swedish researchers or turn to a website with a genealogical discussion group. Distance can be overcome, but it is of course always more difficult to research in a country and culture other than your own.

In most cases it is not difficult to trace your Swedish ancestry. In other cases you run into dead ends and unanswered questions. But for many people this is actually what makes genealogy so fascinating: to solve the riddle, to find the way around the obstacle, to find that other source. It just feels so good when you finally find those answers.

But is the gravestone enough?

Would the brief information on the gravestone in Portland, Connecticut, be enough to trace Adolph Rapp's ancestry in Sweden? In this case it most certainly would, although it helps that his name is rather unusual. He is the only Adolph Rapp born in 1858 who ever emigrated from Sweden. While his wife, Anna Carlson, is one of over a thousand Anna Carlssons, the number of Anna C. Carlssons is smaller; and with her birth year we can further narrow down the number of possibilities.

Even without any more information than this – without any letters or American records – the epitaph on the gravestone would be enough in this case to trace this couple to the right parish and farm in distant Sweden, which, as it turns out, is the same parish for both of them.

About Our Case

In this book we will present some sample cases, showing you how to do the research, step by step. We will show you documents, just like those you can find on the Internet, on microfiche, in copybooks, or as originals. Our idea is to explain in detail what you see, and to translate the Swedish text.

Our main case is Adolph Rapp and his wife Anna Carlson. They represent a typical case of emigration at the end of the nineteenth century. They left Sweden in 1879, the first to leave the parish of Mölltorp in western Sweden.

We will also show examples of very early emigration from Sweden using the Freeman family, who left Sweden in 1838, and Ivar Alexis Hall, who emigrated as a young man in 1851.

An example of relatively late emigration is Oskar Källberg, who came to the United States in 1920.

We have chosen these cases in order to demonstrate typical research problems during each time period.

Before we go into these cases, we will give some general information about Sweden and genealogical research in Sweden. You also need to know some things about the Swedish language and about Swedish names.

Your first step, however, will be to gather all the background information you can here in the United States, looking at any records your immigrant ancestors and their families have left behind. We will discuss this in the next chapter.

CHAPTER TWO

Clues to Your Family's History

To find your ancestors in Sweden you need:

- A name of the person or persons who immigrated into the United States (or Canada) from Sweden, preferably the whole name with the Swe-dish spelling.
- The time of arrival in the United States or departure from Sweden. The more accurate you can be, the better. Preferably you will have the date (day and/or month), or at least the year.
- The name of the place in Sweden from which your ancestor left. A mail address or the name of a city or town, a parish, a village, or farm is very helpful.

If you can find all of this information you should find it relatively easy to trace your family roots. If you have only some of this information, your chances are still good. Even if you only have very limited information, that is still better than nothing. And you at least have a place to start the work.

Here are some ideas about where you may find clues – names, addresses, dates – to your family's history.

Old Relatives

First and most important, talk to your older relatives in the United States. They may have information. Perhaps they have saved letters, other papers or pictures, or they have heard names of people and places in their childhood or from their parents and grandparents. This point can't be stressed enough. Don't take it for granted that older relatives will be around years from now, and don't take it for granted that their children will save old papers and documents. Some people are very quick to throw everything away after their relatives have passed away. Many people have little interest or regard for historical documents or personal papers.

Ask if you can tape the interview with your relative. First and foremost you want to extract all the information you can about "the Swedish link." But ask questions also about the American family: where they lived, what they did, who their friends were and so on. If you get stuck, this kind of information can be very important. It may, for example, lead you to

"Larson's Liten Julita Gård" (Larson's little Julita farm). This sign is posted at the home of Irene Larson in Wonewoc, Wisconsin. Her husband Walt's father and maternal grandparents all came to the United States from the parish of Julita in central Sweden. The parish name is the most important clue. It is in the parish records in Sweden that you find all the facts about your ancestor's family.

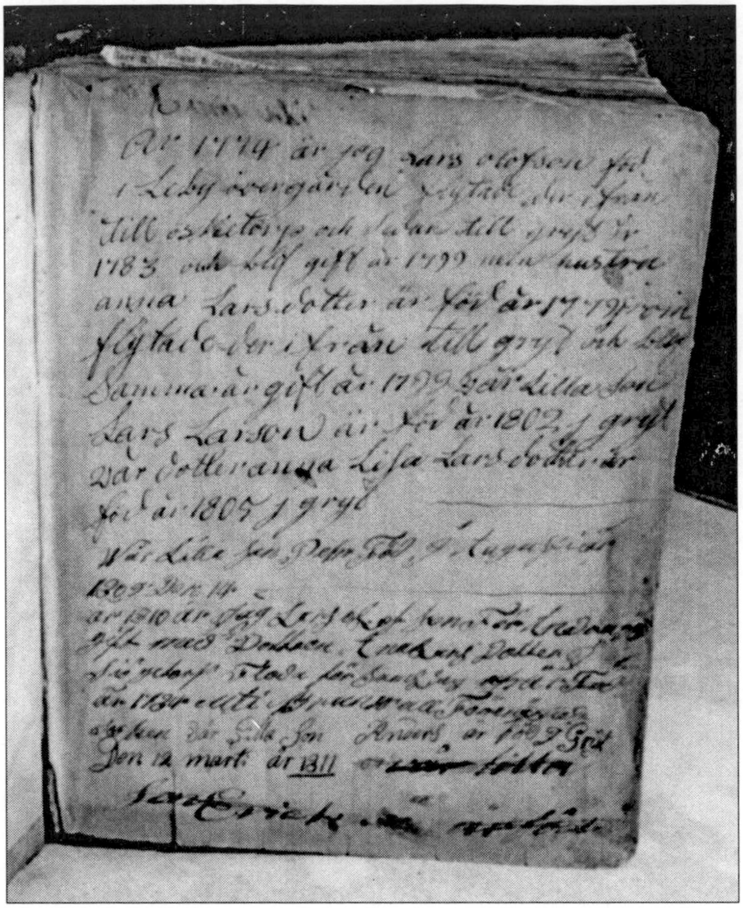

Page one (left):

År 1774 är jag Lars Olofson föd
i Leby övergården flytade der ifrån
Till öskepetorp och sedan till Gryt år
1783 och blef gift år 1799. min hustru
anna Larsdotter är föd år 1779 som
flytade der ifrån till Gryt och blef
samma år gift år 1799. wår lilla son
Lars Larson är föd år 1802 i gryt.
Wår dotter anna Lisa Larsdodter är
Föd år 1805 i gryt ———
Wår lilla son Pehr Föd i augusti år
1809 Den 14. ————————
År 1810 är jag Lars Olofsson För Andan gå(ng)
Gift med Dottren Ana Lars Dotter i
Siögetorp Floda församling och är föd
År 1784 uti Brunwall Förenämda
Socken Vär lilla Son Anders är föd i Gryt
Den 12 marti år 1811

Page two (reverse side):

År 1752 är jag Lisa Jönsdotter
Föd i Leby öwergården blef der
År 1771 gift och flyttade derifrårn till
Öskietorp var der i 4år och sedan till
Gryt blef sedan änkia år 1805
1783

vårlilla son Erick är föd
i Gryt Gulitta soken
den 11 mag år 1820

---

a Lutheran congregation with good church records, where you may find information about a birthplace in Sweden.

But most important: ask about names, dates, and other relevant information. Ask if there are any letters, diaries, paper clippings, photos, or papers. Ask if you can make copies of this material. Never take anyone's originals.

Questions to ask in an interview with older relatives:

- What is your full name, birthplace, and birth date? Where have you lived and what have you done in your life?
- What are your parents' and grandparent's full names, birth dates, and birthplaces? Spelling should be as accurate as possible, and note if the spelling has been changed. Don't forget middle names. Note their residence and occupation.
- Who was, to your knowledge, the person/persons in the family who first immigrated to America? Do you know in which year, or even on what date, they arrived? Do you know by what route they came to America? Do you know where they departed from in Sweden and where they arrived in the United States (or Canada)? If you don't know the exact year, make your best guess.
- Did they all come at the same time, if a whole family or several relatives immigrated?
- Are there any letters, postcards, diaries, pictures, vital records, deeds, or other legal papers in your possession, that may include names and addresses from Sweden or the early days in America?
- Did you ever hear any stories about life in Sweden? Or have you heard any places mentioned? (Sometimes even a vague family story can contain some information that may help you to get ahead in your research.)
- Do you know if the family joined a Swedish congregation in America? If so, do you know the name of it or the location?

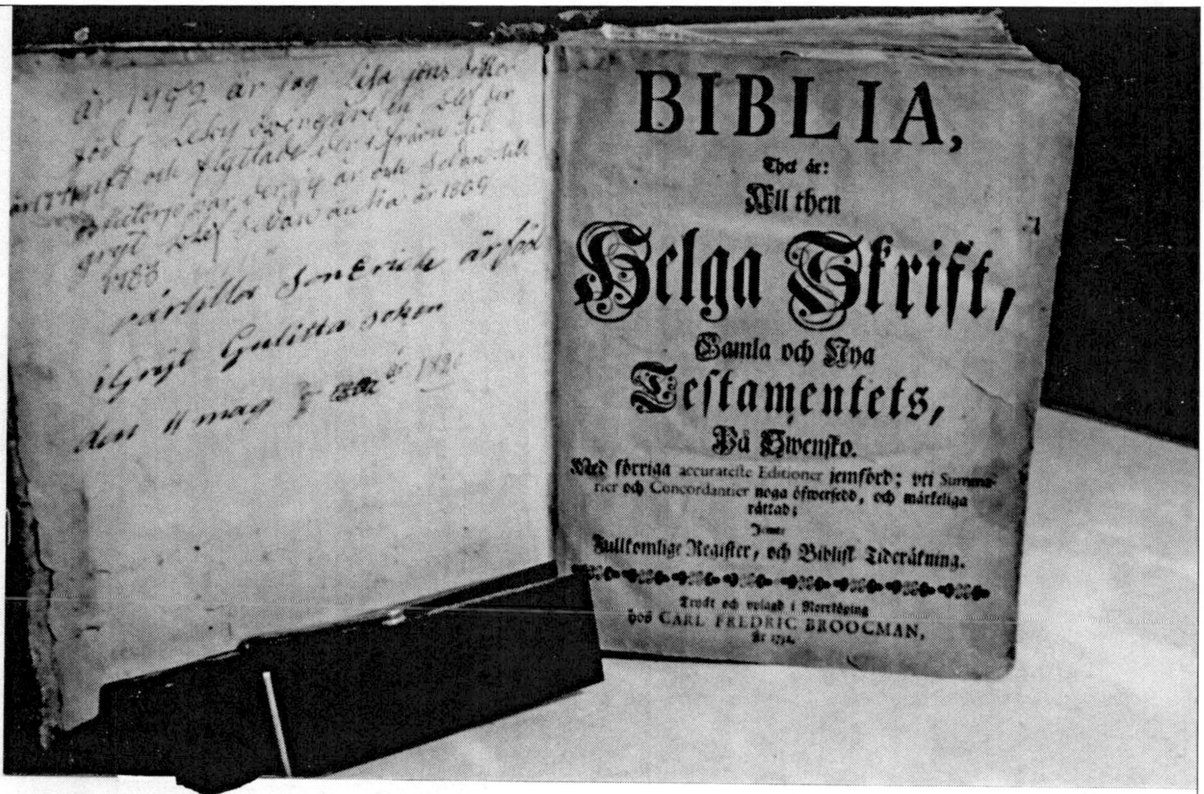

This family Bible once belonged to a family who lived first at the farm Leby Övergården, then moved to the farm Gryt in 1783.
The mother, Lisa Jönsdotter, is a widow, and her son Lars Olofsson first married Anna Larsdotter in 1779.
They had three children: Lars in 1802, Anna Lisa in 1805, and Pehr in 1809.
Lars remarried another Anna Larsdotter in 1810, and they had a son Anders in 1811, and a son Erick in 1820.
The spelling is incorrect in many places, the capital letters seem to be used at random, and it can be difficult to interpret the names if you don't know the area.
We see two parish names: The farm Gryt is in "Gulitta soken", usually spelled Julita, located in Södermanland.
The second wife came from Siögetorp in neighbouring Floda parish (församling).
The Bible now belongs to descendants in Chicago.

Home Sources

Family Bible

Quite often the emigrant family brought a Swedish family Bible along, especially if a whole family moved to the United States. These old Bibles have usually been kept as a treasure. Often there is a list of names on the inside of the cover or on the title page, of the members of the family who owned the Bible, even a short genealogy.

Letters and Postcards

Immigrants often wrote numerous letters to Sweden after they arrived in the new country, to tell about their experiences and out of homesickness. They also received letters in response. Usually there are return addresses on the envelopes, and there may be references to people and places in these letters. Before the era of telephones, people wrote postcards

Old photos give clues

Look at these old photos. There are no names or identifications on them. Someone has written ***farmor*** *(grandmother) on the back of one picture, but even without any names the pictures can be important clues. The photographer's names and addresses indicate the area where the relatives came from. Göteborg is the big city of Gothenburg. Skara is a small town 100 miles northeast of Gothenburg with Sweden's oldest cathedral.*

frequently, and often sent congratulations on birthdays and "name days." These cards can give you valuable information about names and relations, even if you don't find a complete address (postcards usually don't include return addresses). A card may, for example, give you an idea of a birth date, a piece of information that at some point will make it possible to distinguish one emigrant among dozens with the same name.

You may also find similar information in notebooks, diaries, or other personal records. Look for names, birth dates, and addresses.

Photographs

Often the only material left is photographs, either of relatives in Sweden, or of the immigrants themselves, taken after the arrival in the new country or brought along from Sweden. Sometimes there will be whole albums with pictures, and if you are lucky some thoughtful relative has written down the names of the people in the pictures. But often that is not the case.

The pictures were usually taken by a professional photographer in the nearest town. The pictures often have stamps or labels with the name of the photographer, generally including the name of the city. This could be an important clue. At least you have an indication of what part of Sweden your relative came from. With that you can start looking in the records of the parishes around the town of the photographer.

Legal Documents

People tend to save legal documents, such as deeds, wills, estate declarations, and birth and marriage certificates. These documents also may include birthplaces and birth dates. Remember that a birth date might be of critical importance when you have to distinguish between several people with the same name leaving Sweden the same year. The chance that two Emma Anderssons or Per Nilssons had the same birth date is, after all, rather slim.

Sometimes legal documents will give direct clues to a Swedish relative. A will may even give names and addresses of relatives in Sweden at the time.

American Records

Swedish American Church Records

About one-third of the Swedish immigrants ended up in Swedish congregations, primarily Lutheran, but also in the Swedish Covenant Church and Swedish Baptist churches. These churches kept records that were as meticulous as the church records back in Sweden. The Swedish birth parish is usually noted in these records.

Swedish American Church records have been microfilmed and are available at the Swedish Emigrant Institute in Växjö in Sweden and at Swenson Swedish Immigration Research Center in Rock Island, Illinois.

We will look at these Swedish American church records later in the book. Read more on page 65.

Census Records

While the U.S. Federal census records note the country of origin ("Sweden" for the Swedish immigrant), they seldom offer any more precise note of birthplace (city, province, or parish). They are therefore of little help to you. The only possibly helpful information is that they note all the members of the household. This could in some cases be useful, if you can't find that information elsewhere. It is easier to identify a fa-mily when you have all the names of the family members, for example in the ships' manifests in Gothenburg, where most emigrants from Sweden departed. To find information on using census records, consult a regular American genealogical handbook, the American Regional National Archives, or the Family History Centers accociated with the The Church of Jesus Christ of Latter-day Saints. Read more on page 70.

County Courthouse Records

Most U.S. county courthouses have population records. These records usually give the place of birth as "Sweden" for a Swedish immigrant, but sometimes in older records you may find the name of a place or a city. We have, for example, found specific Swedish birthplaces in records in McPherson County (Lindsborg) in Kansas.

Vital Records

Vital records are handled in different ways in different states. Sometimes they are kept on the local level, sometimes they have been handled by a state vital statistics office. In these records you will generally be able to find accurate birth dates.

Probate Records

Probate records, wills, and estate declarations are documents that may include the birthplace of the deceased in Sweden and even the names of relatives in Sweden. Often, probate records are kept in the county courthouse, but in some states there are special probate courts and probate court districts.

Naturalization Records

Naturalization records can be the best way to find accurate information for many difficult-to-find ancestors. Old records are kept in the local courts, but after 1906 the records were kept by the Immigration and Naturalization Service, and are housed at the National Archives in Washington. After two years stay in the United States, immigrants could submit a Declaration of Intent. After another three years they could apply for citizenship. The application can contain information about the birthplace in the old country.

Newspapers – Obituaries

The Swedish American community retained the Swedish language and much of the Swedish culture during the first couple of generations. One important part of this culture was Swedish American newspapers. A large number of newspapers and other periodicals were published. *Svenska Tribunen – Nyheter* in Chicago reached a circulation of 65,000 around World War I. *Svenska Amerikanska Posten* in Minneapolis printed 56,000 copies per issue in 1915. None of the Swedish newspapers were daily. The Swedish American papers have been microfilmed, and the film is available at the Swenson institute in Rock Island and at the Swedish Emigrant Institute in Växjö.

For the genealogist the obituaries in these papers can give information about birth date and birth place in Sweden. The papers can also provide much other valuable information.

The epitaph reads:

Här hvilar
Mrs Anna Peterson
föd i Floda soken
Södermanland län Sverige
den 1st aug 1830
Dog i Hobart
den 6 oct 1906.

Here rests
Mrs Anna Peterson
born in Floda parish
in Södermanlands län in Sweden
August 1, 1830.
Died in Hobart
6 October, 1906.

This gravestone gives information about the birth parish in Sweden, which is quite unusual. Anna Peterson is grandfather's grandmother to Kjell Andersson (one of the authors of this book), and she joined some of her children who had emigrated from Sweden to Hobart, Indiana. The grave is in the cemetery in Hobart.

CHAPTER THREE

THE EMIGRATION FROM SWEDEN TO AMERICA

From 1821 to 1930 more than 1.2 million Swedes emigrated. Most of them left for the United States, but some also came to Canada, Australia, New Zealand, and South America. Almost one out of five returned to Sweden, but one million Swedes stayed for good in their new home countries.

In the 1990 census some 4.7 million Americans, out of a total of 249 million, stated that they had Swedish ancestry. Another 680,000 stated that they were of Scandinavian ancestry, and some of these were of course also "Swedes." In addition there is an unspecified group of people who are not aware of their Swedish heritage.

The number of Swedish descendants in the United States grows much more quickly than the number of Swedes in Sweden, for obvious reasons. The Swedish immigrants of the first generation tended to marry other Swedes. They went to Swedish churches and lived in Swedish neighbourhoods. Their children still mixed with Swedish descendants to a large extent. But by the third and fourth generation, Swedish-Americans were fully Americanized and they began to marry Americans of every creed and race.

Thus the number of people with Swedish ancestry grows rapidly. At the same time the number of young people with only or primarily Swedish ancestry is becoming quite small. Even so, many of these young people feel that it is still important to connect to their great-grandmother's or great-grandfather's country and if possible to plan a trip to go to the place where it all started and hopefully find some relatives in the old country.

In another couple of generations the awareness of ones Swedish heritage may no longer be present, and the ancestry will be so mixed and diluted that it is of little importance.

ONE OUT OF FIVE EMIGRATED

At the time of the great emigration, in the late nineteenth century, Sweden had a population of some five million people. The population growth was rapid and the farmland was scarce. On many small farms there wasn't room for the second or third child to get work and income. Many people had to find a place outside the farm community, either in the growing industry or the expanding cities and towns, or by emigration to another country.

Sweden lost one out of five of its population to emigration. This is a very high percentage, exceeded only by Ireland and Norway among the European countries. Emigration was a big chance for many individuals to get a richer and better life. For many farmers it was an opportunity to get better land to farm. Emigration was also a relief to the Swedish society, where an overpopulated countryside and unemployment was a strain on the economy. In the long run, however, emigration was perceived as a threat by many politicians and intellectuals in Sweden. A countermovement developed to try to persuade people to stay in their mother country.

ECONOMIC FACTORS MOST IMPORTANT

The strongest motive in the emigration was economics. Historians who have analysed this process talk about the push and pull of migration. Bad economic conditions in the old country (Sweden in this case) pushed people away. Good economic conditions in the new country (the United States or Canada) pulled people to them. The first big wave of emigration from Sweden occured in 1867–1868, when the harvest in Sweden was extremely bad. Because of the conditions in these years, the period is sometimes characterized as "the last famine" in Sweden.

There were also other reasons to emigrate besides looking for work and better income. The earliest large group of emigrants from Sweden left in 1846 for religious reasons. A group of religious dissidents under the leadership of Erik Jansson from middle Sweden found a new home in Illinois and founded the communal society of Bishop Hill. Such religious

Gothenburg harbor was, and still is, one of Scandinavia's busiest. The church on the hill, Masthuggskyrkan, was built 1910–1914 and is a landmark for travelers, visible far out at sea. The building in the foreground is the Custom's house, built in 1864, where all the emigrants passed through. The picture was probably taken in the 1930s.

groups of emigrants were rare though. Most Swedish emigrants kept to their traditional Lutheran beliefs and founded traditional congregations in their new homeland.

Reasons for Emigraton

There are many factors considered most important for the Swedish emigration to North America.

The pushing factors:

- The developments within Swedish farming. More efficient methods required fewer people for farming.
- The rapid population growth during the nineteenth century, caused by "the peace, the vaccinations and the potatoes," as expressed by the Swedish bishop Esaias Tegnér. The number of children in each family that survived to adulthood increased and the farms became overcrowded.
- A growing number of landless and poor people in the Swedish countryside.
- The famine in the late 1860s.
- Dissatisfaction with the draft into military service.
- Dissatisfaction with religious intolerance and the total dominance of the state Lutheran church.

The pulling factors:

- The availability of free farmland in the United States (because of the Homestead Act 1862).
- The possibility to get work and make money in the growing American economy.
- The organized propaganda from American states, steamship lines, railway companies and their Swedish agents.
- The letters sent home to Sweden by earlier emigrants. Many also sent tickets back to their siblings and other relatives.

Early Swedish Immigrants

The first Swedes arriving in North America were the colonists of New Sweden along the Delaware River. The colony was founded already in 1638, and a total of about seven hundred to eight hundred Swedes and Finns are believed to have settled in the area. They built a fortress, churches, and Swedish style "log cabins" – creating one of the most important Scandinavian contributions to American culture. The Dutch rather early took over this colony and the British took it from them. The Swedish colony had only a very brief existance, and Sweden never became a colonial power.

Through the next two hundred years few individuals found their way from Sweden to North America, mainly adventurers and people on the run from justice. The first larger influx didn't occur until the 1840s. Some of the first "modern immigrants" from Sweden arrived in Wisconsin. One was Gustaf Unonius from Uppsala. He was an educated man driven by a romantic ideology inspired by Rousseau. He brought his family and a couple of students along and founded a small colony at Pine Lake, Wisconsin. He had been preceded by Mr. Carl Freeman and his sons. We will meet this brave family later in the book (page 116).

Another early immigrant was Peter Cassel who founded the colony New Sweden in Iowa in 1845. He was a farmer and builder. In 1858 the colony had around 500 inhabitants. And, as mentioned, the religious commune of Bishop Hill near Andover in Illinois was founded earlier in the 1840s.

A First Group of Immigrants

The first group of idealistic and religious immigrants were followed by a broader group of immigrants around 1850, who came primarily for economic reasons. For the first time we can talk about a mass movement. This generation of immigrants is described by the Swedish author Wilhelm Moberg in his emigrant books (*The Emigrants, Unto a Good Land, The Settlers*, and *The Last Letter Home*).

Between 1850 and the Civil War some 14,000 Swedes arrived in the United States. Most of them settled in the upper Mississippi river valley, in a number of settlements. The previously mentioned New Sweden in Iowa was one of them; Vasa in southeast Minnesota was another.

This was before modern steamship travel, and immigrants came on small sail ships that also carried cargo, usually iron, which Sweden exported. The trip over the Atlantic took one and a half to two months. The trip could be very rough and quite a few immigrants perished during the voyage.

An emigrant steamship leaves Gothenburg. The flag is the flag of the Union Sweden–Norway. The union broke up in 1905.

Steamships Cut Travel Time

The first big wave of immigrants from Sweden arrived in the United States between 1868 and 1869. The driving forces behind this wave were fourfold: The bad times in Swedish farming with bad harvests three years in a row, 1866, 1867 and 1868, drove people from the countryside to seek new income and escape hunger. The U.S. Homestead Act was passed in 1862 and the prospect of getting free and fertile land was very tempting to smallholders with poor soil in Sweden. The bloody American Civil War was over. Finally, modern steamships were put into service in the North Atlantic. The Steamship Lines were formed and travel time was cut from two months to two weeks.

During these years 120,000 Swedes emigrated to the United States. Most of them ended up in the farming areas in the upper Mississippi valley. Minnesota became the favourite state for Swedes, but many also settled down in Iowa and Illinois. Most of the immigrants were sons and daughters of farmers and ended up in small farm communities in the upper Midwest where the climate and landscape were not so different from Scandinavia.

Emigration was abruptly halted by economics on both sides of the ocean around 1873, America experienced some years of bad economy while Sweden's economy improved markedly. Without the previously mentioned pull and push the immigration from Sweden almost ground to a halt for several years.

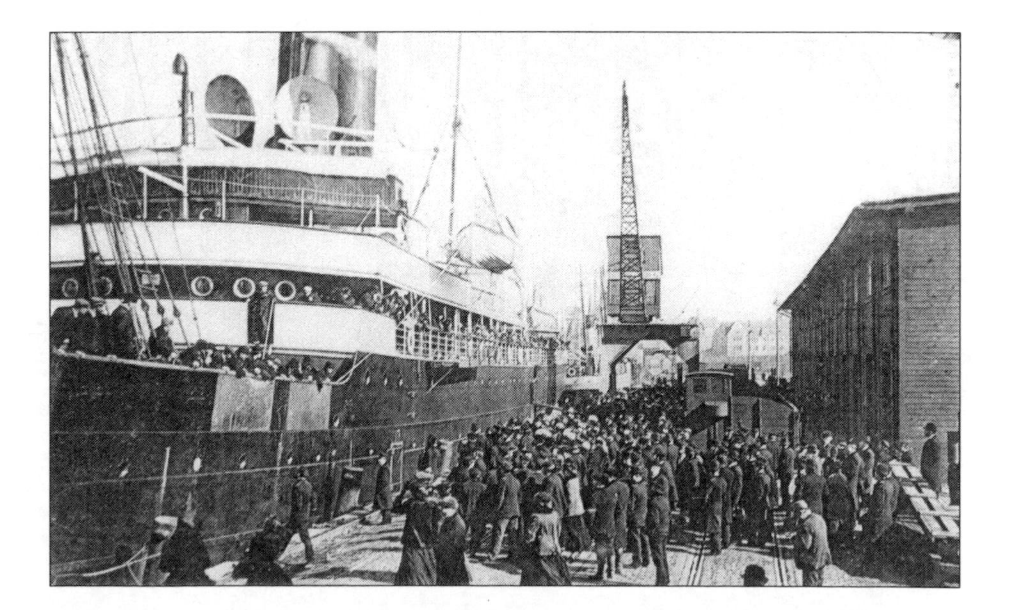

It was a big event when emigrants boarded the ship and bid a last farewell to their friends and relatives.

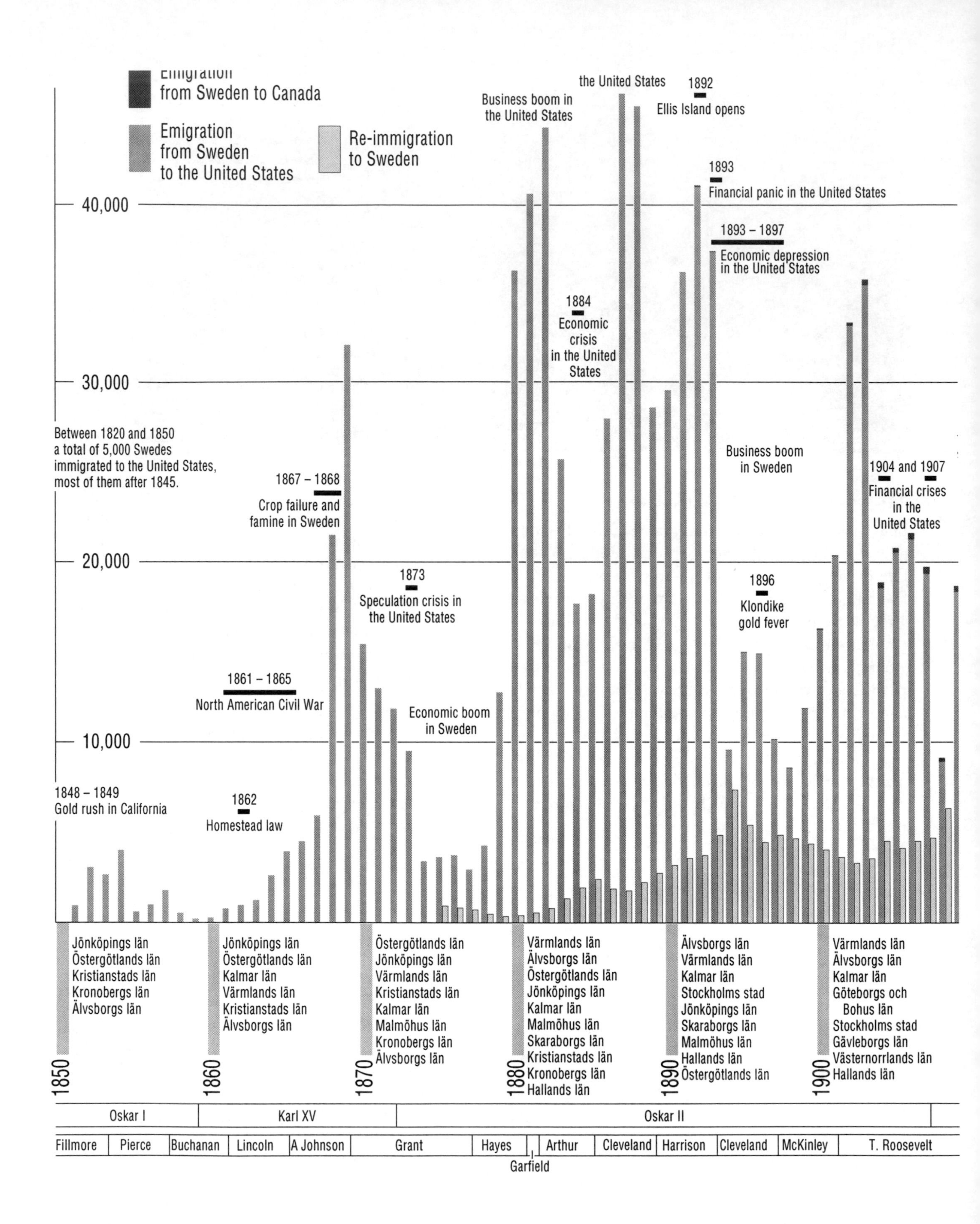
Emigration
from Sweden to Canada
Emigration
from Sweden
to the United States
Re-immigration
to Sweden
40,000
30,000
20,000
10,000
Between 1820 and 1850
a total of 5,000 Swedes
immigrated to the United States,
most of them after 1845.
1848 – 1849
Gold rush in California
1862
Homestead law
1861 – 1865
North American Civil War
1867 – 1868
Crop failure and
famine in Sweden
1873
Speculation crisis in
the United States
Economic boom
in Sweden
Business boom in
the United States
the United States
1884
Economic
crisis
in the United
States
1892
Ellis Island opens
1893
Financial panic in the United States
1893 – 1897
Economic depression
in the United States
Business boom
in Sweden
1896
Klondike
gold fever
1904 and 1907
Financial crises
in the
United States
1850
Jönköpings län
Östergötlands län
Kristianstads län
Kronobergs län
Älvsborgs län
1860
Jönköpings län
Östergötlands län
Kalmar län
Värmlands län
Kristianstads län
Älvsborgs län
1870
Östergötlands län
Jönköpings län
Värmlands län
Kristianstads län
Kalmar län
Malmöhus län
Kronobergs län
Älvsborgs län
1880
Värmlands län
Älvsborgs län
Östergötlands län
Jönköpings län
Kalmar län
Malmöhus län
Skaraborgs län
Kristianstads län
Kronobergs län
Hallands län
1890
Älvsborgs län
Värmlands län
Kalmar län
Stockholms stad
Jönköpings län
Skaraborgs län
Malmöhus län
Hallands län
Östergötlands län
1900
Värmlands län
Älvsborgs län
Kalmar län
Göteborgs och
Bohus län
Stockholms stad
Gävleborgs län
Västernorrlands län
Hallands län
Oskar I
Karl XV
Oskar II
Fillmore
Pierce
Buchanan
Lincoln
A Johnson
Grant
Hayes
Garfield
Arthur
Cleveland
Harrison
Cleveland
McKinley
T. Roosevelt

The Great Emigration from Sweden to North America

The emigration from Sweden and the re-immigration to Sweden as it is reflected in the official statistics in Sweden. The numbers have been compiled from different public sources.

The numbers underestimate the true emigration by about ten percent, for several reasons:

- Migration through foreign ports is not recorded in the statistics. This migration took place through ports in Germany (Hamburg and Bremen), in Denmark (Copenhagen), and in Norway (Kristiania and several others).
- First and second-class passengers were not recorded as emigrants.
- Travelers on cargo ships were not recorded as emigrants.

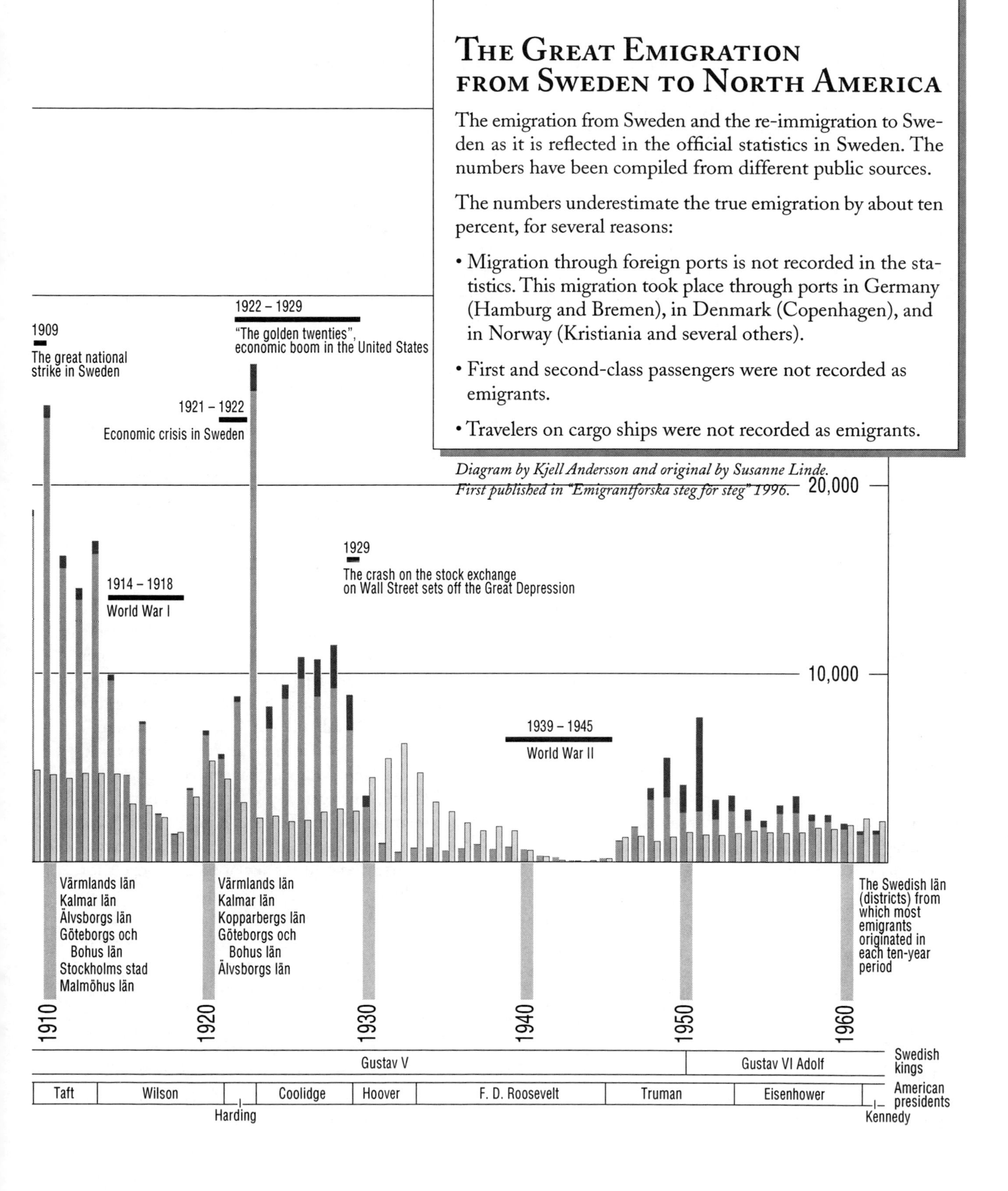

Diagram by Kjell Andersson and original by Susanne Linde. First published in "Emigrantforska steg för steg" 1996.

The Mass Emigration Between 1879 and 1893

The period from 1879 to 1893 is the era of mass emigration from Sweden to the United States. During these fifteen years almost half a million Swedes (485,000 people) left their home country to find a new life in America. Almost all parts of Sweden were affected, even the big cities. The immigrants still ended up, for the most part, in "the Homestead triangle," between Mississippi, Missouri and the Canadian border. In addition to Minnesota, Illinois and Iowa, Swedes also settled in South and North Dakota, Wisconsin, Nebraska, and Kansas. When the land was occupied and it became more difficult to find a free farm many Swedes moved on to mountain states like Montana, Colorado, Utah, and Washington.

In the 1890s emigration slowed down, mainly because the economic growth was good in Sweden. But the Klondike gold rush in 1896 attracted many adventurous Swedes, just as the California gold rush in 1848–1849 had done.

The Swedish City of Chicago

Around the turn of the century, as it became more difficult to acquire farmland in the Midwest, more and more of the Swedes ended up in the fast-growing big cities. Many of these were people from the Swedish countryside who had already tried their luck in big cities in Sweden, and then moved on to North America. Some ended up in the Northeast, in industrial cities in Massachusetts, Connecticut or upstate New York. Many stayed in or around New York City. But first and foremost, they came to Chicago, which now became a gathering place for Swedish-Americans.

Fast-growing Chicago attracted hundreds of thousands of immigrants. Many Swedes were engaged in the building industry as carpenters, masons, and builders. Swede Town, or Andersonville, became a Swedish city within the city, with Swedish stores, churches, restaurants, newspapers, and other Swedish establishments of all kinds. At the turn of the century Chicago was in terms of Swedish population the second biggest Swedish city in the world, bigger than Gothenburg and surpassed only by Stockholm.

Many Swedes Moved On

The late-coming immigrants from Sweden, arriving before the World War I and during the 1920s, spread to even farther parts of the United States and to an increasing extent, Canada. More and more Swedes moved to the West Coast, to northern California and Washington state. Still few Swedes immigrated to the South, Texas being the exception to the rule. The last big year of Swedish emigration was 1923. Sweden had a bad recession in 1921–1922 whereas the American economy took off in the early twenties. With the crash of the stock market in 1929 and the following depression the flow of emigration dried up completely. Instead there was a rather substantial move back in a reimmigration to Sweden from the United States. In the 1950s there was a new, but much smaller flow, but this time mainly to Canada.

Many of the Swedes and their descendants in the United States at the same time moved on from the Midwest to the West Coast states and sunshine states like Florida and Arizona. Today Swedish-Americans are found all over the North American continent.

From Where Did They Come in Sweden?

Almost all provinces (*landskap*) in Sweden were affected by emigration, but in general the poorer forested areas in southern and western Sweden were affected the most. Provinces like Småland, Västergötland, Dalsland, Värmland, and Öland experienced a very heavy emigration. In these areas the farms could not support the large families that were common at the end of the nineteenth century. Often one or two of the younger members of the families bought tickets and left for the United States or Canada. Later they wrote back and sometimes sent money or bought tickets for younger siblings or for their parents to come and join them. This kind of step-by-step emigration by a whole family was quite common. In some areas there were emigrants from every village and farm, and parishes could lose a substantial share of their populations in only a few years.

In later stages of the emigration the big cities and the northern parts of Sweden were also affected. The more productive agricultural provinces in central and southernmost Sweden had the lowest emigration rate.

"On the way to America."
The handwritten text on the postcard is a greeting from Gothenburg at the departure 4 May 1906, from "the Friend E".

The postcard below has the following text: "Here you can see how it looked when Anton departed. Merry Christmas and I hope you get many presents. From your friend Hildur."

Along this street in Gothenburg all the Swedish agents for the steamship lines had their offices, alongside small hotels and cafés. The street's official name was Postgatan, but the popular name was Sillgatan which means Herring Street.

Good for Both Parties

In the 1890s, after the peak of the mass emigration, there was widespread criticism of this exodus of young, able Swedes. The argument was that Sweden was losing some of "its best blood" and human resources. The mood was nationalistic and led to propaganda against emigration.

Was emigration harmful to Sweden? After all, a lot of young people with skills and education left the country. At the same time, the Swedish countryside was crowded and the economy couldn't absorb all of these people. The alternative for many young people would have been unemployment and for the country possibly civil unrest. Emigration was probably good both for Sweden and for North America. For the individuals who emigrated it was a chance to live a new and better life, although not everyone succeeded or enjoyed the new country. About one- tenth of the Swedish immigrants to the United States emigrated once again, and returned back to Sweden.

The steamship companies produced beautiful postcards, as well as maps, posters, brochures, and newspaper ads.

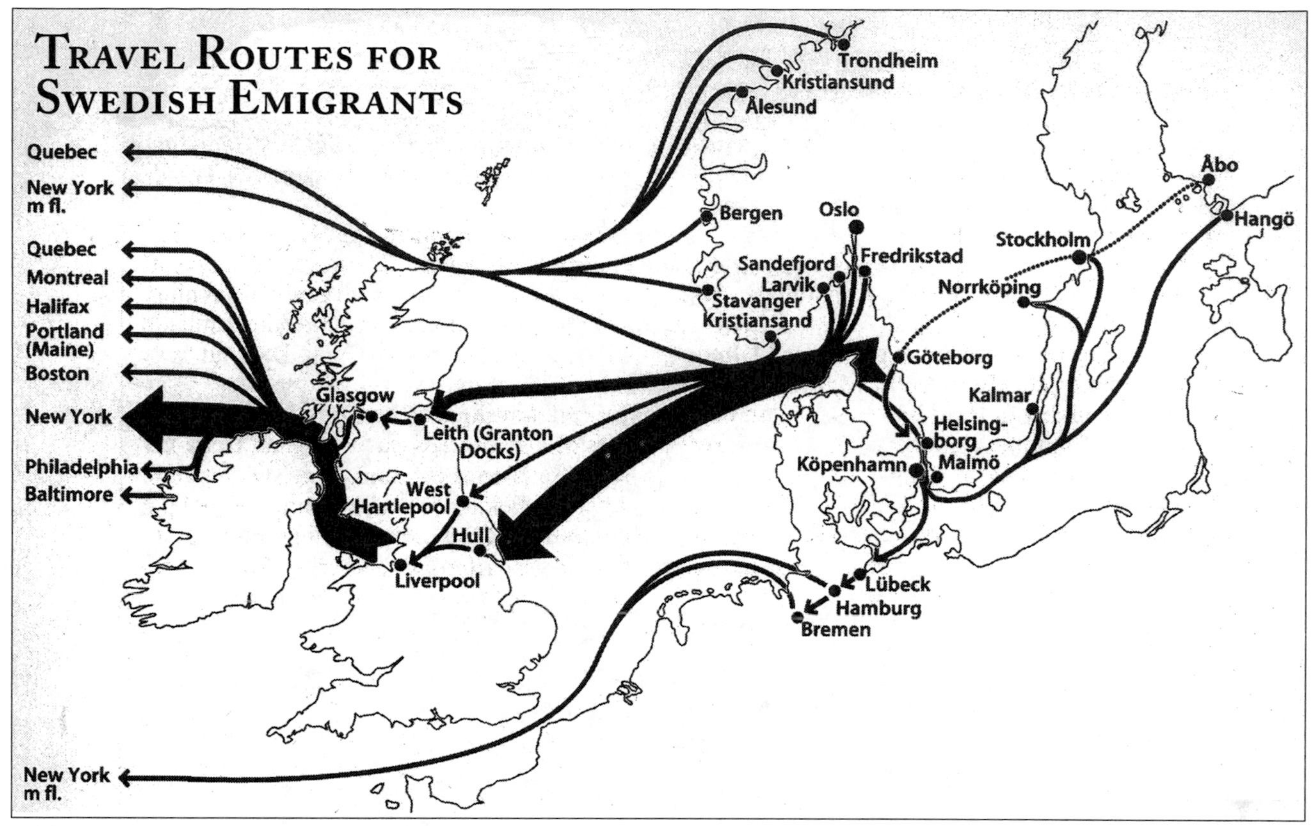

This map shows the different routes used by Swedish emigrants headed for North America. The majority of travelers left from Gothenburg (Göteborg) and arrived in New York. (m fl. means "and others").

The Travel Routes

The early emigrants, before the 1860s, traveled by small cargo ships (sail ships) from several different ports in Sweden, directly to North American ports.

After the American Civil War, emigration was organized by the big steamship companies. The travel route from Sweden almost exclusively went through Gothenburg (Göteborg) on the Swedish west coast. The emigrants traveled by train or other means of transport to this port city. They often stayed in small hotels along Sillgatan (or "Herring Street") before boarding a ship to England. From Gothenburg, the most common route was to take a ship across the North Sea to Hull on the English east coast, and to cross England by train to Liverpool. Most of the big steam liners went from Liverpool to New York. Some Swedes also traveled to Scotland and took a ship from Glasgow. On the American side, some ships also landed in Boston and Quebec.

Swedes from western Sweden sometimes traveled through Norwegian ports like Oslo (called Kristiania before 1925), Bergen, and Trondheim. Emigrants from southern Sweden often chose to travel through Copenhagen (Denmark), Hamburg, or Bremen (Germany).

But the absolute majority, more than a million out of 1.2 million, passed through Gothenburg. An even higher proportion on the American side came through New York.

In 1915 the Swedish American Line (Svenska Amerika-Linjen) was established. With it came the first direct steam ship line between Gothenburg and New York, and after World War I Swedes no longer had to travel through England.

The ticket was usually purchased from a Swedish emigration agent, and was a contract for travel all the way from Gothenburg to a final destination within the United States (for example Chicago, Grand Rapids, or Sioux Falls). The emigration/immigration was highly organized by big companies and other entities with strong economic interests: steam ship lines, railroad companies, and states that were eager to attract young farmers and workers.

All immigrants arriving in New York harbor from 1 January 1892 to 29 November 1954, seventeen million in all, had to pass through Ellis Island before they were admitted into the United States.

The total domination of the travel route from Gothenburg to New York gives us good focal points for our research. Beside the Swedish church records and the American population records we have the ship's manifests in Gothenburg and New York, where most of the emigrants have been recorded.

The immigrant family Hägglund went to "Lundquist photo, Alexandria, Minnesota" to have their picture taken.

CHAPTER FOUR

How to Find the Place of Origin in Sweden

Where did the family come from in Sweden? You might for example find a name of a place in an old letter or a return address on an envelope. Maybe there is a family tradition that your great grandfather came from a certain place in Sweden: "Smolan" or "Tuna." To identify such a place, you need to know some basic facts about Swedish geography.

The word "Smolan" probably stands for the province (or *landskap*) of Småland, a whole region with today close to one million inhabitants, consisting of three districts (*län*) and of several hundred parishes, each with its own separate church records. So, in this case "Smolan" alone doesn't give enough information to help you find the records of your great grandfather. You will need much more accurate and precise information to find the right place — his place of birth or the place he emigrated from.

A return address is much better but does not necessarily lead you to the parish where his church records can be found. With the help of the old address you will, however, have a good chance to find the right archives.

Let us first look at the geography of Sweden and how the country is divided in different ways.

Sweden – a General Picture

Sweden is a little larger than California, around 173,000 square miles, but the population is more like that of Michigan, around nine million people. The northern part is sparsely populated with large areas of evergreen forests, mountains, bog areas and lakes, much like northern Canada. There are a number of rivers, and villages in the valleys along these rivers. Southern Sweden is fertile with a mix of forests and farmland, not unlike parts of Minnesota or New England. Southernmost Sweden, Skåne (Scania), resembles Denmark and northern Germany. It is densely populated and has very good farming conditions. Sweden's big cities are Stockholm on the eastern Baltic coast, with 1.5 million people, and Gothenburg on the west coast, with over half a million people.

Today the majority of Swedes live in cities and towns, and less than a third live in small communities and in the countryside. This was, of course, the reverse a hundred years ago. Until the end of the nineteenth century Sweden was a predominantly agricultural country, with a small part of the population engaged in mining, ironworks, and forest industry. The Swedes have always been a seafaring people, with a large merchant fleet. Industrialization was very quick in the late nineteenth century.

Sweden in earlier times had a violent history, from Viking raids in the tenth century to warring kings, like Gustavus Adolphus and Charles XII, in the seventeenth and eighteenth century. But during the last 200 years Sweden has not taken part in any wars. The last time Swedish soldiers went to war, other than under the U.N. flag, was in 1814. Through the nineteenth century, as a result of peace, improved health (vaccina-

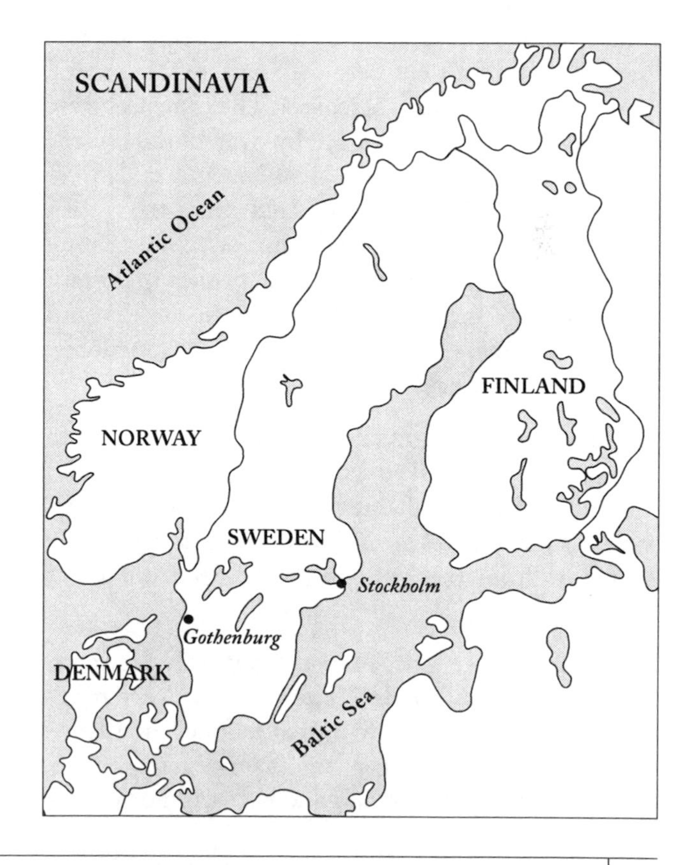

tions), improved nutrition (the po- tatoes' arrival in Sweden), and agricultural reform the population grew rapidly in the Swedish countryside. This population growth was an important factor behind Swedish emigration.

Another typical feature of Sweden is how homogenous the country has been, especially a hundred years ago. Apart from a small minority of Samic reindeer herders in the northern mountains and a small Finnish-speaking group in the far northeast, all Swedes speak Swedish, a Germanic language.

All Swedes were, and most still are, members of the Swedish Lutheran Church, which until the year 2000 was a state church. In fact, membership and adherence to the Lutheran religion was mandatory until the end of the nineteenth century. The church demanded of everyone good knowledge of the catechism and the Bible. As a result, the Swedes very early on knew how to read and write. A strong administration guaranteed that conditions were similar in all parts of the country.

Landskap
Provinces

The twenty-four *landskap* (provinces) today have no administrative or legal significance, but they are important as cultural entities; they also reflect natural geographical or ecological regions. The provinces were originally local "kingdoms" led by strong local leaders. Each landskap had its own local law and trials were held at meetings (*ting*) held in the open at a central place in the landskap. At these meeting elections of leaders (local kings) and other important decisions were made. When Sweden in the eleventh century became a unified country these "kingdoms" became the provinces of Sweden.

Often when immigrants referred to their origin in Sweden they talked about their provinces and saw themselves as inhabitants of a certain landskap, such as Småland, Värmland, and Dalarna (exception: emigrants from the large cities like Stockholm and Gothenburg).

The map to the right shows the Swedish provinces. They vary greatly in size. They are also very different in population. The two smallest ones are mountainous Härjedalen near the Norwegian border, (around 11,000 inhabitants) and the island of Öland, (around 25,000). Skåne, in the south, has a population of more than a million.

Information about the Province/landskap can give a starting point in the research, but is usually not enough.

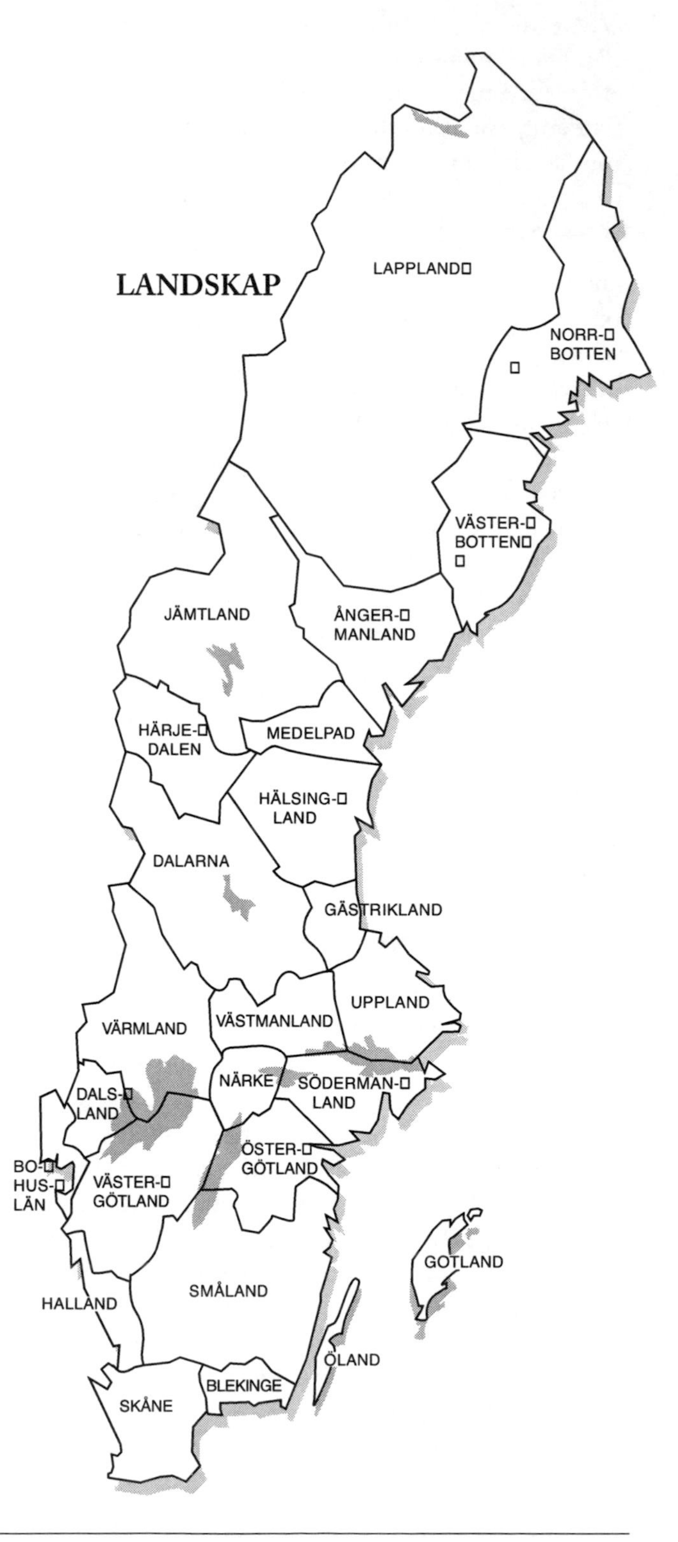

Län
Districts, "counties"

In 1634 the Swedish kingdom was radically reorganized. The old *landskap* gave way to the new *län*. Some of these districts were identical with the old provinces. But in some cases, large provinces were divided into two or three län. Sometimes two landskap formed one län. The purpose of the reform was to form districts of similar size and population. An average-sized län today has around 250,000 to 300,000 inhabitants.

Each of these län was (and still is) led by a governor (*landshövding*) and a regional administration (*länsstyrelse*). Since 1862 there have also been regional parliaments (*landsting*) elected in each län.

This organization and partition of Sweden into län has lasted into modern times. The boundaries of the län were in general the same until around 1970. Since then boundaries have been changed in certain areas and some län have merged.

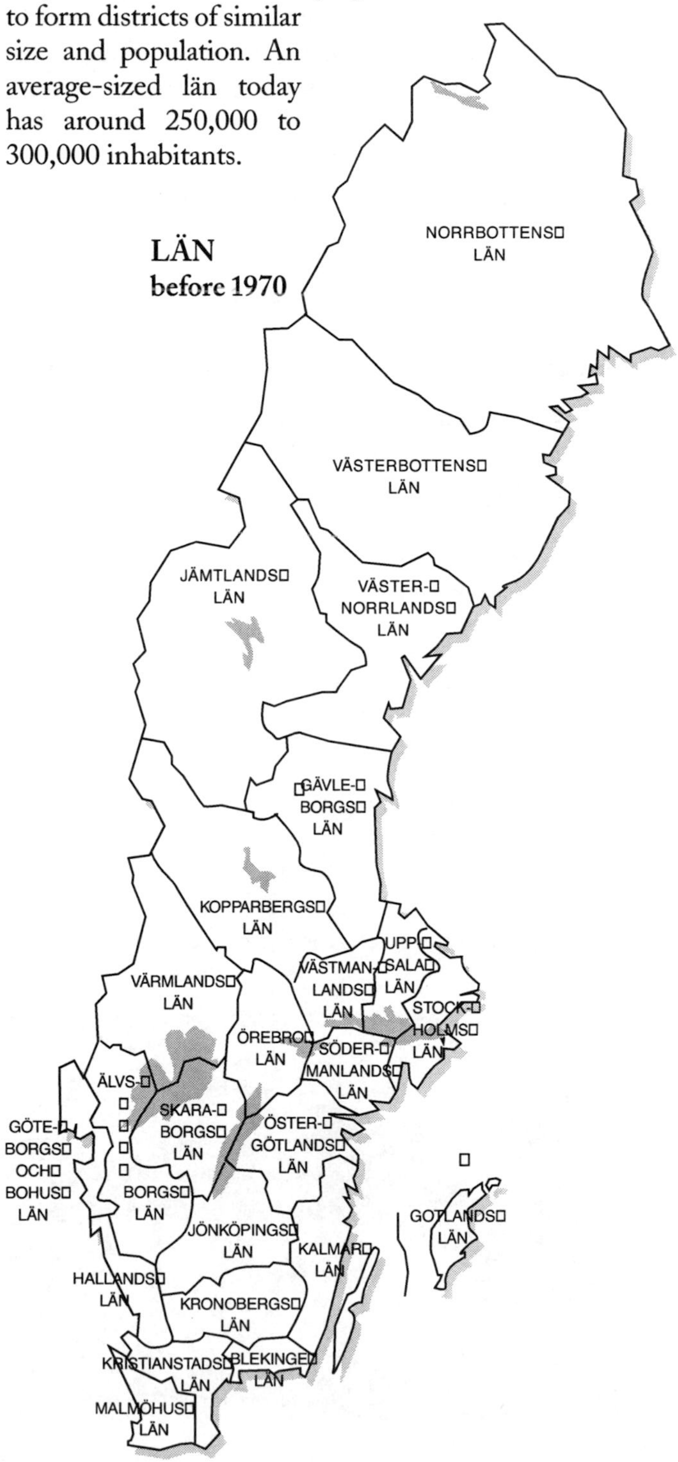

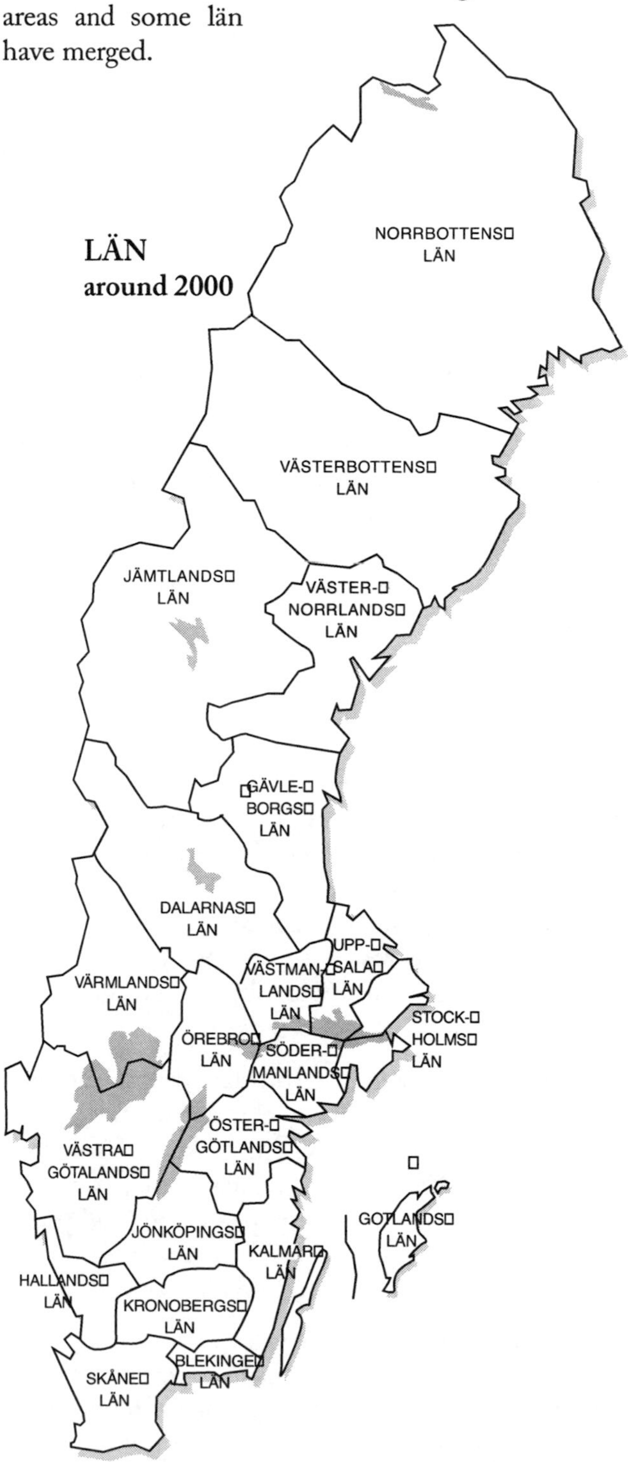

LÄN
before 1970

LÄN
around 2000

For the genealogist it is important to know what län a certain parish belongs to when you want to visit the regional archives (*landsarkiv*). Each of the regional archives collects records from certain län. The current boundaries determine which regional archive a certain parish belongs to. But be aware that while the parish of your origin may have belonged to a certain län historically, it might have been transferred to another län when boundaries changed, which usually affected entire parishes. The important thing is to find the right parish.

Härad
Counties

The Swedish word län is often translated as county. This is not correct. There are in fact Swedish counties, called *härad*. Usually a län consisted of a handful to a dozen of counties (*härad*). The counties were primarily judicial entities, each with a local court that met in a small courthouse three times a year. The cities and towns had their own court-houses. The counties also were administrative units, for tax collection, country sheriffs etc. For your family research, härad is of limited importance, unless you want to look into court records — just in case your forefather left for America to escape justice!

Socken – Församling
Parish

The most important entity for genealogical research is the parish. Church records kept in the local parish church have been the official population records in Sweden, from the late seventeenth century until the present day. The state officially took responsibility for the population records on 1 July 1991. Until that date the Swedish Lutheran State Church had the official responsibility to keep the records.

The Swedish parishes are territorial, which means that they include all people (today church members) living within its fixed boundaries, just like an American township or city. On a regular map, you can still see the boundaries of the parish, and old parish boundaries still in most cases form the basis for the modern partition of Sweden into municipalities.

The parishes were formed in early medieval times, when people in a certain area came together to build a church. In many parts of Sweden, such as in the oldest populated areas along the coasts and around the big lakes in central Sweden, or on the most fertile agricultural plains, the same medieval parishes with their medieval churches still exist. On the island of Gotland, for example, there are ninety-four medieval parishes. Most of the churches were built out of sandstone or limestone during the twelfth or thirteenth century, and they are virtually all still in use.

When forest areas were colonized and new farm areas were cultivated, new parishes were formed, and old parishes were partitioned. At the end of the nineteenth century, at the time of the mass emigration, and before the big industrialization and urbanization, there were around 2,000 parishes in Sweden, and a majority of the population lived in these countryside parishes. Also included in these old parishes were people living in new railroad communities and new industrial places (saw mills, mines, countryside factories). At times, when a place grew to become a bigger town, it was also formed into a parish of its own.

Cities and towns had their own parishes. Small towns usually had one church and constituted one parish, whereas larger towns had several. Sometimes German merchants formed their own parish (congregation), as in Stockholm. Military garrisons in some cases had their own congregations, too.

In some cities there was a separate parish for the people farming the countryside around the town (*landsförsamling*), whereas the city dwellers (burgers, merchants, and artisans) had their own parish.

The term used for the parish was in old times *socken*. The word goes back to a medieval word for "coming together, congregate." Later the term *församling* (congregation) came into use. Both words are still in use, although *församling* today is the official term.

Ransberg Church.

Annex Parishes

When searching for information in the church books it is important to note that some parishes were linked together and had a mutual "administration." The vicar (*kyrkoherde*) was priest in a "mother parish," and there might be a chaplain (*komminister*) in an adjoining "annex parish." The church books have often been kept in common for the mother parish with its annex parish (or annex parishes, as there are sometimes more than one), with separate sections for the different parishes. When you look for the records you may thus find them in the mother parish. How will you know which parishes are linked together? Information can be found in the archives and also on the Internet (through Genline).

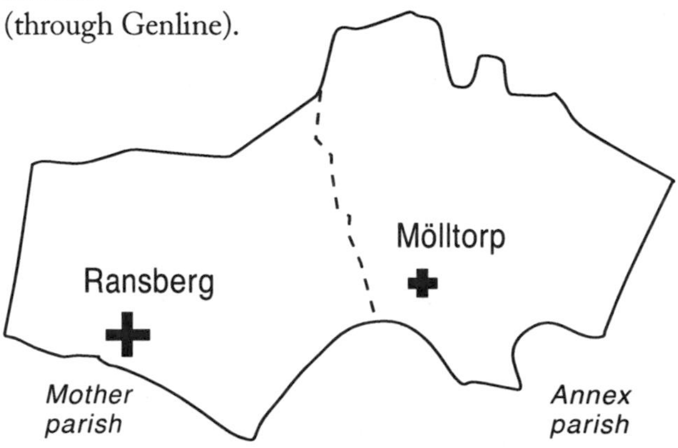

Mölltorp Church, above, looks much like Ransberg Church. They are both quite old. Mölltorp church was probably built in the thirteenth century. The tower was added in the fifteenth century.

Addresses

When you find an address on a letter it doesn't necessarily give you information about the parish. Often the post offices and mail addresses are connected to more modern population patterns than the old parishes. The post office can be located in and named after a small town or village around a railway station, a road crossing, a market place, or a local industry. The parish with its old church will be nearby and the small new community is included in the parish. Sometimes the parish and the post office have a common name, but often the names are different.

You may need to consult a map. Try to get access to a detailed road map where the parish churches are marked and named. In our example the railroad station was Mölltorp. So was the name of the post office. And so was the name of the parish. The church and parish gave the name to the railroad station. Southwest of Mölltorp there is another small railroad station with the name Fagersanna. This was also the location of a post office. Fagersanna is a small community located within the parish of Ransberg. In this case, if you found a letter with the name Fagersanna you would have to look at a map to understand that the community belongs to the parish Ransberg. With a detailed map with parish boundaries you can be sure. To complicate things further: not in every case is the village or community located in the parish with the nearest church. Sometimes the boundaries between the parishes are unpredictable. Then you have to look in the records of several adjoining parishes.

Kommun
Today's Municipalities

At the end of the nineteenth century each parish was also the local municipality or "township." In 1862 the old *socken* was turned into two separate entities – the church community (*församling*) and the civil rural municipality (*landskommun*). During the twentieth century the original 2,000 municipalities (plus towns and cities) have merged step by step into larger local units. Today Sweden has 289 municipalities, with populations varying from around 5,000 to 100,000 or more (the biggest is Stockholm). These modern municipalities (*kommuner*) typically include a city or town and the surrounding countryside, usually several old parishes. The borders follow the old parish boundaries.

Mölltorp's railroad station is not in use any more. The railroad from Karlsborg to Skövde was opened in 1876. Our emigrants Gustaf Adolf Rapp and Anna Christina Carlsson, discussed in detail in chapter seven, probably took the train from this station to Gothenburg.

Part of a small farm village.

Today a lot of people think of themselves as living in their kommun, although most people in the countryside still identify themselves as parishioners and know in which parish they reside. And the population records still name the parish beside the kommun. When you try to find current relatives in Sweden it is sometimes helpful to know the name of the kommun as well as the parish (and the län or landskap).

Names of Farms and Villages

In Sweden individual farms always have their individual names, often of very old origin, dating back to the Iron Age (the Viking age) or early medieval times. Sometimes there are names for whole villages, where the individual farms may have their own names (like Kvarngården, "the mill farm," or Norrgården, ("the Northern farm"). Swedish farm villages are usually small, compared to the large villages in many European countries. In many areas of Sweden there weren't any villages at all, but only single farmsteads.

If you have a name of a farm, in a letter or in a note, in a diary or on a photo, but no name of a parish, nor a mail address or a name of a nearby town, it may still be possible to trace the place. There are directories with all farms and villages listed. One was edited by Carl Martin Rosenberg and printed in 1883. It is in five volumes and was reprinted in 1982. The title of the book is *Geografiskt-Statistiskt handlexikon öfver Sverige* by C. M. Rosenberg, and it gives the geographic composition of Sweden at the time when the emigration was at its peak. The book is available at many archives and research institutions, as well as on microfilm from SVAR (more about SVAR on page 51).

In many cases there are numerous farms with identical names. The name Torp is one example. The word today means "smallholding", but is believed to have once had a wider meaning, that of a dwelling place in general, or a village. In Rosenberg's book there are 177 places with the name Torp, plus thirty-nine with the similar name Torpa. Most of these places are single farms or villages. A few are larger estates. Three places named Torp and five named Torpa are parishes. It's like the Anderssons — just too many with the same names.

Of course more modern directories of places are available at archives and libraries. One is *Svensk ortförteckning*, published by the Post office.

Rote [root-eh]

This term is often used in church records. Each parish was divided into several *rotar* (plural of *rote*). And the farms were entered in the book "rote by rote." The term was also used when farms kept the soldiers. Two or more farms (a rote) had the responsibility to maintain a soldier. See more about how the soldiers and their upkeep was organized on page 85.

When reading the records *rote* can be translated as "a group of farms" or "a part of a parish" used for administrative purposes. Also the towns were divided into *rotar*. In this case a good translation would be "ward."

Blocks and Street Numbers

The numbering of houses in Sweden is somewhat different than in the United States. The houses are given uneven numbers, starting with 1 (1,3,5,7...), on one side of the street and even numbers on the other side of the street (2,4,6,8...), with the numbering starting from the city center outward. Quite often apartment houses have several doors, numbered with letters (1A, 1B, 1C). The bottom floor is usually "bv" (*bottenvåningen*) or "n b" (*nedre botten*). The letters "ö g" (*över gården*) stand for the rear house in a city. Each block has a name and each lot within the block has a number. In the records these names and numbers are often given.

In Summary

Any kind of name is a clue: it may be a province, district, town, parish, village, farm, or street. And it should be noted. The very best is to find the parish name right away, but the other names can also lead in the right direction.

Cities in Sweden

▲ = capital of län
† = cathedral city

Sweden had, at the most, 133 cities or towns with a city charter. Some date back to medieval times, the youngest were chartered as late as 1951. Since 1970 no difference is made between cities and other municipalities — they all have the same name (*kommun*). Here are the traditional cities and towns with their location. The letters (within brackets) are often used to identify län. The letters were earlier used on the number plates of cars; an A-car came from Stockholm.

Stockholms stad (A)

Stockholm ▲ †

Stockholms län (B)

Djursholm
Lidingö
Nacka
Norrtälje
Nynäshamn
Sigtuna
Solna
Sundbyberg
Södertälje
Vaxholm

Uppsala län (C)

Enköping
Uppsala ▲ †
Öregrund (B before 1971)
Östhammar (B before 1971)

Södermanlands län (D)

Eskilstuna
Flen
Katrineholm
Mariefred
Nyköping ▲
Oxelösund
Strängnäs †
Torshälla
Trosa

Östergötlands län (E)

Linköping ▲ †
Mjölby
Motala
Norrköping
Skänninge
Söderköping
Vadstena

Jönköpings län (F)

Eksjö
Gränna
Huskvarna
Jönköping ▲
Nässjö
Sävsjö
Tranås
Vetlanda
Värnamo

Kronobergs län (G)

Ljungby
Växjö ▲ †

Haga Nygata, a street in Göteborg (Gothenburg) around the turn of the century 1900.

Kalmar län (H)

Borgholm
Kalmar ▲ (†)*
Nybro
Oskarshamn
Vimmerby
Västervik

Gotlands län (I)

Visby ▲ †

Blekinge län (K)

Karlshamn
Karlskrona ▲
Ronneby
Sölvesborg

Kristianstads län (L) – today part of Skåne län

Hässleholm
Kristianstad ▲
Simrishamn
Ängelholm

Malmöhus län (M) – today part of Skåne län

Eslöv
Helsingborg
Höganäs
Landskrona
Lund †
Malmö ▲
Skanör–Falsterbo
(originally two separate towns)
Trelleborg
Ystad

Hallands län (N)

Falkenberg
Halmstad ▲
Kungsbacka
Laholm
Varberg

* Kalmar has a cathedral, and there was a Kalmar diocese from 1678 until 1915.

Göteborgs och Bohus län (O) – today part of Västra Götalands län

Göteborg ▲ †
Kungälv
Lysekil
Marstrand
Mölndal
Strömstad
Uddevalla

Älvsborgs län (P) – today part of Västra Götalands län

Alingsås
Borås
Trollhättan
Ulricehamn
Vänersborg ▲
Åmål

Skaraborgs län (R) – today part of Västra Götalands län

Falköping
Hjo
Lidköping
Mariestad ▲
Skara †
Skövde
Tidaholm

Värmlands län (S)

Arvika
Filipstad
Hagfors
Karlstad ▲ †
Kristinehamn
Säffle

Örebro län (T)

Askersund
Karlskoga
Kumla
Lindesberg
Nora
Örebro ▲

Västmanlands län (U)

Arboga
Fagersta
Köping
Sala
Västerås ▲ †

Kopparbergs län (W) – today Dalarnas län

Avesta
Borlänge
Falun ▲
Hedemora
Ludvika
Säter

Gävleborgs län (X)

Bollnäs
Gävle ▲
Hudiksvall
Sandviken
Söderhamn

Västernorrlands län (Z)

Härnösand ▲ †
Kramfors
Sollefteå
Sundsvall
Örnsköldsvik

Jämtlands län (Y)

Östersund ▲

Västerbottens län (AC)

Lycksele
Skellefteå
Umeå ▲

Norrbottens län (BD)

Boden
Haparanda
Kiruna
Luleå ▲ †
Piteå

To be continued

Cities on Postcards

Skara is the cathedral city of the diocese where Mölltorp and Ransberg are located. The cathedral is one of Sweden's oldest; the first church was built in the eleventh century.

Skövde is one of the nearest cities to Mölltorp and Ransberg. The main railroad between Stockholm and Gothenburg passes through the city.

Kungsbacka on the west coast south of Gothenburg used to be a small town but has grown into a suburban community that is a part of the metropolitan area.

Cities in Alphabetical Order

Alingsås (P)
Arboga (U)
Arvika (S)
Askersund (T)
Avesta (W)
Boden (BD)
Bollnäs (X)
Borgholm (H)
Borlänge (W)
Borås (P)
Djursholm (B)
Eksjö (F)
Enköping (C)
Eslöv (M)
Eskilstuna (D)
Fagersta (U)
Falkenberg (N)
Falköping (R)
Falun (W)
Filipstad (S)
Flen (D)
Gränna (F)
Gävle (X)
Göteborg (O)
Hagfors (S)
Halmstad (N)
Haparanda (BD)
Hedemora (W)
Helsingborg (M)
Hjo (R)
Hudiksvall (X)
Huskvarna (F)
Härnösand (Y)
Hässleholm (L)
Höganäs (M)
Jönköping (F)
Kalmar (H)
Karlshamn (K)
Karlskoga (T)
Karlskrona (K)
Karlstad (S)
Katrineholm (D)
Kiruna (BD)
Kramfors (Y)
Kristianstad (L)
Kristinehamn (S)
Kumla (T)
Kungsbacka (N)
Kungälv (O)
Köping (U)
Laholm (N)
Landskrona (M)
Lidingö (B)
Lidköping (R)
Lindesberg (T)
Linköping (E)
Ljungby (G)
Ludvika (W)
Luleå (BD)
Lund (M)
Lycksele (AC)
Lysekil (O)
Malmö (M)
Mariefred (D)
Mariestad (R)
Marstrand (O)
Mjölby (E)
Motala (E)
Mölndal (O)
Nacka (B)
Nora (T)
Norrköping (E)
Norrtälje (B)
Nybro (H)
Nyköping (D)
Nynäshamn (B)
Nässjö (F)
Oskarshamn (H)
Oxelösund (D)
Piteå (BD)
Ronneby (K)
Sala (T)
Sandviken (X)
Sigtuna (B)
Simrishamn (L)
Skanör-Falsterbo (M)
Skara (R)
Skellefteå (AC)
Skänninge (E)
Skövde (R)
Sollefteå (Y)
Solna (B)
Stockholm (A)
Strängnäs (D)
Strömstad (O)
Sundbyberg (B)
Sundsvall (Y)
Säffle (S)
Säter (W)
Sävsjö (F)
Söderhamn (X)
Söderköping (E)
Södertälje (B)
Sölvesborg (K)
Tidaholm (R)
Torshälla (D)
Tranås (F)
Trelleborg (M)
Trollhättan (P)
Trosa (D)
Uddevalla (O)
Ulricehamn (P)
Umeå (AC)
Uppsala (C)
Vadstena (E)
Varberg (N)
Vaxholm (B)
Vetlanda (F)
Vimmerby (H)
Visby (I)
Vänersborg (P)
Värnamo (F)
Västervik (H)
Västerås (U)
Växjö (G)
Ystad (M)
Åmål (P)
Ängelholm (L)
Örebro (T)
Öregrund (C) (B before 1971)
Örnsköldsvik (Y)
Östersund (Z)
Östhammar (C) (B before 1971)

Letters within brackets show in what län the city is located.

The two most prominent Swedes. Queen Silvia came to Sweden from Germany in 1976, when she married, and her maiden name was Sommerlath. King Carl XVI Gustaf's royal family name is Bernadotte. He is a descendant to a French general who was elected crown prince of Sweden in 1810. So they both represent the hundreds of thousands of Swedes belonging to immigrant families with foreign family names.

CHAPTER FIVE

Swedish Names and Swedish Spelling

The most common types of family names in Sweden today are the "son-names" (Andersson, Johansson, Persson etc). Today they are used as true family names, which in itself is rather confusing, as so many have the same last names. Look in the Stockholm telephone directory — there are 42 pages of Anderssons and 37 pages of Johanssons! There are 162 Eva Anderssons in Stockholm alone. Of course not all of these Anderssons and Johanssons are members of the same family.

Andersson Eva Konsulent. Nykroppag. 25 FARSTA 604 8
Andersson Eva Grafiker Nynäsv. 28 D NYNÄSHAMN 520 2
Andersson Eva Nytorgsg. 11 A 643
Andersson Eva Oaxen HÖLÖ 551 5
Andersson Eva Observatorieg. 21 30
Andersson Eva Odelbergsv. 26 ENSKEDE GÅRD 649
Andersson Eva Olshammarsg. 54 BANDHAGEN 749
Andersson Eva Otto Bondes v. 72 ÅKERSBERGA 540 6
Andersson Eva Poppelv. 11 HUDDINGE 449
Andersson Eva Läkarsekr. Porlabacken 22 BANDHAGEN 647
Andersson Eva Prästvik 2A Pl 261 DROTTNINGHOLM 759
Andersson Eva Rapsodiv. 220 SKOGÅS 771
Andersson Ewa Robert Anbergs v. 27 SÖDERTÄLJE . 550 8
Andersson Eva Roslagsg. 6 21
Anderson Eva Russinv. 14 FARSTA 604
Andersson Eva Råstav. 8 A SOLNA 83
Andersson Eva Rörstrandsg. 26 33
Andersson Eva S:t Eriksg. 37 B 652
Andersson Eva Saltarö 6 VÄRMDÖ 571 6
Andersson Eva Sandfjärdsg. 10 ÅRSTA 91
Andersson Eva Serenadv. 12 NACKA 718 2
Anderson Eva o. Göran Vallström Sidensvansv. 26 SOLLENTUNA 35
Andersson Eva Sjöbjörnsv. 14 18
Andersson Eva Skarpgränd 7 TÄBY 768
Andersson Ewa Skogsbacken 29 SUNDBYBERG 28
Andersson Ewa Skolrådsv. 14 HANINGE 742
Andersson Eva Skvadronsbacken 61 SUNDBYBERG 733
Andersson Eva o. Jan Skärblackav. 8 ENSKEDE 81
Andersson Eva Skönviksv. 283 ENSKEDE 647
Andersson Eva o. Gösta Skönviksv. 294 ENSKEDE 647
Anderson Eva o. Håkan Smala Gränd 3 21
Andersson Eva Spireabågen 47 HÄSSELBY 38
Andersson Eva o. Rolf Dahlqvist St. Gungans v. 9 ENSKEDE 39
Andersson Eva Stagneliusv. 42 656
Andersson Eva Starrgränd 34 SOLLENTUNA 754
Andersson Eva o. Jan Bollemo Stationsv. 6 HUDDINGE 711
Andersson Eva Stenbrottsv. 26 A HUDDINGE 711
Andersson Ewa Stigtomtav. 3 ÄLVSJÖ 86
Andersson Eva Strindbergsv. 9 A SÖDERTÄLJE 550 3
Andersson Eva Stupv. 6 TUMBA 530 3
Andersson Eva Stupv. 8 TUMBA 530 3
Andersson Eva Störtloppsv. 24 HÄGERSTEN 88 8
Andersson Eva Fru Stöttingsgränd 4 HÄGERSTEN 88 5

Excerpt from a Swedish telephone directory.

The "son-names" are so-called patronymic names. Nils Andersson was "Nils, Anders' son" (the son to Anders). If Nils had a son, he would consequently be a Nilsson. If he had a daughter she would be a Nilsdotter (dotter = daughter). The patronymic names were used in this way until about 100 to 150 years ago.

See illustration on the next page.

When the priest made his entries in the church records he always made them in this manner, until these names became family names. A family at the beginning of the nineteenth century might consist of a man, Anders Olofsson; his wife, Sara Jonsdotter; and their children Cajsa, Johan, and Lisa. The children would have no last names noted in the church books, but as adults they would be known as Cajsa Andersdotter, Johan Andersson, and Lisa Andersdotter.

Later on, during the twentieth century, a similar family would probably have the common family name Olofsson, both males and females. The parents and their three children would be: Anders and Sara, Cajsa, Johan, and Lisa Olofsson.

The change from patronymic names to family names has taken place with differing speeds in different parts of Sweden. The old practice was kept longer in more traditional areas. The patronymic naming system is still in use on Iceland, and in the Icelandic phone book the names are listed according to first names.

Note that the Swedish son-names traditionally always were spelled with a double s. The reason is simple. The first s is the genetive s, just like in English, expressing ownership or possession. The second s is the s in "son" (Andersson and Nilsson should actually have three s's, since the names Anders and Nils also end with an s). When Swedes moved to America they often dropped one s, for practical reasons. Many Swedes in Sweden today also spell such names with just one s, although this is not logical.

Note that the Swedish patronymic ending is always "son", never "sen." In Denmark the regular patronymic

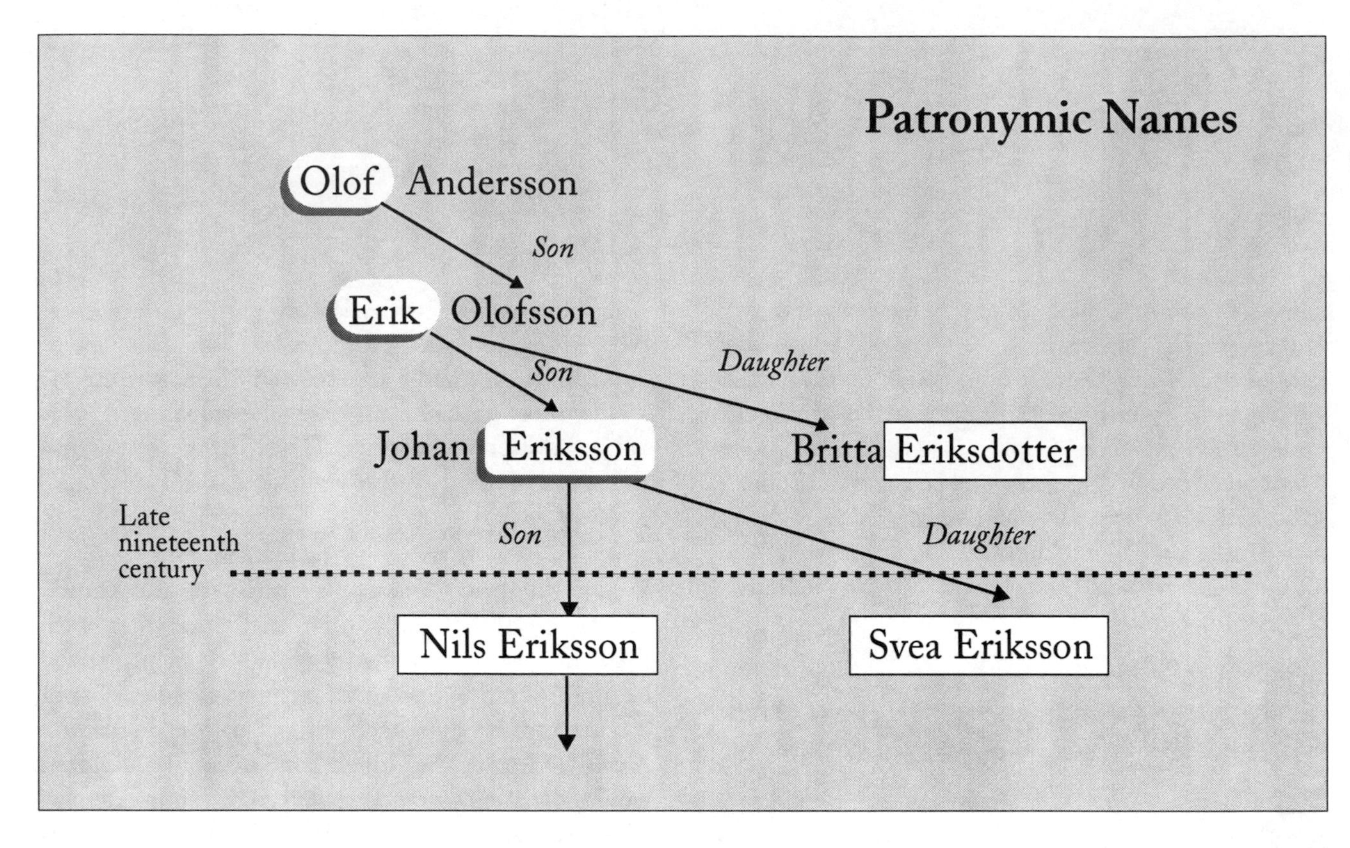

is "sen." In Norway, "sen" is more common although "son" also occurs frequently. The Icelandic names end with "son" or "dotir." A Swedish "sen" has probably immigrated from Norway or Denmark to Sweden. An American "son" is in often of Swedish, and sometimes of Norwegian or Icelandic descent, whereas a "sen" is usually of Danish or Norwegian descent. But note, there are also Scottish and British Andersons and Johnsons! There is also a relatively large Swedish speaking minority in Finland, with son-names.

The Most Common Son-names

The numbers given after the names are the number of pages for each name in the Stockholm phone book (each page contains about 350 entries).

Andersson	42.5
Karlsson, Carlsson	40.5
Eriksson, Ericsson	39.5
Johansson	37.5
Nilsson	26
Larsson	23
Pettersson, Peterson	21
Gustavsson, Gustafsson	21
Olsson	20.5
Jonsson	16.5
Jansson	15.5
Persson, Pärsson	15.5
Svensson	14.5
Hansson	7.5
Jakobsson, Jacobsson	6.5
Bengtsson	5
Magnusson	5
Mattsson, Matsson	5
Olofsson	4
Danielsson	4
Fredriksson	4
Axelsson	3.5
Jönsson	3

Some names are more common in certain regions. In southern Sweden (Skåne) Jönsson, Månsson, and Pålsson (Paulsson) are much more common than in other parts of Sweden.

The large numbers of these names show that names like Anders, Karl, Erik, Johan, Nils, Lars, Petter, Gustaf, and Olof (Olle) were very common in the Swedish countryside at the middle and end of the nineteenth century. You will also frequently find these names in every church register from this time. Beware! It's easy to get lost among all these men and boys named Anders, Petter, or Erik — as well as among all the girls and women called Anna, Kristina, or Johanna.

Different Forms of Son-names

Many of the son-names can appear in different spellings and forms. Johannes, Johan, and John are just different versions of the same name. The same is true of the patronymic names based on these variations. Different versions are often found in different church books and other records pertaining to the same person and written by the same priest.

Here are some of the variations on some common names (the colon ":" was used in records to shorten the name):

Johansson – Jaensson, Jansson, Jeansson, Joansson, Johannesson, Johnsson, Joh:son, Jonasson, Jonsson, Jönsson, (J:son, Hansson)

Mattiasson – Mathiasson, Mattesson, Matthiasson, Mattisson, Matsson

Olofsson – Olausson, Olovsson, Olsson, Olzon, Ol:son

Pettersson – Pedersson, Persson, Petersson, Petrusson, Pet:son

Different Forms of First Names

First names also appear with many variations. Anders and Andreas, for example, could be used as different spellings for the same name. Here are some other examples:

Anna – Aina, Anita, Ann, Anne, Anette, Annie, Annika, Anny

Britta - Birgit, Birgitta, Brigitta, Brit, Brita

Catarina – Cajsa, Cari, Carin, Carna, Catharina, Catrin, Kajsa, Kari, Karin, Karna, Katarina, Katinka, Katrin

Christina – Christin, Christine, Kerstin, Kirsti, Kristin, Kristina, Kristine, Stina

Elisabet – Betty, Elise, Elsa, Else, Lisa, Lisbet, Lisken

Johan – Jaen, Jan, Janne, Jean, Jens, Joan, Joen, Johannes, John, Jon, Jonas, Jöns (Hans)

Margareta – Greta, Maggie, Maret, Margit, Marit, Marta, Märta

Maria – Maj, Maja, Mariana, Marianne, Marie, Marika, Marja, Mary, Mia (Majken)

Olof – Ola, Olaus, Olav, Olle, Oluf

Petter – Peder, Pehr, Pelle, Per, Petrus, Peter, Pär

Family Names

Among certain groups in traditional Swedish society other kinds of names were used rather than the son-names discussed above.

The nobility, which never consisted of more than one percent of the population, had special noble names, such as Bonde, af Trolle, von Rosen, and Drakenberg. The family name was usually adopted when the man was raised to knighthood by the king. Some of the nobility came to Sweden from other countries: Denmark, Germany, the Baltic countries, and Poland. You can find the nobility listed in certain printed calendars, like *Adelskalendern* (The Peerage) published by Riddarhuset (the Noble House).

This is the shield for the noble family von Hall.

Priests often adopted names with Greek or Roman endings (-ander, -ius) formed from the names of the parishes where they served or their birthplaces (Fallander, Bolander, Ekselius, Morelius, etc).

Very few noble people emigrated. A few priests did, and some served in the Swedish Lutheran churches in America.

Soldiers were given names when they were contracted, even if they had regular patronymic names before.

These soldier names sometimes expressed a personal quality like Stark (strong), Rapp (quick), Hurtig (dashing, brisk), or Fager (good looking). Some names were military, like Pantzar or Kula (bullet). The names could also be associated with the place where the soldier served, like Loberg, who was a soldier for Logården. Soldier's names can be confusing. Often a new soldier at the same place would be given his predecessors name, even if they were not related. The name was usually given by an officer of the regiment when the soldier was contracted.

Burgers (in the towns) and artisans sometimes had names connected to their trades or professions. However, this was not as common as in England or Germany, where names like Miller (Müller), Fisher (Fischer), Smith (Schmidt), Schumacher, and Bauer are very common.

Many townspeople and others who didn't want to be perceived as "common folks" or wanted to distance themselves from the peasants adopted special family names. The name was an important social marker.

During the nineteenth century more and more people took their own family names. There was no legislation regulating this and many families took the same names. Some were quite common, such as Lindberg, Berggren, Lundberg, Lundgren, Lindkvist, Lindström etc. The famous movie director Ingmar Bergman and the actress Ingrid Bergman share one of these common names, but are not related. Many of these names are composed of features of nature, and these types of family names are sometimes called "nature names." The names are just combinations of nature features; the combinations don't necessarily make sense, as with Dalberg, which is composed of "dal" (valley) and "berg" (mountain). These names have been used all over Sweden and they cannot be used to trace the ancestry to a specific region or area.

Here is a list of the meaning of such components:

Common Primarily First Parts of Nature Names

Al	alder
Alm	elm
Ask	ash
Asp	aspen
Bjur	beaver (old word)
Björk	birch
Björn	bear
Bo	nest, living place
Bok	beech
Bro	bridge
By	village, shower
Ceder	cedar
Ed	place where boats were pulled around a waterfall or from one lake to another
Ek	oak

+ = EKBERG

Gran	fir (tree)
Grön	green
Hag	pasture (hage)
Hall	see Häll (old meaning)
Hammar	mountain, rock (old meaning)
Hassel	hazel
Hed	moor
Häll, Hell	flat rock
Hult	forest (old meaning)
Hägg	bird cherry
Hög	high
Käll	spring (källa)
Lind	linden
Ljung	heather
Lönn	maple
Malm	ore, sand area
Nor	narrow straight
Nord, Norr	north
Ny	new
Näs	isthmus, point
Ros, Rosen	rose
Sand	sand
Sjö	lake
Skog	forest
Sund	strait
Svan	swan
Söder	south
Törn	thorn
Val, Wal	whale
Väst, West, Wester	west

Vik, Wik	bay
Å, Åh	small river
Åker	field
Ås	ridge
Älv, Elv, Elf	big river
Äng, Eng	meadow
Ö, Öh	island
Öst, Öster	east

Common First or Second Halves of Nature Names

Berg	mountain
Borg	burg, castle
Blom	flower (blomma)
Bäck, Beck	creek
Dal, Dahl	valley
Fors	rapids
Holm	little island (holme)
Mark	ground, field
Lund	woods
Löv, Löf	leaf
Sten	stone
Strand	beach
Ström	stream
Vall, Wall	pasture

Common Primarily Second Halves of Nature Names

Blad	leaf
Fält	field
Gren	branch
Kvist, Qvist	twig
Man	man
Rot	root
Stedt	place

Sometimes a single word can make up the whole family name, like Blom (flower), Brant (steep hillside), Falk (falcon) or Holm (little island).

In the last century name changes have been regulated by law and switching from son-names to other names has been encouraged by the authorities. After all, it is not practical to have hundreds or thousands of people with identical names and a majority of the population with just a handful of common son-names. Today, if you adopt a new family name, it has to be a truly new name, one that is not carried by any other family. Today at marriage it is also possible for the wedded couple to use either spouse's last name. This way the number of "son-names" gradually decreases.

Names From Other Countries

Immigration has also introduced new names to Sweden. The seventeenth century saw an influx of iron workers from the Netherlands. In the following centuries traders, entrepreneurs, artisans, and artists came from Holland, France, Italy, England, Scotland, and many other countries. In the twentieth century Sweden needed labour from southern Europe (Italy, Greece, Yugoslavia, and Turkey), and later gave refuge to large groups of refugees from the Middle East, Eastern Europe, the Balkans, and Africa.

Throughout history, people from Finland have settled in Sweden through the history, since Finland was part of Sweden until it was conquered by Russia in 1809. In the sixteenth and seventeenth century Finnish farmers took up slash and burn farming in the mid-dle Swedish forest areas. Other Finns worked in Stockholm as servants and labourers. During the twentieth century Finnish workers came in tens of thousands to work in Swedish industry. All these immigrants brought their names to Sweden and many of these names have been kept by the families.

Old and New Spelling

Around the turn of the twentieth century Swedish spelling was reformed and some old practices were abandoned. These changes can sometimes make it difficult to find a name in a register, directory, biography, or dictionary.

- In the old spelling the v-sound was written fv inside a word, and hv at the beginning of a word. In the new spelling the f and h were dropped.
  Example: öfver (over) was from now on spelled över. Hafva (have) changed to hava. Hvad (what) was changed to vad.
- At the end of words the v-sound was spelled f, and after the reform v.
  Example: af (by, off) became av. Löf (leaf) became löv. In family names f is still sometimes used instead of v. The name Lövgren can be spelled Löfgren or even Lööfgren.

These changes were made in 1906. Some other changes had already been made around 1889:

- In some cases e was substituted with ä.
  Example: embetsverk (governmental agency) was changed to ämbetsverk. Enka (widow) was changed

to änka. In names of persons and places this can be a problem. Älvsborgs län was spelled Elfsborgs län. In some cases people and companies still spell in the old fashion, which adds a quaint quality.

- In old spelling qu or qv was sometimes used instead of kv. As of 1906 only kv was used and the letter q was practically taken out of use.
  Example: qvinna (woman) was always spelled kvinna.
- In some names Q is still sometimes used, like Qvarnström (kvarn = mill).
- Another change was that gt sometimes changed to kt.
  Example: magt (power, might) became makt. The combination dt was changed to single t or double tt. These changes are not so common in names.

Some Examples of Old and New Spelling

All of these examples are names of parishes from the area around Mölltorp (Skaraborgs län).

Old spelling	New spelling
fv – v	
Sköfvde	Skövde
Hofva	Hova
hv – v	
Hvarf	Varv
f – v	
Grefbäck	Grevbäck
Hvarf	Varv
e – ä	
Bellefors	Bällefors
Elgarås	Älgarås
qv (qu) – kv	
Qvänum	Kvänum
gt – kt	
(no examples)	

Sometimes other alterations occur. Grevbäck is also named Gredbäck. The parish Varola is often written Valora (or Warola – Walora).

Alteration of Swedish Names by Immigrants to America or Canada

When the Swedes settled in the United States and Canada they quite often changed their family names, sometimes the spelling, but often the pronunciation as well. Some families adopted a completely new family name. The purpose was to make the names easier to use in the new environment. The double s in the son-names was quickly dropped. Nilsson became Nelson, Svensson became Swanson, Andersson became Anderson, and so on. Here are some other typical changes:

Bengtsson – Bentson, Benson
Eriksson – Erickson
Grönlund – Greenlund (grön = green)
Johansson – Johnson
Kjellström – Callstrom
Ljungkvist (or Ljungquist) – Youngquist
Pärsson – Pearson
Sjöberg – Seeberg or Seaberg (sjö = sea, lake)
Söderberg – Soderberg (söder = south)

The Swedish letters å, ä, ö turned into a and o. Typical Swedish letter combinations like tj, kj, lj and gj were dropped or changed. A c was often inserted before k: ik and ek often became ick and eck.

Also first names could be altered, "Americanized," and often shortened. Johannes and Johan became John, Valdemar became Wally, Gustaf became Gus, Fredrik became Fred, Maria became Mary and so on. If the first name was odd or difficult to use in the new environment the second name could be used instead, or a completely new name was adopted. Therefore, always be sure to note both first and second names.

Good to Know About the Swedish Language and Swedish Spelling

There are twenty-eight letters in the Swedish alphabet: ABCDEFGHIJKLMNOPQRSTUVXYZÅÄÖ

Å, Ä, and Ö are treated as separate letters and stand for distinctive and separate vowel sounds. They are not an "umlaut" like in German. Forget all comparison to German. Swedes don't see any connection between A and Ä or O and Ö. They are just as separate as E and I. Ä is close to E, and Å is close to O, in pronunciation.

The vowels are often pronounced in a very different manner than in English.

The Q is almost never used, except in a few last names. The same goes for Z.

W is not treated like a separate letter, and can be used alternately with V. The English w-sound does not exist in Swedish and a written W is pronounced like a V. In lists, directories, phone books, and dictionaries V and W are listed together under the same section.

C is sometimes used instead of K in names. Karlsson – Carlsson provides the most common example. This rarely occurs with geographical names.

The combination tj and the letter k before a "soft vowel" (e, i, y, ä, ö) is pronounced like a very soft ch-sound (like the German ch in ich).

Standardized Swedish Spelling

A compulsory school was introduced in 1842, but there were schools in most parishes even before that, and most Swedes already knew how to read and write in the eighteenth century. However, spelling varied greatly in the eighteenth century and earlier. If you study church records before 1840 you will find that spelling was very individual, and it will often be a challenge to interpret both handwriting and spelling. Different priests used different spelling.

In 1801 the Swedish Academy published a spelling guide which, for the first time, gave standardized Swedish spelling rules. But not until 1874 were these spelling guidelines adopted by the academy as an official Swedish dictionary. The Swedish Academy still publishes the dictionary that defines what is standard Swedish.

TAB. IX.

Model af Cursiv Skrift N°4.

25

Latin and German Writing

Two major types of handwriting were in use during the eighteenth and nineteenth centuries: Latin (or Classic) and German. Many varieties and individual styles were used, but as schools became more common handwriting became more and more standardized. The Latin style is usually easy to interpret, whereas the German style can be difficult, at least at the beginning.

In 1794 Carl Beckman published a short instruction for proper handwriting (*Grunderne til skrif-konsten*). It includes ten pages showing different styles and alphabets. This page (to the left) shows how to write the letters in cursive German handwriting. The original page is larger.

Name Calendars and Name Days

Swedes celebrate name days. 8 July is, for example, the Kjell day, and Per has his name day on 1 August. The name days go back to the medieval Saint's calendars. The name calendar has been revised at certain intervals to include more modern names and exclude names that have gone out of use. Lately the calendar has been changed to include more than one name for each date. The name days are celebrated almost like birthdays. Friends can get together for a cup of coffee and cake on a name day, and greeting cards and presents can be given.

Certain name days had, historically, special interest attached to them in the old farming society. If the rye had formed ears on the Erik day (18 May), then there would be new bread on the Olof day (29 July). *Om Erik ger ax så ger Olof kaka* (If Eric gives ears, then Olof gives cake). Similarly, if it were frost and cold (below freezing point) on Anders' day (30 November), it would be mild with sloppy weather on Christmas. The opposite was also true: a mild Anders' day predicted a cold Christmas. Midsummer's Eve was on Johannes' day on 24 June. Indian summer in Sweden is called *Brittsommar* (Britt's summer) after the Birgitta day, 7 October. Michael's day, 29 September, was the day when a farm hand could change his employment. The end of September and beginning of October were also the time of fairs and markets. The farmer often let his job be directed more by the calendar than by the weather.

Here is an old calendar from 1850, the days of the early emigration from Sweden. The calendar lists all the traditional name days, and the positions of the moon and the planets, sunrises and sunsets, all for Stockholm (59 degrees, 20.5 minutes north). The month of July was also called hay-month (*hö-månad*). Note that Christina's name day was on 24 July. The Anna day is on 9 December. The six days from 19 July until 24 July are called the women's week (*fruntimmersveckan*), because of the name days: Sara, Margareta, Johanna, Magdalena, Emma, Kristina. During these days a lot of Swedish women celebrate their name days. The cal-endar also shows the movements of the sun, the moon and the planets, and even predicts the weather. On 22 July the "rotting month" (*rötmånad*) began, the period of late summer when food and other products would more easily rot and decay.

JULIUS,

Dagar			Mån.	Upp	Wäderleken	G.st.
1	M	Aron	♓	11.53	Regn	Jun. 19
2	T	Mar. Besök.	♓	f. m.	(☉ Fjärmast	20
3	O	Anatolius	♈	0. 8	◑ kl. 7.11 e. m.	21
4	T	Ulrica	♈	0.23	Warmt	22
5	F	Melcher	♈	0.40	och	23
6	L	Esaias	♈	1. 2	Solrök	24
		Om Phariseernas Rättfärdighet, Matth. 5.				
7	S	★ 6 e. Tref.	♈	1.30	★ 3 Böndagen	25
8	M	Kilian	♊	2. 9	Claes)	26
9	T	Cyrillus	♊	Ned	● kl. 3.40 e. m.	27
10	O	Canutus	♋	9.28	☾ Närmast	28
11	T	Eleonora	♋	10. 2	☊ Solrök	29
12	F	Herman	♌	10.27	—	30
13	L	Joel	♌	10.47	—	Jul. 1
		Om Christi Förklaring, Matth. 17.				
14	S	★ 7 e. Tref.	♍	11. 4	Phocas	2
15	M	Apostl. Deln.	♍	11.20	Mulet	3
16	T	Reinhold	♎	11.36	◐ kl. 7.54 f. m.	4

☉ Dag.	Upp T.m.	Midd. T.m.	Ned T.m.	☉ Dag.	Upp T.m.	Midd. T.m.	Ned T.m.
1	2.51	12.3	9.15	9	3. 1	12.5	9. 8
3	2.53	12.4	9.14	11	3. 4	12.5	9. 5
5	2.55	12.4	9.12	13	3. 7	12.5	9. 2
7	2.58	12.5	9.10	15	3.11	12.6	8.59

Hö-Månad.

Dagar			Mån.	Ned	Wäderleken	G.st.
17	O	Alexius	♎	11.53	Solrök	5
18	T	Fredric	♏	f. m.	—	6
19	F	Sara	♏	0.13	Regn	7
20	L	Margaretha	♏	0.38	Klart	8
		Om de falska Propheter, Matth. 7.				
21	S	★ 8 e. Tref.	♐	1. 9	Johanna	9
22	M	Magdalena	♐	1.48	(Rötm. början	10
23	T	Emma	♑	2.37	☉ i ♌	11
24	O	Christina	♑	Upp	○ kl. 6.36 f. m.	12
25	T	Jacobus	♑	9.11	☾ Fjärmast) ☋	13
26	F	Martha	♒	9.30	Klart	14
27	L	7 Sofware	♒	9.47	—	15
		Om den otrogne Gårdsfogden, Luc. 16.				
28	S	★ 9 e. Tref.	♓	10. 2	Botwid	16
29	M	Olof	♓	10.16	Warmt	17
30	T	Abdon	♓	10.31	—	18
31	O	Helena	♈	10.46	—	19

☉ Dag.	Upp T.m.	Midd. T.m.	Ned T.m.	☉ Dag.	Upp T.m.	Midd. T.m.	Ned T.m.
17	3.14	12.6	8.56	25	3.30	12.6	8.41
19	3.18	12.6	8.52	27	3.35	12.6	8.36
21	3.22	12.6	8.49	29	3.39	12.6	8.32
23	3.26	12.6	8.45	31	3.43	12.6	8.27

CHAPTER SIX

Where to Find Your Sources

The basis for research into the family history in Sweden is the local church archives. These "church books" are kept at the regional archives around the country. They are available on microfilm and microfiche and are currently also being published on the Internet. By 2005 all the historic local church archives, registers before around 1895, will be available on the Internet through Genline.

In this chapter we will tell you where to find the records you need for your research. First we will describe the church books, then the regional archives. After that we will describe the services offered by Genline. Then we will give information about microfilm and microfiche and list some institutions where you can get help and do your research.

The Role of the Local Church

The Swedish priests were both religious and secular leaders in the local community. They preached on Sundays, baptized and performed weddings and funerals, and took care of all the other obligations of priesthood. But they were also the leaders of the local community. The priest was the chairman of the "parish meeting" and the "parish board," the local communal institutions where the common issues of the parish were discussed and decided. All parishioners had a right to participate. Minutes were kept, and were saved in the church books.

The priest was also a representative of the government on the local level. He helped keep records of taxes and conscriptions of troops. During the frequent wars he was obliged to speak in favor of the war effort. The sermons were used as a means of information and propaganda by the state and the regional governors. The pulpit was the main channel for information before newspapers and other mass media were established.

In summary: the Swedish State Lutheran Church was an important and completely integrated part of the strong Swedish centralized national state. It was also an important part of longstanding local self-governance.

The Church Books

One of the priest's main functions was to keep records of the population. This obligation was regulated in the Church law of 1686, where it was stated that the priest was to keep records of all people moving in and out of the parish as well as the births and baptisms, deaths and burials, banns and marriages. Registers were also kept of the household examinations, where all the parishioners were asked about their knowledge of the Christian faith. These household examination records became the main population registers, because they included all parishioners and gave a total overview of the whole population, village by village, farm by farm. Today they are the main source for genealogical research in Sweden.

Later in the book we will present examples out of different Swedish sources and give further information about the different types of books and records in the church archives.

The church books were kept by the priest at the church, in the vestry, or at the vicarage, usually in a large chest. Different priests were naturally more or less meticulous in their record keeping. From time to time the bishop would travel around the parishes in the diocese to make inspections (so called visitations), and he then would check to see that the records were in good order.

Complete Records

As a rule the Swedish church records are of very good quality, and they are quite complete. Most Swedish churches are old stone structures and fires have been relatively rare. Sweden has not been at war since 1815 nor has it been invaded by foreign troops since the early sixteenth century, with the exception of some border regions or coastal areas. As a result, most records are available. Not all parishes have records from 1688 onward, when the church law was in effect. In many cases the series start later, or they are incomplete. Sometimes the different types of records were kept in a common book. Occasionally there are much older books, dating from as early as 1608.

When church books have been destroyed or damaged, the reason is usually fire. Sometimes they are badly damaged by water from flooding or leaks. Mice can also be a threat to old books. When church records are lost or damaged you can usually find genealogical information in tax records or land records. In general, the information obtained this way is not as detailed as the information in the church books.

At the end of this book you will find a list of the few parishes where the church records have been lost or destroyed.

The Regional Archives

All the church records from before 1895 have long been kept in the regional archives, and are kept there under safe conditions. They have been microfilmed and copied. Only in exceptional cases will an amateur researcher get access to the original books. Research is regularly done on microfilm or in copybooks or via the Internet.

The Swedish church kept the official Swedish population records until 1 July 1991. When this task was transferred from the state church to the taxation authority in 1991 all the records between 1895 and 1991 also had to be delivered to the regional archives. This has been a big undertaking and the work is now largely done. These records are also being microfilmed.

Sweden has nine regional archives in all, each with its own district, usually comprising one or several "län." There is also a National Archive in Stockholm, but all of the books of importance to the amateur genealogist are kept in the regional archives.

The regional archives also maintain other types of records of importance to genealogical research, such as tax records, land records, and court records.

The Nine Regional Archives and Their Districts

These are the nine regional archives and their districts:

Location – City	District (län)
Göteborg (Gothenburg)	Västra Götalands län (Göteborgs och Bohus län, Älvsborgs län, Skaraborgs län)
Härnösand	Norrbottens län, Västerbottens län, Västernorrlands län, Gävleborgs län
Karlstad	Värmlands län
Lund (Malmö)	Skåne län (Malmöhus län, Kristianstads län), Blekinge län, Hallands län
Stockholm (Stockholms stadsarkiv)	Stockholms län
Uppsala	Södermanlands län, Örebro län, Västmanlands län, Uppsala län, Dalarnas län (Kopparbergs län)
Vadstena	Östergötlands län, Jönköpings län, Kronobergs län, Kalmar län
Visby	Gotlands län
Östersund	Jämtlands län

Former names of län in brackets.
See also page 31.

In Stockholm the city archives (*Stockholms stadsarkiv*) has the same function as a regional archive. The city archive in Malmö has the role of regional archive in the city of Malmö in cooperation with the regional archives in Lund.

Microfilm

Between 1948 and 1963, The Church of Jesus Christ of Latter-day Saints (the Mormons) microfilmed 100 million pages out of the Swedish archives. The 61,000 rolls of films include all the church books before 1895, court records and estate declarations before 1860, tax records before 1860, land records before 1750, emigrant records and military records before 1900. These microfilms are kept by the church in Salt Lake City, and they are available to the public for research. A copy of the film was also donated to the Swedish state and is kept by the National archives. From this copy film further copies have been made.

Today most research is done on microfiche, and increasingly on scanned images published on the Internet. The Swedish National Archives has a special department named SVAR (*Svensk Arkivinformation*) that produces, handles, lends, sells and publishes images from the Swedish archives to researchers and libraries. Up till recently the major activity was production of microfiche. But SVAR now has discontinued the production of microfiche, and all new production is of scanned images. The old microfiche stock has been sold to the public. Still microfilm and microfiche is available at libraries, archives and research centers throughout Sweden, but microfiche of the historic church records can no longer be purchased from SVAR. Each regional archive has copies of the microfilm from its own region. The same is often also true for local libraries. SVAR's catalog, produced to list the available microfilm, still gives a very good picture of what records are available, parish by parish (see page 56). The catalog can be accessed on SVAR's website.

The microfilm is of course also available at the Family History Library and through the 3,500 Family History Centers throughout the world, operated by The Church of Jesus Christ of Latter-day Saints. In Sweden these centers keep microfilm of the records from the region. Genealogists can order microfilm from the Family History Center nearest to them, and the film will be sent directly to the center for their use. It takes a few weeks to get the microfiche, which means that long-distance research can become time-consuming.

Genline – Swedish Church Records on the Web

A quick and practical alternative to ordering microfiche is to access the church records directly on the Internet. A private Swedish company, Genline, publishes the Swedish church records on the Internet, and the entire collection is now available. The film used for this publication is the Mormon microfilm, the copies owned by the National Archives in Sweden. Genline has developed an efficient method to scan the microfilm. The company has also developed a program, Genline FamilyFinder®, by which you can easily search and find the documents from individual parishes and years. The program itself is an excellent index to the enormous number of church archives and documents.

Through Genline you can get access to each individual page from every church book from every parish in Sweden, from the earliest books until around 1897. Genline now also scans and publishes later church records, up to 1937. These records will eventually be available for all of Sweden. For details, see Genline's website. So you can conduct your research from your own computer, without the delay caused by waiting for microfiche in the mail. And you don't have to visit a Family History Center or an archive in Sweden. Everything can be done from your own home.

There is of course a cost, an annual or monthly fee, but this cost is small compared to the cost of renting or buying microfiche or traveling to your sources. Consider also the convenience and time saved.

Is the picture quality good enough? The scanned microfilm is sometimes murky or vague, as may also be the case with the original documents. At the scanning Genline tries to adjust the quality of the pictures. With the program you can also make blow-ups, adjust the light, and in other ways manipulate the picture to get the best image possible. You need a good computer and a reasonably fast modem. Broadband is helpful, but it is not necessary to use the program. The technical features of the program have been developed to guarantee that most users will be able to access and use the pictures with good quality.

Is there information in the program in English? Yes, but you will still need assistance in understanding what's written in the books. For that reason we wrote this book.

Beside Genline other alternatives are now introduced on the web. AD OnLine has a service similar to Genline's. But unlike Genline the website is so far only in Swedish. AD OnLine's images are scanned from new digital pictures in color taken of the church records. The Swedish National Archives (SVAR) will step by step publish historic documents on its website, e.g. population records from after 1895 and old tax records (*mantalslängder*). Both AD OnLine and SVAR charge a fee similar to that of Genline for

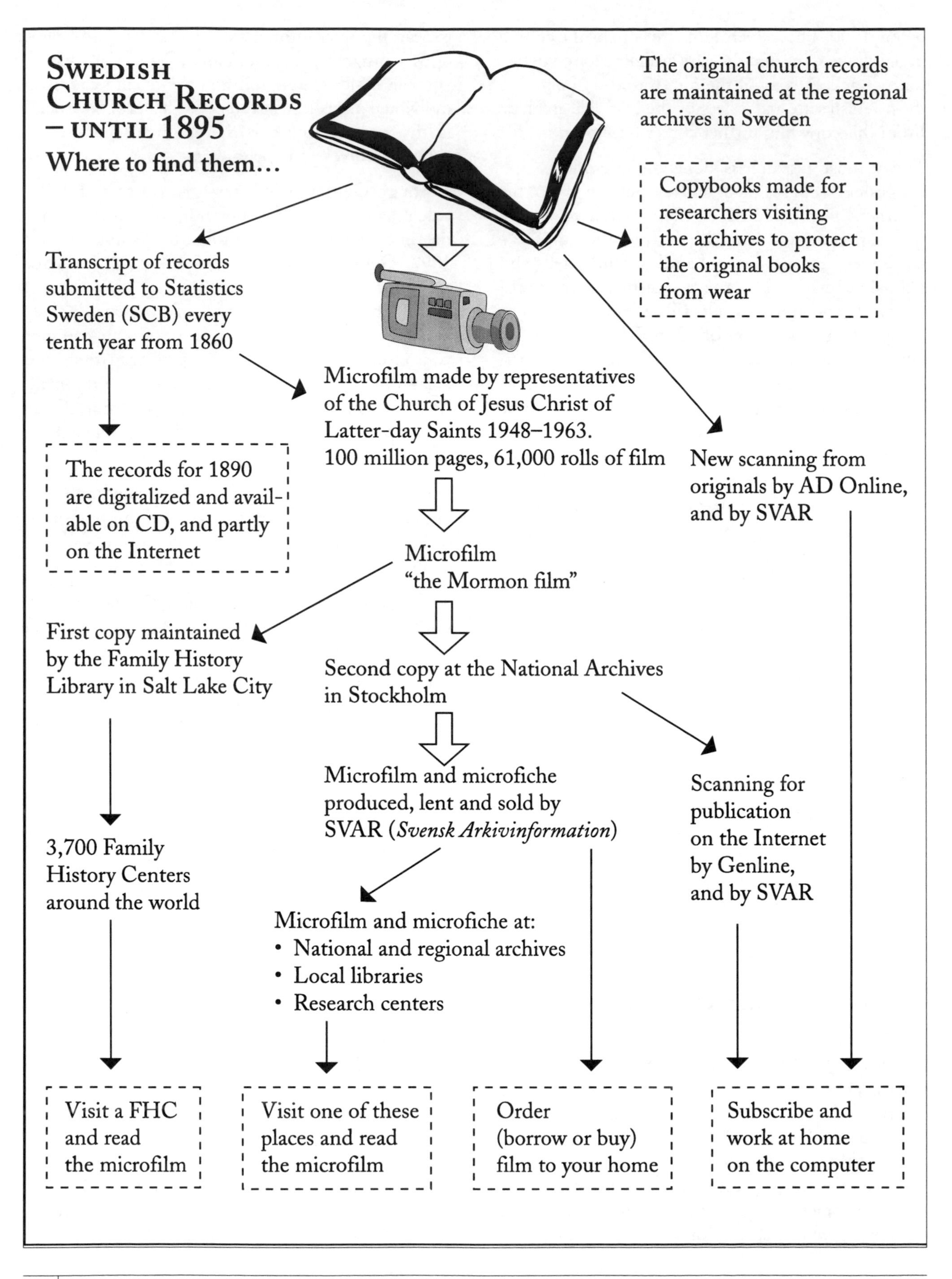
Swedish Church Records – until 1895
Where to find them…
The original church records are maintained at the regional archives in Sweden
Copybooks made for researchers visiting the archives to protect the original books from wear
Transcript of records submitted to Statistics Sweden (SCB) every tenth year from 1860
The records for 1890 are digitalized and available on CD, and partly on the Internet
Microfilm made by representatives of the Church of Jesus Christ of Latter-day Saints 1948–1963.
100 million pages, 61,000 rolls of film
New scanning from originals by AD Online, and by SVAR
Microfilm
"the Mormon film"
First copy maintained by the Family History Library in Salt Lake City
Second copy at the National Archives in Stockholm
Microfilm and microfiche produced, lent and sold by SVAR (Svensk Arkivinformation)
Scanning for publication on the Internet by Genline, and by SVAR
3,700 Family History Centers around the world
Microfilm and microfiche at:
• National and regional archives
• Local libraries
• Research centers
Visit a FHC and read the microfilm
Visit one of these places and read the microfilm
Order (borrow or buy) film to your home
Subscribe and work at home on the computer

access to the digital databases. In the coming years we will probably see a fast growth in the amount of records available on the web.

To Summarize – Where Do You Find the Sources?

The information needed is primarily to be found in the Swedish church records. They are available:

1. In the nine regional archives in Sweden. You can travel there for your research, but you will not be able to study the original books.
2. On microfilm or microfiche. These can be read at a number of archives and libraries, and they can be rented or purchased. The microfilm is also available at the regional archives and at the Family History Centers.
3. On the web through Genline.

Research Centers in Sweden

There are a number of research centers in Sweden where researchers can work with Swedish microfilm and also get help from experienced personnel. SVAR, the unit within the Swedish National Archives that produces microfiche, has a research center in Ramsele in the interior of northern Sweden. In Leksand, located in Dalarna in the middle of Sweden, there is a "House of Genealogy" (*Släktforskarnas hus*), geared especially to the Swedish-American researchers.

The Swedish Emigrant Institute (*Svenska Emigrantinstitutet – Utvandrarnas hus*) in Växjö, also in southern Sweden, has a large research department and maintains the microfilm of the Swedish-American church records. It also has a lot of Swedish microfilm, especially of records from the Småland region. The Emigrant Institute has large collections of emigrant memorabilia, a standing exhibition, and a library. There is also an emigrant institute (*Emigrantregistret*) in Karlstad in western Sweden. We strongly recommend that you, as a descendant of Swedish emigrants, visit the Swedish Emigrant Institute.

If you travel to Sweden and plan to stay for an extended time you can do your own research at one of these institutions. We suggest that you contact them beforehand and study their home pages to make certain that they can give you the help you require. Be aware that there are also fees to use the facilities. You may also want to book lodging in the area. See more in the chapter "Prepare for a trip to Sweden." See also the addresses at the end of the book.

Official Records and Right of Access

Sweden has a unique legislation for freedom of speech and free access to public documents; in part, this legislation dates back to 1766. The general rule is that all documents handled or possessed by public institutions are open to the public. The only exceptions are to protect privacy and certain types of public interest, such as national security. There is, in fact, a special legislation for the protection of privacy. The general rule is that sensitive personal information can be closed for seventy years. The definition of sensitive information is rather narrow, and most information in the public records, such as birth date, marriage partner, even taxed income, is available to anyone. Passport applications with photos are also open. Protected is, for example, information about personal health and social benefits.

The principle of public access to information is an important reason why the Swedish archives have such an abundance of information. For more than two hundred years detailed records concerning many aspects of the citizens' lives have been kept and been public.

If you ask for information in public archives and public institutions the general rule is simple: you shall have access to the information without delay, and without needing to give specified reasons. It is up to the keeper of the records to give reasons *not* to give you the information.

Research Centers in the United States

The United States has several research centers for studies of Swedish immigration to the United States. The most important is the Swenson Swedish Immigration Research Center in Rock Island, Illinois. It is located at Augustana College, the oldest of the Swedish-American colleges.

The Swenson Center is named after Birger and Lyal Swenson, whose donations made it possible to start the center in 1980. Birger Swenson came to the United States at the age of sixteen from Sweden, and went to school at Augustana College. He worked as a publisher and promoted Swedish literature and culture in America.

The Swenson center has microfilm copies of all

the Swedish-American church records, and of Swedish-American organizations and newspapers. The microfilm of the Swedish-American church records (around 2,000 microfilms) must be studied at the center and cannot be borrowed. The microfilm of Swedish-American newspapers (around 1,500 films) can be obtained by other libraries through the Augustana College Library. The center also has microfilm for some private manuscript collections and city directories from Chicago.

The Swenson center can be a good starting point if you lack leads and clues to your background in Sweden.

North Park College in Chicago has archives mainly concerning Swedes in Chicago and Swedes belonging to the Covenant Mission Church (today the Evangelical Covenant Church). North Park College is located in "Swedetown" in Chicago.

There are also many Swedish institutes, museums, and historical and genealogical societies in the United States and Canada that specialize in Swedish-American immigration and culture. These organizations can offer assistance to genealogists interested in learning more about Swedish research.

Genealogical Societies

There are a number of local genealogical societies throughout Sweden. You can find their addresses through the national organisations *Svenska Släktforskarförbundet* or *Genealogiska föreningen*, and the website *Rötter* (roots).

One way to enquire about lost relatives is to contact the genealogical societies in the area where you believe the family originated and give them all the information you have. They can post your request for information on their websites and ask around in their societies. With good luck there might be Swedish researchers who have run into your emigrating relatives.

For addresses to genealogical societies in Sweden see the end of the book.

Good Websites

The website *Rötter* (roots) has general information about genealogical research in Sweden and a large number of links.

The website of the National Archives has links also to all the regional archives and to SVAR, where you can obtain information about microfilm.

The web has opened up new possibilities to do research, find information and prepare for a trip. In the genealogical field what you need is a good starting point with many good links. Most Swedish websites have at least some information in English.

For websites' addresses see the end of the book.

What Church Records Contain

We have stated over and over that the most essential sources for the genealogist researching Swedish ancestry are Swedish church records. But what does a typical church archive consist of? Let us look at one example: the parish of Mölltorp, where Gustaf Adolf Rapp and Anna Christina Carlsson came from and presumably were born.

The original church books from Mölltorp are stored at the Regional Archives in Gothenburg. This has long been the case for all the older books, from before 1895. They are stored at the Regional Archives according to their districts (see page 50). Now also the new books, from the period 1895 to 1991, will be delivered to the regional archives around the country, and Mölltorp's new books will be kept at the Regional Archives in Gothenburg.

How the Church Records Are Listed

All Swedish church records have been listed in the same manner. Each category of records has a specific letter. Household examination rolls are listed under A, moving records under B, birth and christening records under C, etc. However, sometimes certain records are included in another book. The "volume number," like AI:8, always refers to one specific book.

Mölltorp in the Catalog in Gothenburg Regional Archives

Mölltorp R

Tid	BESTÄLLES MED		Anmärkningar
	Volymbeteckning	Film nr	
HUSFÖRHÖRSLÄNGDER			
1768-1783	Mölltorp A I: 1		
1783-1820	" A I: 2		
1821-1837	" A I: 3		
1838-1847	" A I: 4		
1843-1860	" A I: 5		
1849-1864	" A I: 6		
1860-1873	" A I: 7		
1874-1887	" A I: 8		
1887-1898	" A I: 9		
IN- OCH UTFLYTTNINGSLÄNGDER			
1734-1753	Mölltorp C: 1.		
1768-1849	Ransberg B: 1		Luckor 1771-1776, 1783-1800.
1783-1801	Mölltorp A I: 2		Lucka 1797-1798.
1850-1868	Ransberg B: 2		Utflyttningslängd.
1850-1868	" B: 3		Inflyttningslängd.
1869-1895	Mölltorp B: 1		
FÖDELSE- OCH DOPBÖCKER			
1689-1752	Mölltorp C: 1		
1753-1849	" C: 2		
1783-1845	" C: 3	Ej mikrokort	Kladd. Lucka 1788-1789.
1845-1869	" C: 4		Kladd.
1850-1895	" C: 5	Ej mikrokort	
LYSNINGS- OCH VIGSELBÖCKER			
1689-1795	Mölltorp C: 1		
1797-1849	Ransberg E: 1		
1850-1868	" E: 2		
1854-1855	Mölltorp A I: 6		
1869-1895	" E: 1		
DÖD- OCH BEGRAVNINGSBÖCKER			
1689-1797	Mölltorp C: 1		
1798-1849	" C: 2		
1839-1845	" C: 3		Kladd.
1845-1869	" C: 4		Kladd.
1850-1895	" F: 1		

The catalog in the Regional Archives in Gothenburg lists all the records and documents in the Mölltorp parish archive. At left you see parts of the catalog, with the records that are most valuable to the genealogist. In addition to these records there are also records of confirmations, different kinds of supplements, statistical reports, minutes, and accounts for the parish council and the poor relief board, etc.

Translation

Husförhörslängder =
household examination rolls

In- och utflyttningslängder =
in- and outmoving records

Födelse- och dopböcker =
birth and baptism records

Lysnings- och vigselböcker =
records of banns and marriages

Död- och begravningsböcker =
death and burial records

For each of these records there are several books (volumes) in the archive, and each book covers a period of several years. Some of the oldest books include several types of records. The volume C:1 contains both moving records, birth records, marriage records, and death records in the same book, beginning in 1689. The household examination roll starts from 1768, which is rather late compared to many other parishes.

Mölltorp in the SVAR Catalog

The catalog from SVAR (*Svensk Arkivinformation*) is a listing of the microfilm, on microfiche cards, available through this department of the National Archives of Sweden. The catalog includes all the important records, but it doesn't include all of the documents in the Mölltorp parish archive that can be found in the regional archive (as some of them have not been microfilmed). But, in addition to the books found in the catalog from the regional archives, it also lists microfilm from other sources, such as the records maintained by Statistics Sweden (*Statistiska Centralbyrån, SCB*).

We recognize the volume numbers (first column) and years (second column) from the regional archives' catalog on the previous page. There is also a microfiche number (*kortnummer*, third column). The last column shows the number of microfiche for each type of record and each volume. Altogether the Mölltorp parish records fill 121 microfiche cards.

MÖLLTORP 121

Tidigt särskilda böcker för Karlsborg. 1831 utbrutet Vanäs (Karlsborgs garnisonsförsamling), 1885 utbrutet Karlsborg
Tingslag: .-1890 Valla, 1891-1947 Vadsbo södra, 1948-1970 Vadsbo, 1971- Mariestads tingsrätt.
Pastorat: Ransberg.

Husförhörslängder. 57
AI: 1-9 med ortregister

AI: 1	1768-1783	512066	3
AI: 2	1783-1820	512067	3
AI: 3	1821-1837	512068	4
AI: 4	1838-1847	512069	2
AI: 5	1843-1860	512070	4
AI: 6	1849-1864	512071	6
AI: 7	1860-1873	52469	9
AI: 8	1874-1887	52470	10
AI: 9	1887-1898	G00661	16

Utdrag ur församlingsböcker 3

SCB	1900	CB2534	1
SCB	1910	CB2795	1
SCB	1920	CB4474	1

Böcker över obefintliga

AI: 8	1874-1887
AI: 9	1887-1898

Inflyttningslängder 4

C: 1	1734-1753		
	1768-1770		
Se: Ransberg B: 1			
	1777-1782		
Se: Ransberg B: 1			
AI: 2	1783-1796		
AI: 2	1799-1801		
	1801-1849		
Se: Ransberg B: 1			
	1850-1868		
Se: Ransberg B: 3			
B: 1	1869-1895	G00662	4

Utflyttningslängder

C: 1	1734-1753
	1768-1770
Se: Ransberg B: 1	
	1777-1782
Se: Ransberg B: 1	
AI: 2	1783-1796
AI: 2	1799-1801
	1801-1849
Se: Ransberg B: 1	
	1850-1868
Se: Ransberg B: 2	
B: 1	1869-1895

Födelse- och dopböcker. 14

C: 1	1689-1752	512072	4
C: 2	1753-1849	512073	7
C: 4	1845-1869	512074	3
Kladd			

Utdrag ur födelseböcker 12

SCB	1860-1897	CA9041	5
SCB	1898-1920	CK2052	7

Konfirmationsböcker

AI: 2	1799-1800

Lysnings- och vigselböcker. 2

C: 1	1689-1795		
	1797-1849		
Se: Ransberg E: 1			
	1850-1868		
Se: Ransberg E: 2			
AI: 6	1854-1855		
E: 1	1869-1895	514087	2

Utdrag ur vigselböcker 4

SCB	1860-1897	CA9042	2
SCB	1898-1920	CK2053	2

Död- och begravningsböcker. 3

C: 1	1689-1797		
C: 2	1798-1849		
C: 4	1845-1869		
F: 1	1850-1895	512075	3

Utdrag ur dödböcker 11

SCB	1860-1897	CA9043	3
SCB	1898-1920	CK2054	8

Emigranter befolkningsstatistik 1

	1865-1874	CE0701	1

Bilagor till flyttningslängd. 1

HII: 1	1849-1858	512076	1
1850-1856 saknas			

Räkenskaper för kyrka. 9

LI: 1	1737-1822	512077	3
LI: 2	1746-1835	512078	4
LI: 3	1785-1830	512079	2

Räkenskaper för fattigvård

LI: 1	1772-1822

Mölltorp in Family History Library

Microfilm copies of Swedish church records are also available through the Family History Library (FHL). You can search in the Family History Library Catalog online (www.familysearch.org). The database is enormous in size. The collection includes more than 2.2 million rolls of microfilm, with records of hundreds of millions of people from all around the world.

We made a "place search" on Mölltorp and within seconds had a full list of all the records from the church archive in Mölltorp that are available on microfilm and can be ordered to any one of the 3,700 Family History Centers (see below). The list is similar to the list from SVAR, but it is not identical. The FHL has its own numbering system, different from SVAR's. The records from Statistics Sweden (SCB) are not available there, but you can find them under "län" and civil registration. The church archive from Mölltorp in FHL fills ten 16 mm microfilms.

We also made a "surname search" on the name Rapp, and found 39 matching titles. It doesn't seem likely that any one of these references concerns our Rapp family.

Family History Library Catalog

Sida 1 av 2
(Page 1 of 2)

Title
Kyrkoböcker, 1689-1898

Subjects
Sweden, Skaraborg, Mölltorp - Church records

Film Notes
Note - Location [Film]
Förteckning över Mölltorps kyrkoarkiv - FHL INTL Film [249013]
Husförhörslängd 1768-1864 AI:1-6 - FHL INTL Film [249013]
Husförhörslängd 1860-1887 AI:7-8 - FHL INTL Film [519319]
Husförhörslängd 1887-1898 AI:19 - FHL INTL Film [1848592 Item 3]
Födde 1689-1849 C:1-2, 1845-1869 C:4 - FHL INTL Film [249014]
Vigde 1689-1795 C:1 - FHL INTL Film [249014]
Vigde 1798-1849 E:1 filmat med Ransberg sn. - FHL INTL Film [249018]
Vigde 1850-1868 E:2 filmat med Ransberg sn. - FHL INTL Film [518515]
Vigde 1854-1855 AI:6 - FHL INTL Film [249013]
Vigde 1869-1895 E:1 - FHL INTL Film [249014]
Döde 1689-1849 C:1-2, 1845-1869 C:4, 1850-1895 F:1 - FHL INTL Film [249014]
In- och utflyttningsl. 1734-1753 C:1 spr.år - FHL INTL Film [249014]
In- och utflyttningsl. 1783-1796, 1799-1801 AI:2 - FHL INTL Film [249013]
In- och utflyttningsl. 1850-1868 B:2-3 filmat med Ransberg sn. - FHL INTL Film [518514]
In- och utflyttningsl. 1869-1895 B:1 - FHL INTL Film [1848592 Item 4]
In- och utflyttningsl. 1850-1868 B:2-3 filmat med Ransberg socken - FHL INTL Film [1794528 Items 3-4]
Inflyttningslängd 1768-1770, 1777-1782, 1801-1849 B:1 filmat med Ransberg socken - FHL INTL Film [249017]
Utflyttningslängd 1768-1772, 1774-1782, 1801-1849 B:1 filmat med Ransberg socken - FHL INTL Film [249017]
Sockenstämmoprotokoll 1694-1763 C:1, 1735-1804 C:2 - FHL INTL Film [249014]
Konfirmationsl. 1799-1800 AI:2 - FHL INTL Film [249013]
Kyrkoräkenskapsbok 1695-1756 C:1 - FHL INTL Film [249014]
Kyrkoräkenskapsbok 1737-1822 LI:1, 1746-1835 LI:2, 1785-1830 LI:3 - FHL INTL Film [249015]

Mölltorp in Genline

Genline uses the same microfilm as SVAR and Family History Library for its publication on the Internet. Genline has scanned the microfilm. To find the parish and place, in our case Mölltorp in Skaraborgs län, we have two alternatives: Look under "Parishes" on Genline's website. The parishes are listed by county, and for each parish there is a list of all the church records available. For each volume we get the years the book covers, the official volume number, and Genline's own ID number.

The catalog is also an integrated part of the search program, Genline FamilyFinder®. When we search we automatically get the volumes, numbers and sequences. If we run into problems finding a certain place we can use a help program, GIDx.

How Genline FamilyFinder® Works

Genline gives you an opportunity to work with the original documents on your own computer through an online subscribtion to Genline's services. For current prices and other conditions consult Genline's home page. All the historical Swedish church records are today available on Genline. Within a few years all church records until 1937 will also be available. With "historical" we mean the records from before 1895. For Mölltorp it is the same records that are available through Family History Library and SVAR.

When you become a registered user with Genline you get a username and a password. Use these to log in.

When you have logged in you will get a search window. You can now choose between "sequences" and "GIDx". We choose "sequences" to look for a certain document: the birth record from Mölltorp the year Anna Christina Carlsson was born, 1855. We will later see that this information is available in the church records in Zion Lutheran Church in Portland, Connecticut. In this Swedish-American church book there is even a note that Mölltorp is located in "Skbl," Skaraborgs län.

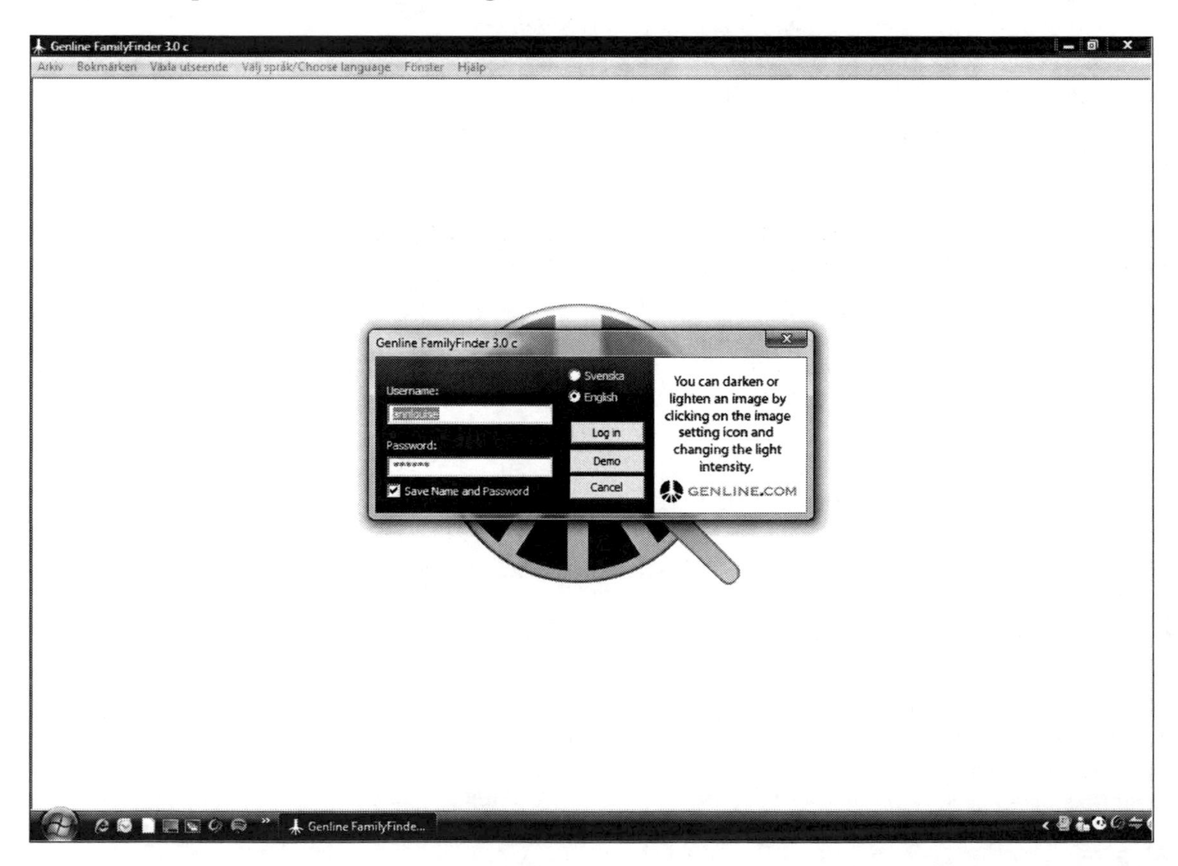

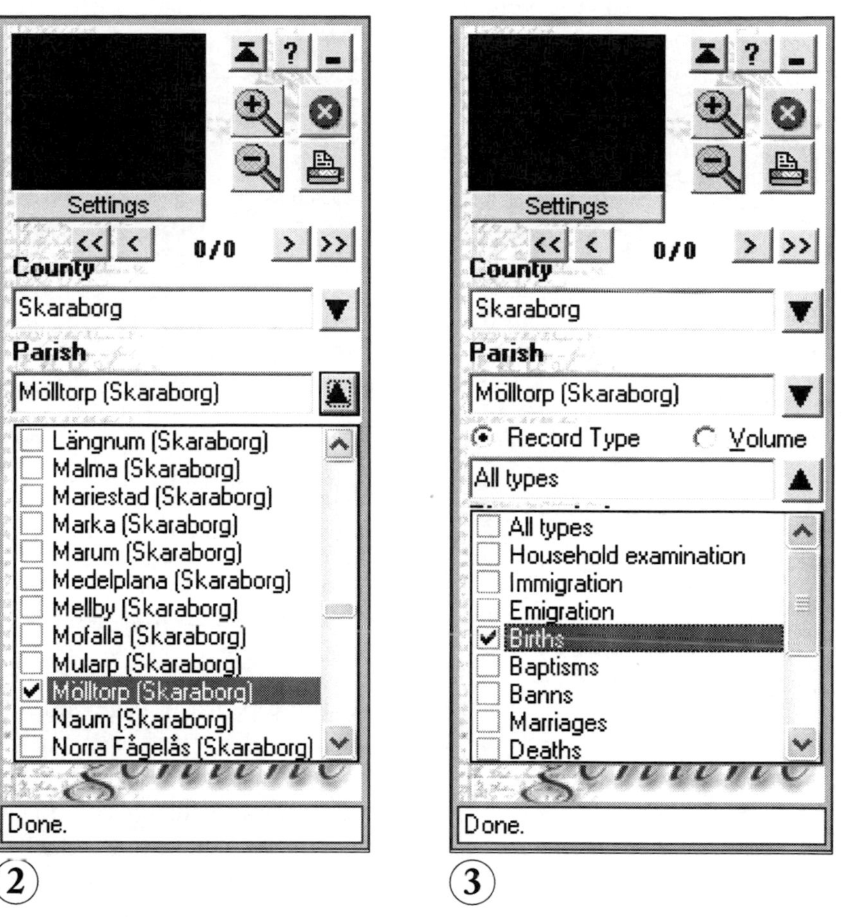

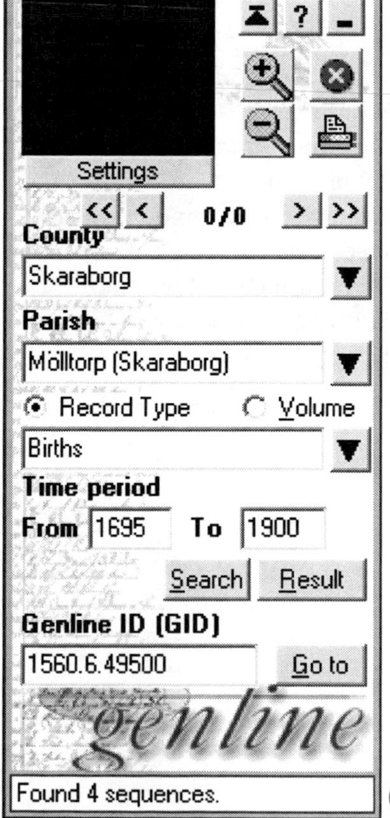

Let Us Search Step by Step:

1. Find the right län, in Genline FamilyFinder® called county. All the Swedish län are listed. Select Skaraborg.
2. Find the right parish. All the parishes in Skaraborg are listed in alphabetical order. Find and select Mölltorp.
3. Find the right kind of records. Mark record type and select "Births."
4. You can also select a certain time period. In this case you might prefer to see all the birth records.
5. You can now push the button "Search."

You get a list of the birth records for different time periods. You can see that there are records in three different volumes (books), C:1, C:2, and C:4. The third book (C:4) has two different Genline ID-numbers. It is divided into two different films. This book has both births and deaths.

Search results

GID	Volume	Year	Type
1554.12	C:1	1689-1752	Births
1554.13	C:2	1753-1849	Births
1554.14	C:4	1845-1869	Births,Deaths
1554.16	C:4	1845-1869	Births,Deaths

5

4

5

Search results

GID	Volume	Year	Type
1554.6	AI:1	1768-1783	Household examination
1554.7	AI:2	1783-1820	Household examinatior
1554.8	AI:3	1821-1837	Household examinatior
1554.9	AI:4	1838-1847	Household examinatior
1554.1C	AI:5	1843-1860	Household examinatior
1554.11	AI:6	1849-1864	Household examinatior
1554.1	AI:7	1860-1873	Household examinatior
1554.2	AI:8	1874-1887	Household examinatior
1554.3	AI:8	1874-1887	Household examinatior

When you make a similar search for household examination rolls you get a list of nine different books.

You select the book you want, for the right time period, and you are ready to start your search. We will not here explain in detail how the work is done.

At the top of the page you have a number of symbols (buttons) that enable you to work with the documents. You can select pages in the book or you can go through the book page by page. You can zoom in on details and enlarge certain parts of the page. You can adjust the darkness of the picture to get the best contrast. You can improve the picture quality with "image improvement", erasing spots and clearing up the picture. You can print pages if you find it easier to read them that way.

In addition to the "search sequence" feature GFF also offers the possibility to search for a place or to search for a person in the church records. The result of this search depends on the availability of published and transcribed material. Transcribed content will become more and more available relative to the amount of transcriptions contibuted by Genline's users. For more information about these features and how to use them, visit Genline's website at www.genline.com.

You are now ready to start your research.

Research Centers

Web-addresses are listed in the back of the book. Look at the homepages to get current information about hours of operation, mailing addresses, fees, reservations, etc.

All of these research centers offer research service to help you find your Swedish roots. Contact them by e-mail or regular mail.

The House of Emigrants – The Swedish Emigrant Institute (Utvandrarnas hus – Svenska Emigrantinstitutet) Växjö

This is the leading research center for Swedish emigration, with archives, library, and a museum. Founded in 1965, it is located in the cathedral city of Växjö, in Småland, the province with the largest total number of emigrants. Maintains the Swedish-American church archives on microfilm. Has a fixed price package for research into an emigrant's family, identifying parents, siblings, and basic facts.

Swedish American Center in Karlstad

Located in central Karlstad, the capital of Värmland, a province with large emigration. The center specializes in research about American emigration and registration of emigrants. The Regional Archives of Värmland is at the same location. Has a fixed price for a "start package" to find your Swedish roots.

The House of Genealogy in Leksand (Släktforskarnas hus) Leksand

Located in the traditional town of Leksand by lake Siljan, in Dalarna province, in a busy and beautiful tourist region. Geared towards service to amateur researchers. Many Swedish-American visitors. Hotel nearby. Promises quick response to overseas enquiries. Can create whole family charts at fixed prices.

The Research Center of Jörn (Demografiska databasen i Jörn) Jörn

This research center is mainly geared towards academic studies in demography, using Swedish church records, and is a part of Umeå University, though located in the small inland town of Jörn. Some of these records are being registered and digitalized. If you have ancestors from the areas around the cities of Skellefteå, Sundsvall, or Linköping, you might find them in the database Indiko. The research center creates family charts and research at fixed prices.

The National Archives in Arninge (Riksarkivet – Arninge) Arninge

This facility is part of the National Archives, but is located in a northern suburb of Stockholm (the National Archives' main building is in central Stockholm). At Arninge the most interesting material for family research is the copies of church records every tenth year from 1860 until 1945, and documents about emigrants from 1860 until 1947, in the archives of Statistics Sweden (SCB). A complete set of Swedish microfilm is also available. The research center is very busy and you have to arrive early in the morning to be certain to get a research table.

SVAR Research Center (SVAR's forskarcentrum) Ramsele

This research center is located in the interior of northern Sweden, in the small town of Ramsele (Ångermanland province), beautifully situated by a river. All Swedish microfilm is available. Excellent modern facilities and lodging in the area. If you visit the center you can get personal guidance. For research service there is a fixed hourly charge. You can also order a complete family tree. For details see the website.

Research Help on the Web

There are several possibilities to get help on the Internet, at different websites.

Disbyt is a department under DIS (Computer Genealogy of Sweden). "Byt" stand for exchange. You can ask questions and submit information about your own research. Disbyt has a database of 19.3 million records of Swedes born before 1909. Each record can represent one or more individuals.
You can reach disbyt on www.dis.se/dbyt

Anbytarforum is a service run by the Swedish Genealogical Society. It is a forum for discussion where you can pose questions, ask for help by other genealogists when you come to a dead end, identify photographs, and so on. The language is Swedish, but as most Swedes understand and read English it is possible to post queries in English as well.
The web-address is: http://aforum.genealogy.se/discus/

Genline's *Bygdeband* ties genealogy with local heritage research allowing these two groups of researchers to easily share information with each other. Bygdeband is a social networking archive making it possible for local heritage societies to add digitalized material into an online archive.
Visit www.genline.com for more and up-dated information about Bygdeband.

Emiweb is a similar service for emigrant research, where you can share information on emigrants and publish documents. The web-address is www.emiweb.se.

The National Archives and the Regional Archives

All of these public archives have similar kinds of services and opening hours as the research centers. They accept commissions to do research, and charge an hourly rate. They have excellent research facilities with microfilm and libraries, and a very knowledgeable staff.

They are usually located in the central parts of the cities. The National Archives in Stockholm has its most valuable records stored deep underground. The archives in Uppsala and Vadstena are located in the old provincial royal castles in these cities. The regional archives in Gothenburg has the largest collections of emigrant records.

Do not hesitate to make a visit to the nearest one of these archives when visiting Sweden. The staffs at the regional archives are the people with the most extensive knowledge about the records and the research facilities within the region.

Besides microfilm, the research centers, archives and libraries usually give you access to computers where you can work with Genline FamilyFinder and other databases without extra charge.

CHAPTER SEVEN

The Rapp Family in U.S. Sources

Our main research case in this book is the Rapp family. You have already seen the gravestone in the cemetery in Portland, Connecticut.

Let us imagine that we are the descendants of Gustaf Adolph and Anna Christina Rapp. We know that they came from Sweden. We know their birth years from the stone.

From older relatives we also know that they belonged to a local Swedish congregation. One of our first research measures would be to check with this congregation and find out if there are any records in which we can find more information about where they came from in Sweden.

The congregation is Zion Lutheran church in Portland. It is still a very active congregation and we can get good help to search in the old records.

Note 1:

The purpose of this search is to find out if the priest has noted certain basic facts, like the birthplaces in Sweden, or at least the places they left from in Sweden. An accurate immigration year would also be helpful. If we don't already know our ancestors' birth dates, those are also important to find out. All of these facts are helpful when we move on to the Swedish records.

Note 2:

The records from the congregation are usually still kept at the local church. If we live nearby the easy way is to make a visit. Usually congregations will help with en- quiries by mail or e-mail.

ADOLPH RAPP
1858 — 1935
ANNA C. CARLSON
HIS WIFE
1855 — 1926
C. ROBERT
1880 — 1904
RAPP

Swedish-American Congregation Records on Microfilm

Most of the records of Swedish-American congregations have been microfilmed. The microfilms were made by the Swede Lennart Setterdahl between 1968 and 1979. He traveled all over the United States and Canada and visited 2,000 congregations. He was able to film records from 1,659 U.S. and 72 Canadian congregations. The records from congregations within the Lutheran Augustana synod and the Swedish Mission Covenant churches were filmed to almost 100 percent. About half of the records within Methodist, Baptist, and other Swedish churches were also filmed. It has been calculated that these microfilms include about three million people.

The microfilms are available at the Swenson Institute at Augustana College in Rock Island, Illinois, as well as at the Emigrant Institute in Växjö, Sweden; they cannot be borrowed. The records are not available through the Family History Library or SVAR, but a catalog of the congregations and the archives is available on microfilm.

See map of the Swedish-America congregations on page 68–69.

The Rapp Family in Portland

As mentioned the Rapp family belonged to the Zion Lutheran Church in Portland, Connecticut. This congregation was part of the Augustana synod, the Swedish Lutheran church in the United States. The church records have been microfilmed and are available for genealogical research. Let's look at the church register and see if we can find any references to the Swedish background.

The Church Register

The oldest church register in Zion Lutheran Church was started in 1874 and was used until 1903. Each family was entered as it joined the congregation. We find the Rapp family on page 38 in the register as seen below.

Zion Lutheran Church, Portland, Connecticut

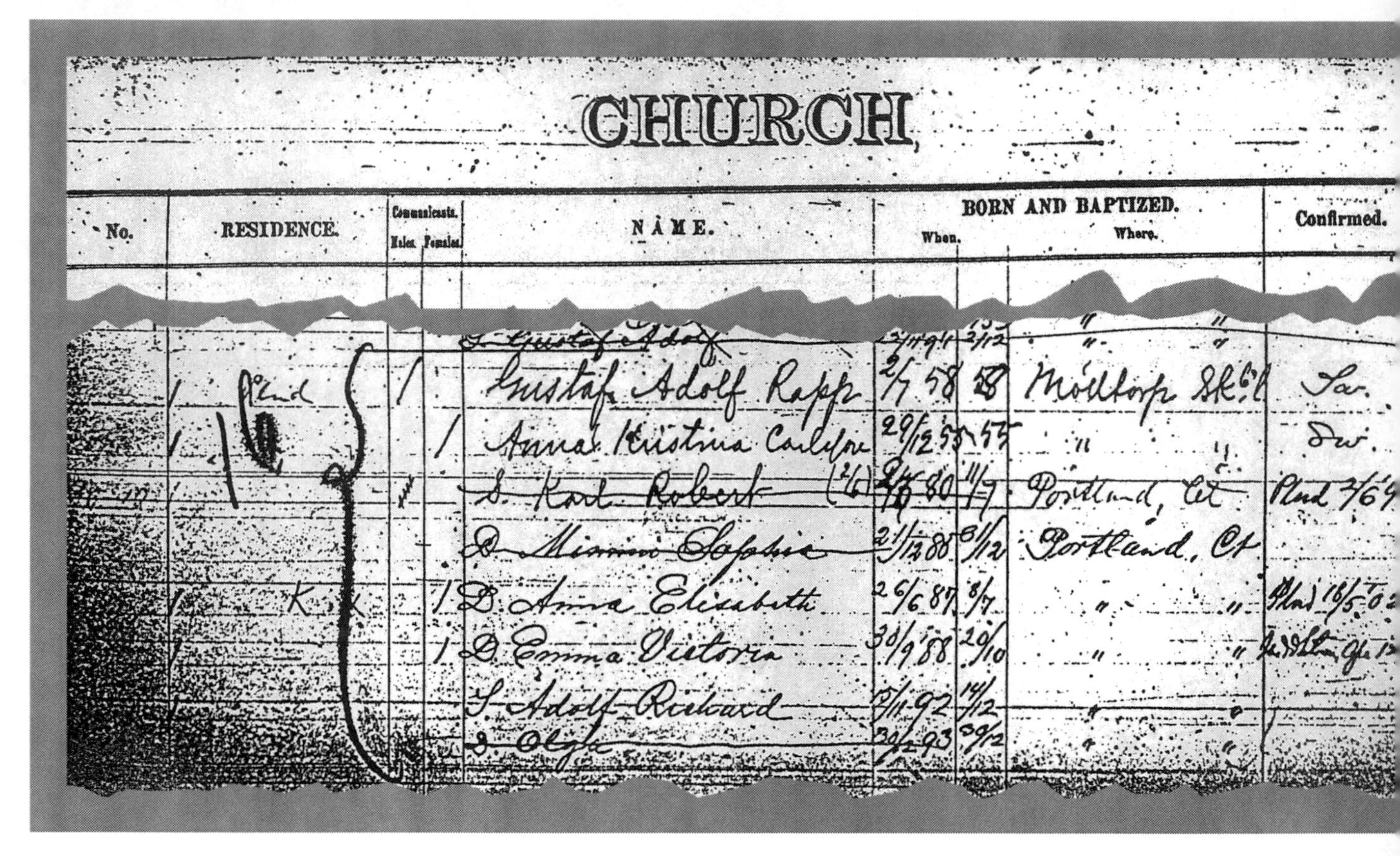

CHURCH

No.	Residence.	Communicants Males	Communicants Females	Name.	Born and Baptized When.		Born and Baptized Where.	Confirmed.
				~~S. Gustaf Adolf~~	2/11 91	3/12	" "	
1	Plnd	1		Gustaf Adolf Rapp	2/7 58		Mölltorp Sk:l	Sw.
1			1	Anna Kristina Carlsson	29/12 55	55	" "	Sw.
				~~S. Karl Robert~~	2/8 80	11/7	Portland, Ct	Plnd 7/6
				~~D. Minnie Sophie~~	21/12 88	8/12	Portland, Ct	
1			1	D. Anna Elisabeth	26/6 87	8/7	" "	Plnd 16/5
			1	D. Emma Victoria	30/9 88	29/10	" "	
				~~S. Adolf Rickard~~	17/11 92	14/12	" "	
				~~D. Olga~~	30/2 93	29/12	" "	

What Can We See on This Page?

The family consisted of eight members: the father, Gustaf Adolf Rapp, the mother, Anna Kristina Carlsson, and their six children.

Our primary interest is the parents:

Gustaf Adolf Rapp was born on *2* July 18*58*, and his birthplace is given as *Mölltorp Skb:l.* He was confirmed in *Sw*(eden) and married on *7* November 18*79*. He arrrived in America in 18*79* from *Mölltorp*.

His wife *Anna Kristina Carlsson* was born on the *29* December 18*55*. All the other date and place details are identical to her husband's; they share the same birthplace, confirmation date, marriage date, and date of arrival in the United States.

continued

We are lucky in several respects:

1. We have a family that is listed and registered in a Swedish American church record. These records are usually well kept and they generally give accurate information about a person's Swedish origins. The priest was probably also a Swedish immigrant, and he knew how to spell the Swedish names (of people and places).
2. We get information about the Swedish parish where the parents were born and with that we can go directly to the church records of this parish, which are now available on the Internet.

The abbreviation *Skb:l.* stands for Skaraborgs län, one of Sweden's twenty-four administrative provinces ("counties").

In this case we don't need any more sources to find our way to the Swedish records. If we could only find the date of arrival in the United States, we would need to look into the ship's manifests at the arrival port (almost always New York) and/or at the departure port in Sweden (almost always Gothenburg).

38

REGISTER.

Knowledge.			Married.	Received.	No. of Certificate.	Arrived in America.		Arrived in this Place.		Removed.		REMARKS.
Reading.	Reciting.	Understanding.				Where From.	When.	Where From.	When.	Where To.	When.	

Where Do We Go from Here?

We can now go to the Swedish church records, and look for the parish Mölltorp in Skaraborgs län. There we can expect to find the church register that can give us information about Gustaf Adolf Rapp's and Anna Kristina Carlsson's families.

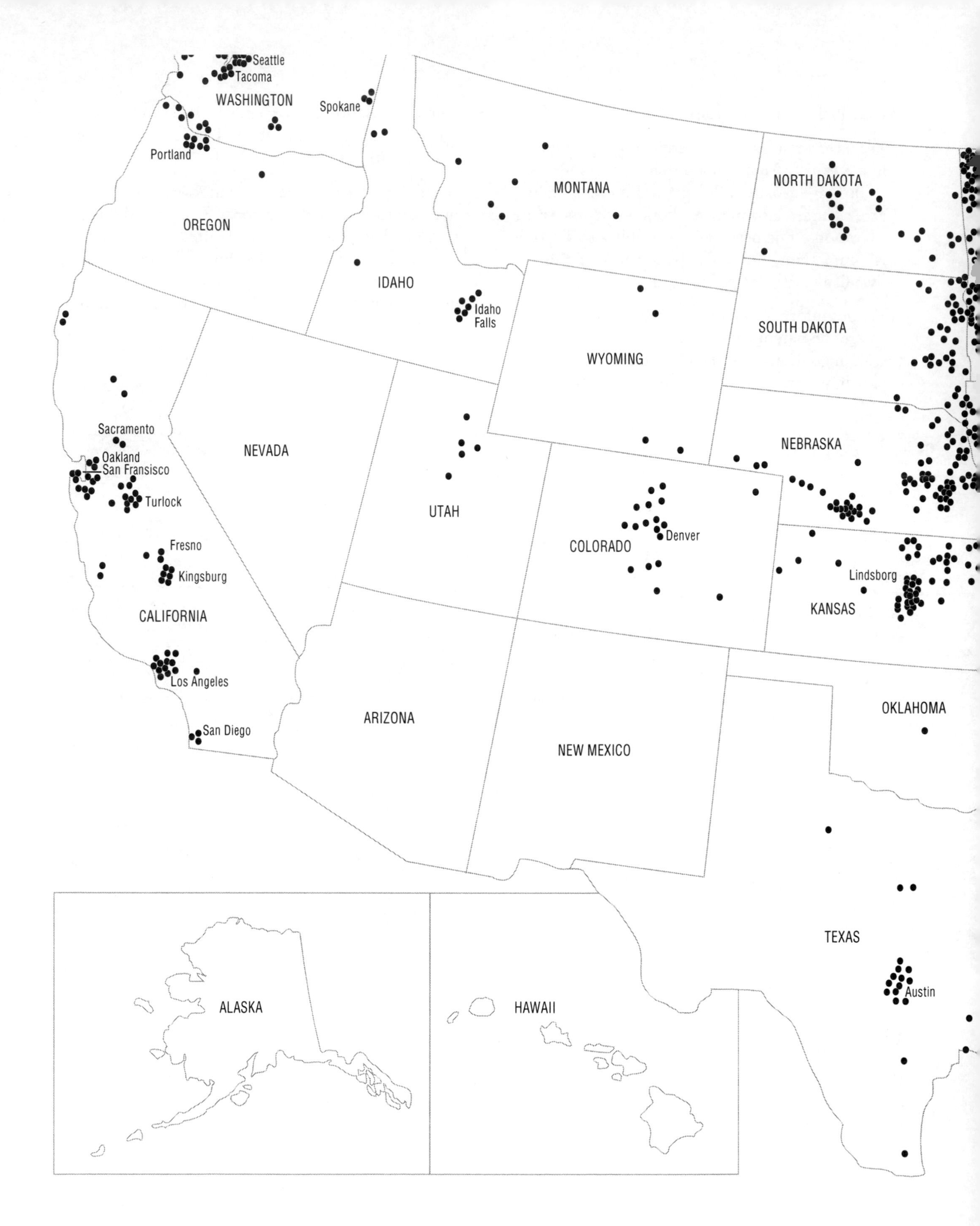
Seattle
Tacoma
WASHINGTON
Spokane
Portland
OREGON
MONTANA
NORTH DAKOTA
IDAHO
Idaho Falls
SOUTH DAKOTA
WYOMING
NEVADA
Sacramento
Oakland
San Fransisco
Turlock
UTAH
NEBRASKA
COLORADO
Denver
Fresno
Kingsburg
Lindsborg
KANSAS
CALIFORNIA
Los Angeles
San Diego
ARIZONA
NEW MEXICO
OKLAHOMA
TEXAS
Austin
ALASKA
HAWAII

Swedish-American Congregations in the United States

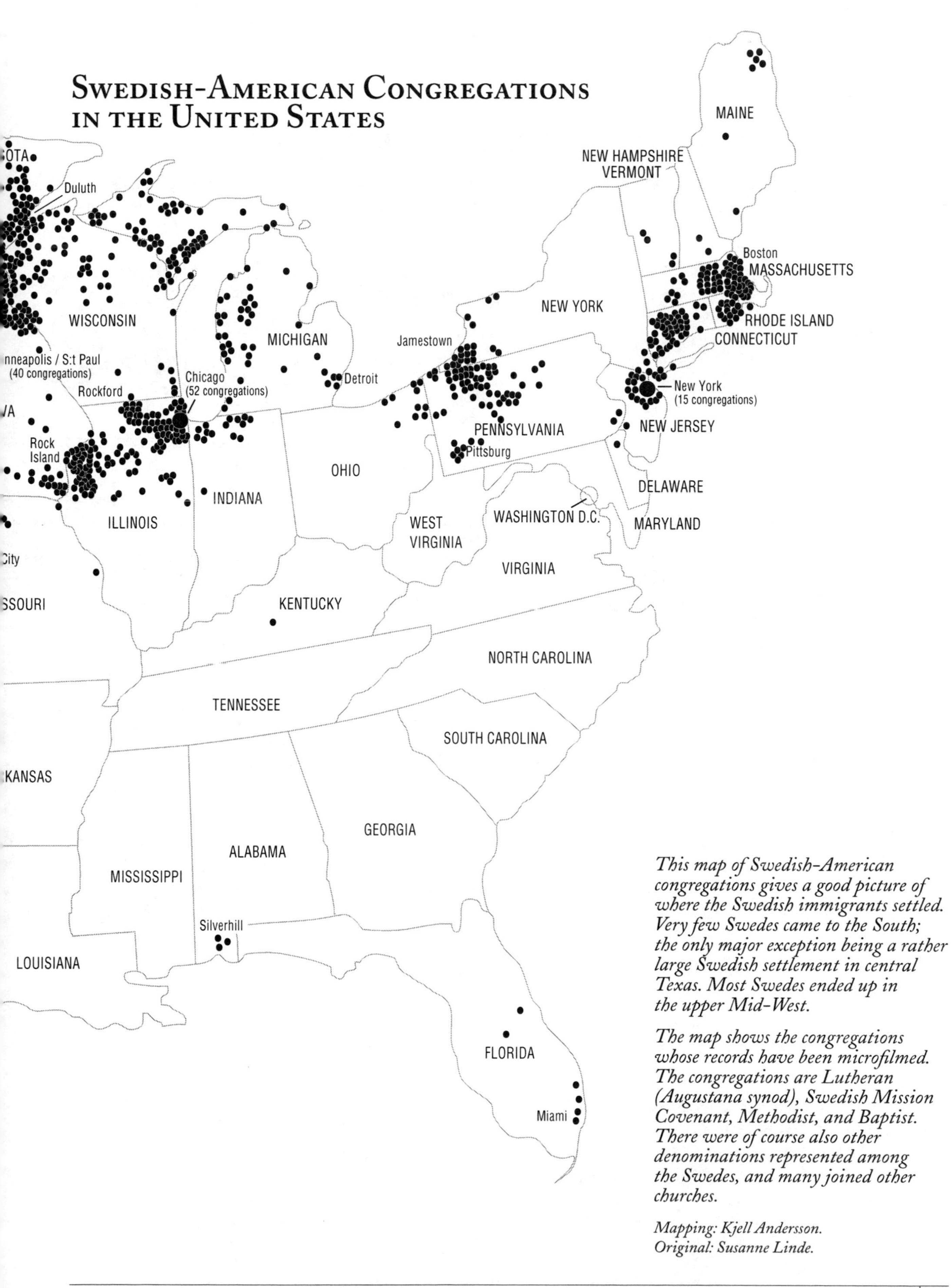

This map of Swedish-American congregations gives a good picture of where the Swedish immigrants settled. Very few Swedes came to the South; the only major exception being a rather large Swedish settlement in central Texas. Most Swedes ended up in the upper Mid-West.

The map shows the congregations whose records have been microfilmed. The congregations are Lutheran (Augustana synod), Swedish Mission Covenant, Methodist, and Baptist. There were of course also other denominations represented among the Swedes, and many joined other churches.

Mapping: Kjell Andersson.
Original: Susanne Linde.

The Rapp Family in the U.S. Federal Census 1900

As a comparison with the church register on page 66–67, we show the Rapp family in the U.S. federal census in 1900 (below). The census schedule is much less detailed than the church register. We can also see that some of the information in this record is wrong, or misleading.

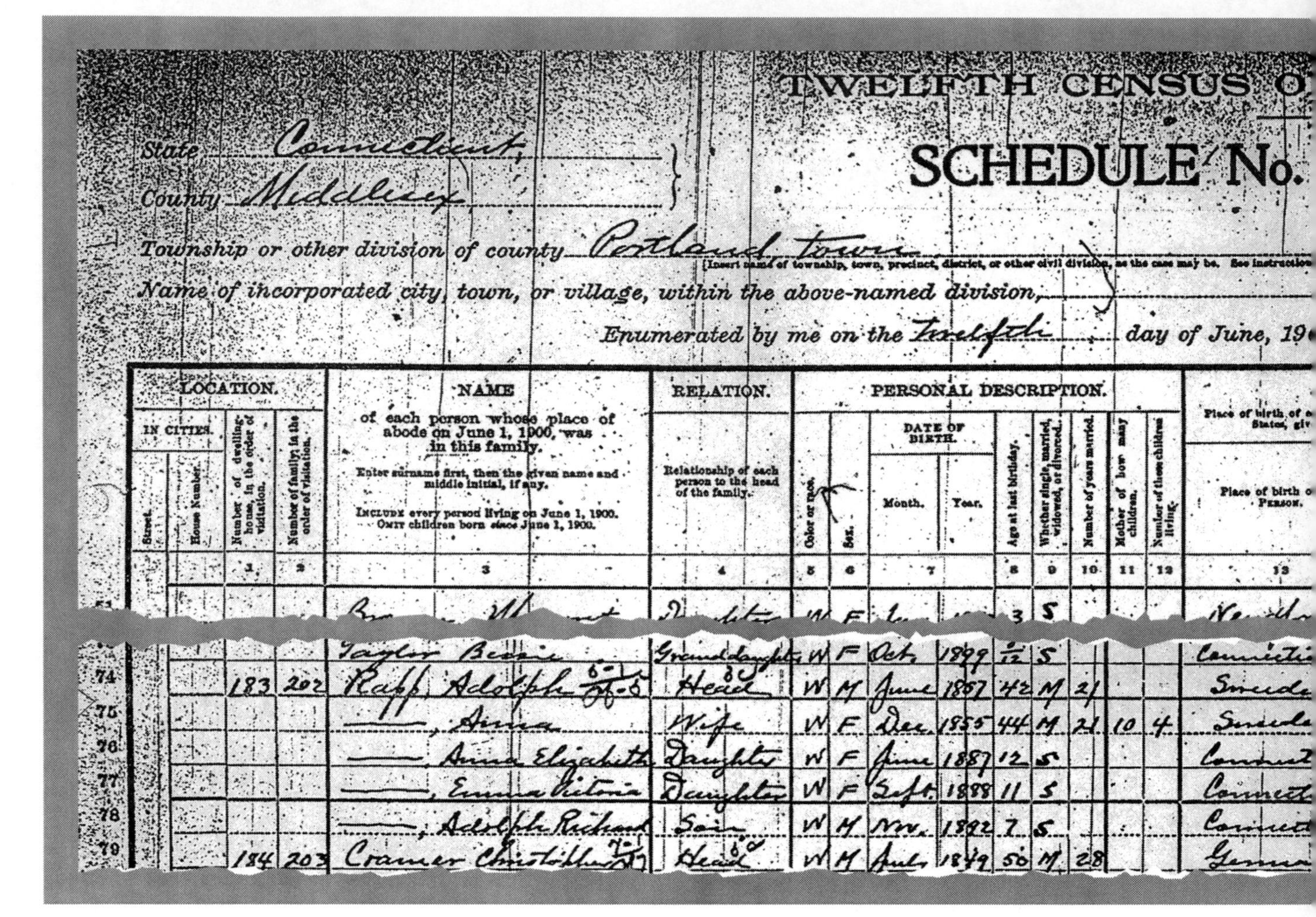

TWELFTH CENSUS O[F]

SCHEDULE No.

State Connecticut

County Middlesex

Township or other division of county Portland town (Insert name of township, town, precinct, district, or other civil division, as the case may be. See instructions)

Name of incorporated city, town, or village, within the above-named division,

Enumerated by me on the Twelfth day of June, 19[00]

	LOCATION. IN CITIES. Street	House Number	Number of dwelling house, in the order of visitation	Number of family, in the order of visitation	NAME of each person whose place of abode on June 1, 1900, was in this family.	RELATION. Relationship of each person to the head of the family	Color or race	Sex	DATE OF BIRTH. Month	Year	Age at last birthday	Whether single, married, widowed, or divorced	Number of years married	Mother of how many children	Number of these children living	Place of birth of each person
			1	2	3	4	5	6	7		8	9	10	11	12	13
					Taylor, Bessie	Granddaughter	W	F	Oct.	1899	7/12	S				Connecti
74			183	202	Rapp, Adolph	Head	W	M	June	1857	42	M	21			Swede
75					——, Anna	Wife	W	F	Dec.	1855	44	M	21	10	4	Swede
76					——, Anna Elizabeth	Daughter	W	F	June	1887	12	S				Connect
77					——, Emma Victoria	Daughter	W	F	Sept.	1888	11	S				Connect
78					——, Adolph Richard	Son	W	M	Nov.	1892	7	S				Connect
79			184	203	Cramer, Christopher	Head	W	M	Aug.	1849	50	M	28			Germa

What Can We See in These Records?

Adolph and *Anna Rapp* live with two daughters, *Anna Elisabeth* and *Emma Victoria*, and one son, *Adolph Richard*. Adolph's and Anna's second names are not given.

Birth year, birth month, and age are given, but not birthday. Adolph was born in *June* of *1857* and Anna was born in *December* of *1855*. He is *42* years old, and she is *44*. All of these facts are consistent with the information in the church register except for Adolph's birth year, which was noted as 1858 in the church register.

Adolph and Anna have been married for *21* years. Thus they must have married in 1879. Anna has had *10* children of which *4* are living at the time of the census. The place of birth for each of Adolph, Anna, and their parents, is *Sweden*. No specific city or place in Sweden is given.

The year of immigration to the United States is noted as *1880*, and the number of years in the United States is *20*. From the church register we know that this is wrong. The church register says that they arrived in America from Mölltorp in 1879.

We also get the impression that they married in Sweden, as they had been married for twenty-one years but lived in the United States for only twenty years. As we shall see later they immigrated first and got married upon arrival in the United States.

In this case we would probably be able to find Adolph Rapp in the Swedish records even with this faulty information, since his name is unusual. If he had been one of hundreds of Anderssons or Nilssons our task would have been much more difficult.

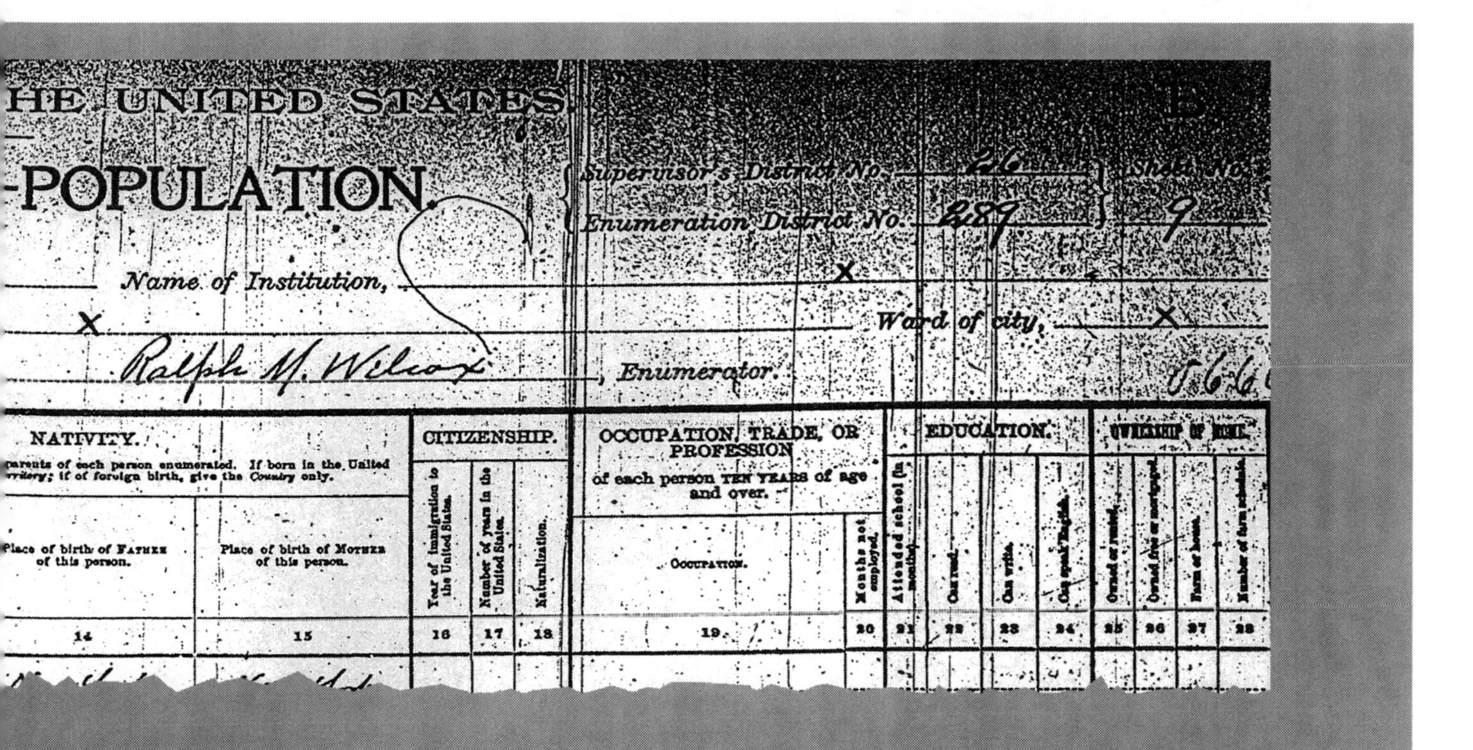

HE UNITED STATES

-POPULATION

Supervisor's District No. 26

Enumeration District No. 289

Sheet No. 9

Name of Institution, X

Ward of city, X

Ralph M. Wilcox, Enumerator.

NATIVITY. — parents of each person enumerated. If born in the United ...; if of foreign birth, give the Country only.

Place of birth of Father of this person. (14)

Place of birth of Mother of this person. (15)

CITIZENSHIP. — Year of immigration to the United States. (16) — Number of years in the United States. (17) — Naturalization. (18)

OCCUPATION, TRADE, OR PROFESSION of each person TEN YEARS of age and over. — Occupation. (19) — Months not employed. (20)

EDUCATION. — Attended school (in months). (21) — Can read. (22) — Can write. (23) — Can speak English. (24)

OWNERSHIP OF HOME. — Owned or rented. (25) — Owned free or mortgaged. (26) — Farm or house. (27) — Number of farm schedule. (28)

The U.S. Federal Census

A U.S. Federal census is taken every ten years. The earliest census is from 1790. All records have been saved except the ones from 1890, which were destroyed by fire in 1921. The census schedules are available on microfilm through the U.S. National Archives and the Family History Library. They are also available online at Ancestry.com. This is the most convenient way to access these data sets all at once. You can also make a name search. In Sweden you can find U.S. census records from states with large Swedish immigrant populations at the Swedish Emigrant Institute in Växjö. The census records are made public seventy-two years after they were recorded. The 1930 census was made public in 2002.

There are special indexes to the census records based on the way a name sounds rather than the way it is spelled. These Soundex indexes are very helpful to find a certain person in the extensive records.

Ship's Manifests in New York and Other Ports

Almost every immigrant has been recorded in the ship's manifests in the American arrival ports. Ninety percent or more of the Swedish immigrants arrived in New York harbor. It is today possible to access many of these manifests on the Internet, and they are all available on microfilm. There are also extensive indexes, which can help you to find your ancestors in the lists. The main problem with this source is that the place of origin within Sweden is often not recorded. This is the case with Anna Carlsson and Gustaf Adolf Rapp, as with most of the earlier immigrants.

We know that the young couple, Gustaf Adolf and Anna, arrived from Sweden in 1879. After some searching we find the couple in a passenger list for the steam ship Germania, arriving from Liverpool on 8 September 1879 as seen below.

Passenger List for Germania 8 September 1879

District of New York.—Port of New York.

I, Charles Wm Kennedy Master of the Germanic do solemnly, sincerely, and truly swear that the following List or Manifest, subscribed by me, and now delivered by me to the Collector of the Customs of the Collection District of New York, is a full and perfect List of all the Passengers taken on board the said Steamer Germanic at Liverpool from which Port said Steamer Germanic has now arrived; and that on the said List is truly designated the age, the sex, and the occupation of each of the said Passengers, the part of the vessel occupied by each during the passage, the country to which each belongs, and also the country of which it is intended by each to become an inhabitant; and that said List or Manifest truly sets forth the number of said Passengers who have died on said voyage, and the names and ages of those who have died.

So help me, God.

Sworn to this 8th Septbr 1879 } Chas Wm Kennedy

before me.

List or Manifest of all the Passengers taken on board the Germanic whereof Chas Wm Kennedy is Master, from Liverpool burthen 5008 tons.

	Names.	Age Years	Age Months	Sex	Occupation.	The Country to which they severally belong.	The Country of which they intend to become inhabitants.	Died on the Voyage.	Part of the Vessel occupied by each Passenger during the Voyage.
357	Anna Carlson	23		F	Servant	Sweden	U. S. A		Steerage
8	G. A. Rapp	21		M	Miner				
9	Victor Anderson	20							
360	Lars Anderson	37							
1	Hilma	11		F	Child				
2	Anders Larsson	40		M	Sailor				
3	C. Krafoe	19							
4	Inga Jons	50		F	Servant				

What Can We See in This Document?

Anna Carlson, age *23*, is noted as *Servant* and comes from *Sweden*. There is no name of a place or town in Sweden.

G. A. Rapp, age *21*, and *Victor Anderson*, age *20*, are recorded right after her. The two men are recorded as *Miners*. It is quite common that trades and occupations are wrong in these records.

They have all traveled as steerage passenger, or third class.

Note that *Carlson* and *Anderson* are spelled the American way with a single s.

Passenger Lists with More Detailed Information

During the 1890s and the first decade of the twentieth century immigration became more and more regulated and, as a result, passenger lists contain more and more information. If we look in lists after 1903 we will regularly find information about the place of origin within Sweden. Below we show one such list from New York with Swedes arriving on a ship from Copenhagen.

Passenger List for Oscar II, 10 July 1905

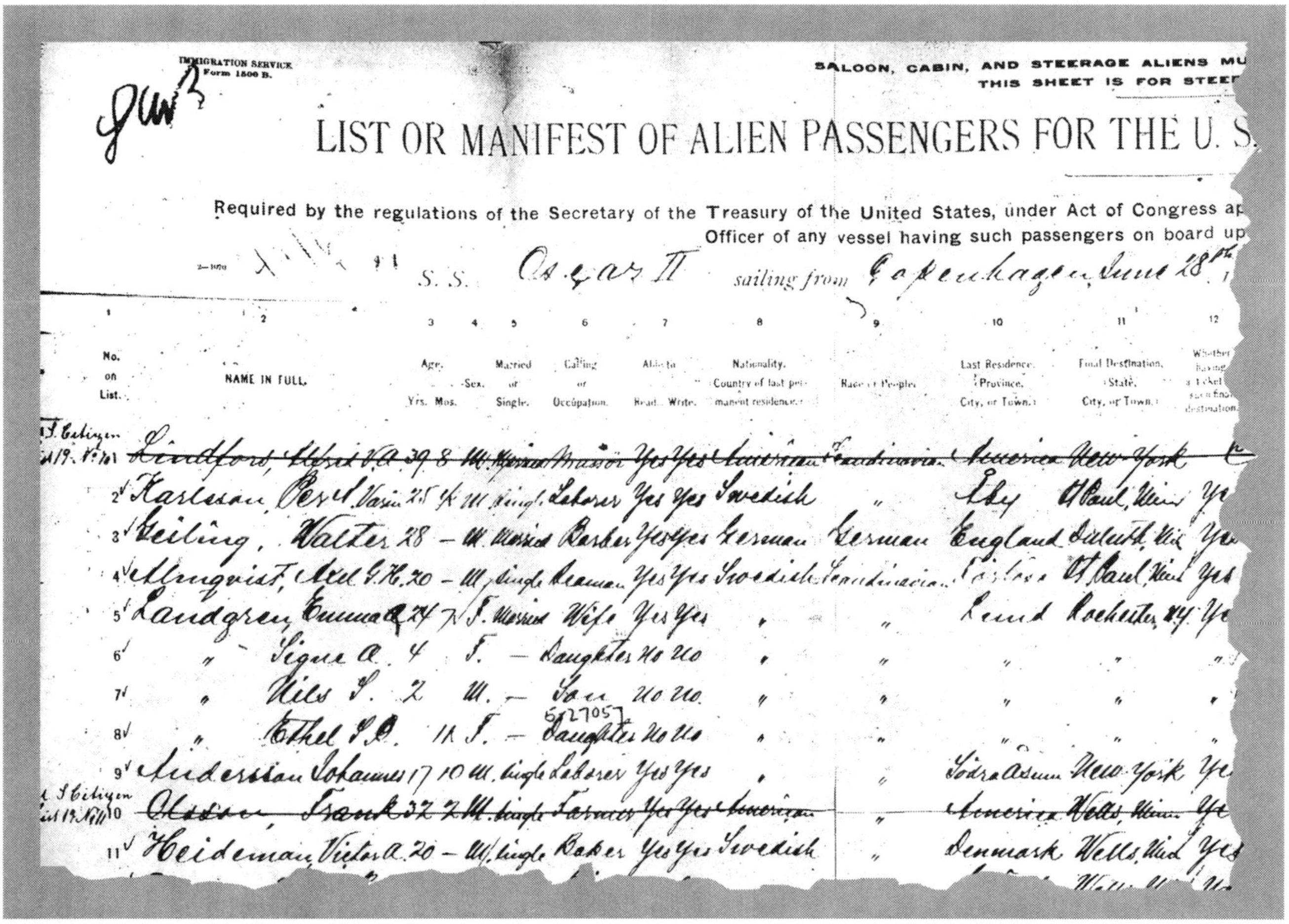

What Can We See in This Document?

The woman *Emma A. Landgren*, age twenty-four years and seven months (*24 7*), and *married*, is of *Swedish* nationality and of *Scandinavian* "race or people." She comes from *Lund* and is travelling to *Rochester N.Y.* She is accompanied by her three children: *Signe*, *4* years old, *Nils*, *2* years old, and *Ethel*, *11* months old.

We can guess that she was joining her husband in Rochester, as she is noted as *wife*.

Ship's Manifests, Passenger Lists

There are many terms in use for passenger records. Passenger records have been kept in the American ports since 1820. In 1819 the American legislators for the first time tried to regulate immigration. The purpose was to guarantee better conditions on board the ships. These early records are called *Ship's Manifests* or *Customs Passenger Lists*, and have been kept in the ports from 1820 until the late 1890s, e.g., in New York until 1897. The lists include some 20 million immigrants, and they have been microfilmed and are available through the National Archives and the Family History Library on microfilm. They are also published on the Internet by Ancestry.com. Indexes are being produced and it is possible to search by name for certain periods.

Besides New York the main immigration ports were Boston, Philadelphia, Baltimore, and New Orleans.

The information in these older passenger lists is usually not sufficient to trace an ancestor. Usually, only the name of the country of origin is given, but no province, city, or parish name.

In 1893, 1903, 1906 and 1907 the U.S. legislation on immigration was progressively tightened with more and more information required from the immigrants, and consequently the passenger lists became more detailed. After 1903 we can usually find information about the place of origin in Sweden, and also the destination within the United States.

From around 1900 the name of the passenger record is changed to *Immigration Passenger List*. The original Immigration Passenger Lists filled in by the immigration officers have been destroyed, but there are copies on microfilm.

Between 1855 and 1890 the immigrants to New York passed through Castle Garden at the tip of Manhattan. From 1 January 1892 the immigrants arrived at the new Ellis Island facility. Ellis Island was in use until 1954, and in the first thirty-two years, until 1924, more than 16 million immigrants passed through this "Gateway to America." Today Ellis Island is a museum and research center for immigrant research. The Immigrant Passenger Lists are available through Ellis Island's website. Searching for an ancestor and viewing the images of the lists is free. But there is a charge if you want to get a copy.

You can search for your ancestor in the indexes to the lists. These indexes, as well as the indexes to the older ship's manifests, have been made by volunteers. The handwriting in the records is often difficult to read. Names are also misspelled in the records. And sometimes they have been misunderstood by the person making the index. So, when you read the names of the places of origin in Sweden, of Swedish towns and parishes, be aware that there are many possibilities to get the names wrong. Use your imagination. Read the document and try to think of alternative interpretations if you get stuck.

CHAPTER EIGHT

Gustaf Adolf Rapp's Family

Leaving Mölltorp

There is only one parish named Mölltorp in all of Sweden, and it is located in Skaraborgs län, in the western part of the country. We can easily find Mölltorp in the Genline FamilyFinder program and get directly to the right records.

Let's start by looking in the moving records for 1879. The parish priest kept a separate book listing people who moved in and out of the parish. The list of people moving out of the parish in 1879 (below) contains 112 people. At the very end of the list we find our people.

Mölltorp Moving Records 1879 (B:1)

(Utflyttningslängd)

för .... Församling.

Års-numer.	Inskrifnings-dag.	Folio uti Förhörsboken.	De utflyttades namn, stånd, embete, yrke.	Ställe hvarifrån utflyttad	Ort hvarthän utflyttad (socken i Län, Stad.)	Mankön.	Qvinkön.
110	6/12	345	Dr. Per Joh. Andersson	d:o	Töftedal	1	
111	18/12	129	Dr. Gust. Adolf. Rapp	[illegible]	N. America	1	
112	19/12	288	P. Anna Christina Carlsd.	[illegible]	d:o		1

Table Column Heads

The table's column heads translate as the following:

Års-nummer	Yearly number (number of entry)
Inskrivningsdag	Day (date) of entry
Folio uti Förhörsboken	(Folio) page in examination roll
De utflyttades namn, stånd, embete, yrke	Name, estate or class, office, trade of the movers
Ställe hvarifrån utflyttad	Place from which (they) moved
Ort hvarthän utflyttad (socken i län, stad)	Place to which (they) moved (parish in county, city)
Mankön	Male sex
Qvinkön	Female sex

What Can We See on This Page?

Let's analyze the entries in detail:

Number *111*, entered on 18 December (*18/12*) 1879, to be found in the household examination roll (the primary church register) on page *139*, *Drg.* (drängen = the farmhand) *Gust.* (Gustaf) *Adolf Rapp*, from *Nya Hulan* (name of farmstead), moving to *N. Amerika* (North America), *1* male.

Number *112*, entered on 19 December (*19/12*) 1879, to be found in the household examination roll on page *188*, *Pig.* (pigan = the maid) *Anna Christina Carlsdr.* (Carlsdotter), from *Skäfverud* (name of farmstead), moving to *do.* (dito = the same, as above), *1* female.

We now know on what pages in the church records we can find more about Gustaf Adolf's and Anna Christina's families. We also know the names of the farms where they lived.

Note 1:

Kristina is here spelled Christina. Spelling of names varied a lot, and can vary from book to book. To be sure that we have the same person we always have to check other records, to compare birth dates, parent's names, etc. She is also entered with her last name Carlsdotter, not Carlsson (see more about Swedish names on page 41).

Note 2:

Dräng and *piga* in old times usually meant "young unmarried man" and "young unmarried woman," and thus could stand for the son and daughter in a family. Later on the meaning changed to "farmhand" and "maid."

Note 3:

The date of moving is given as the *18th* and *19th* of December. We know that the couple was married on 7 November (not in Mölltorp), and that they arrived in the United States in 1879, which is impossible if they left Sweden late December. The truth is that they had left Gothenburg already on 22 August, which we will see in the ship's records (page 110).

The explanation for the erroneous entries in these church books is probably that the priest didn't get the information about their move until the end of the year, and added them at the end of the moving records. At the end of the nineteenth century no permit or even passport was needed to leave Sweden.

Where Do We Go from Here?

Let's look at Gustaf Adolf Rapp's family at the farmstead Nya Hulan on page 139 in the Mölltorp parish household examination roll (*husförhörslängd*).

Moving Records

According to the church law of 1686 the parish priest was obliged to make notes of people who moved in and out of the parish. Moving records were kept more or less completely through the eighteenth century. During the nineteenth century they become accurate and complete in all parishes. The purpose of these records was to control the large migration of people primarily for taxation reasons. The moving records were kept chronologically, that is by year and in the order of dates, and the people moving into the parish and out of the parish were usually noted seperately, but sometimes in the same book. In the Swedish church archives the moving records are placed under the letter B (as described on page 54).

The Rapp Family at Hulan

On page 139 in the household examination roll (*husförhörslängd*), shown below, we find Gustaf Adolf Rapp's family, his parents and siblings.

The name of the family is given as Hulan, not Nya Hulan. (Nya means New; maybe there was an old and a new farmstead).

Mölltorp Household Examination Roll 1874–1887 (AI:8)
(Husförhörslängd)

139

½ Hulan.

	Personernas namn, stånd, embete, yrke och näringsfång (backstugu-, inhyses- och fattighjon), nationalitet (om främmande), lyten (svagsinta, blinda, döfstumma).	Födelse- År.	mån. och dag.	Ort (socken i län, stad.)	Äktenskap. Gift.	Enkling eller Enka.	Koppor.	Flyttad från socken i län, stad, el. pag. i husförhörsbok.	År, månad och dag.	Inflyttnings-attestens n:r.
	Arr.									
1	M. Anders Gustaf Rapp f.d. Korporal	34	19/1	Ramsberg						
2	H:u Charlotta Eriksd:r	39	25/2	d:o						
	Mannens barn i förra giftet:									
3	S. Gustaf Adolf	58	2/7	d:o						
4	S. Johan Herman	60	15/9	d:o						
5	D. Emma Sofia	64	4/7	d:o						
	Gemensamt barn									
6	D. Alida Josefina	69	8/11	d:o						
7	D. Agda Maria	74	8/10	Mölltorp						

Table Column Heads

Personernas namn, stånd, embete, yrke och näringsfång	The persons' name, state, position, profession and trade
(backstugu-, inhyses- och fattighjon)	(crofter, dependent tenant and pauper)
nationalitet (om främmande)	nationality (about strangers)
lyten (svagsinta, blinda, dövstumma)	deformities (feeble-minded, blind, deaf-and-dumb)
Födelse- År. mån(ad) och dag	Birth- Year, month, and day
Ort (socken i län, stad)	Place (parish in län, city)
Äktenskap. Gift. Enkling eller Enka.	Marriage. Married. Widower or widow.
Koppor	Smallpox

What Can We See on This Page?

The name of the farm is here given as *Hulan.*

The family consists of seven members, the parents and their five children.

Arr. (arrendator = leasing farmer)

M. (mannen = the man) *Anders Gustaf Rapp, f. d. Korpralen* (f.d. – före detta = former corporal), born on 19 January *(19/1)* 18*34*, in the parish of *Ransberg.*

H:n (hustrun = the wife) *Charlotta Eriksd:r* (Eriksdotter), born on 25 February *(25/2)* 18*39*, *d:o* (dito, also in Ransberg).

Mannens barn i förra giftet (the man's children in former marriage):

S. (sonen = the son) *Gustaf Adolf*, born on 2 July *(2/7)* 18*58* in *Ransberg*. In the column "moved" we can see that he is noted as moved to *N. Amerika* on 18 December *(18/12)* 18*79*.

Flyttat till (socken i län, stad el. pag. i husförhörsboken).	År, mån. o. dag.	Utflyttnings-attestens n:r.	
314	85		1
			2
N. Amerika	79 18/12		3
			4
N Amerika	80 9/10		5
			6
			7
			8

Notes 1–4: See next page. ⟶

Where Do We Go from Here?

We can look at Gustaf Adolf Rapp's birth records in the Ransberg parish birth records.

There we will also find the name of his mother.

We can look in an older household examination roll to find when the family moved into Mölltorp from Ransberg, and learn when Gustaf Adolf's mother died. We can also find her in the death and funeral records.

We can continue to the examination roll in Ransberg and we can look in the marriage records in Ransberg to find the marriage between Gustaf Adolf's parents.

By moving backwards in time and zigzagging between different kinds of church records we can add pieces to the puzzle. We will probably find that most of the ancestors of Adolph Rapp lived in a rather limited area, in a few parishes around Mölltorp. Most of them were probably farmers, smallholders (small farmers), or soldiers.

Table Column Heads (continued)

Flyttad	Moved
från / till socken i län, stad, el(ler) *pag. i husförhörsbok*	from / to parish in län, city, or page in household examination roll
År, månad och dag	Year, month and day
Inflyttningsattestens n:r. (nummer)	Number of the moving certificate (moving in)
Död	Dead
Utflyttningsattestens n:r. (nummer)	Number of the moving certificate (moving out)

Note 1:

We now have clear proof that this is the right Gustaf Adolf Rapp, since the birth date is the same as given in the U.S. records. He was, however, born in the parish of Ransberg, not Mölltorp as noted in the church register in Zion Lutheran church. If we had looked directly in the birth record of Mölltorp we would not have found him.

Note 2:

We can see that his six years younger sister Emma Sofia left for America a year later. She probably joined her brother in Connecticut. This kind of sideline fact can be helpful in identifying people when we are uncertain. The brother Johan Herman died in 1876 when he was only fifteen years old.

Note 3:

Charlotta Eriksdotter is Gustaf Adolf's stepmother, not his mother. To find the mother we have to look the family up in the Ransberg records.

Note 4:

The father was a former corporal, a soldier. This explains the family name. Rapp (meaning "quick") was a typical soldier's name. Soldiers were often given names reflecting such characteristics, or names referring to the farm and village where they served, instead of their original patronymic names. Sweden had a military system based on professional soldiers living in cottages or at smallholdings near the farms and villages responsible for their upkeep.

We're not positive this is the right Hulan (today's Östra Hulan). There were possibly more houses in the Hulan-area at the end of the nineteenth century.

Household Examination Roll

The household examination roll is the main church register of the Swedish church. The book lists everyone of the residents of the parish, area by area, village by village, farm by farm, household by household. Similar rolls in towns and cities list the residents block by block, house by house, household by household. In the church archives you will find these records under the letter A.

The purpose of the roll was to list the entire population in order to hold examinations to determine everyone's knowledge of the cathecism. These examinations were held in the homes of farmers around the parish, and at these events the priest would ask questions and ask people to recite or read out of the books – the Bible and Luther's Cathecism. People were expected to know the cathecism, with Luther's explanations and the Swedish priest Swebelius' further explanations by heart. There were columns where the priest would enter grades for each person. By studying these records researchers have found that there were widespread reading skills in Sweden already in the eighteenth century, both among men and women.

At the end of the nineteenth century the name of the record was changed to "Parish book" (*Församlingsbok*) and the emphasis was on keeping a population record. The Swedish Church was a state church and retained the responsibility for keeping the official population records until 1 July 1991.

How to Find the Place (Hulan)

hd, Mofalla sn. Gård vid Mullsjön.
Hulan *i Skaraborgs län, Kåkinds hd, Sventorps sn.* Gård.
Hulan *i Skaraborgs län, Skånings hd, Saleby sn.* By.
Hulan *i Skaraborgs län, Skånings hd, Vinköls sn.* By.
Hulan *i Skaraborgs län, Vadsbo hd, Hofva sn.* By vid sjön Skagern.
Hulan *i Skaraborgs län, Vadsbo hd, Mölltorps sn.* Gård med qvarn vid Gälsjön, tillhörande Gälsebo.
Hulan *i Skaraborgs län, Vadsbo hd, Undenäs sn.* Gård nära Stora Bocksjön; tillhörande Bengtstorp.
Hulan *i Skaraborgs län, Valle hd.* Gård i Öglunda sn.
Hulan *i Skaraborgs län, Vartofta hd, Brandstorps sn.* By nära Vettern.
Hulan *i Skaraborgs län, Vartofta hd, Daretorps sn.* Gård.
Hulan *i Skaraborgs län, Åse hd.*

The Rapp family lived at the farm Hulan. In the moving record the name Nya Hulan was also used. How do we find a certain farm within the parish?

The farm is listed within a *rote*, or a ward, in the household examination roll. The bigger parishes were divided up into a number of these wards. On a map you can localize what part of the parish made up this rote by the names of the farms in the church book.

There are of course maps of different types. The best are the detailed "economic maps" showing all the farms and properties within their boundaries. The properties have names and numbers that usually correspond with the names given in the church books. But this is not always the case. Especially small places like cottages, single houses, and smallholdings are sometimes without names on the maps.

These maps can be either historical or current. You can search the historical maps in libraries and archives or at the archives of the land registry (*Lantmäteriet*). Currents maps are sold through Lantmäteriet: its website is www.lantmateriet.se. On its site you can look at Swedish maps and zoom in on details, even before you buy a map.

For Skaraborgs län an old economic map from 1877–1882 has been reprinted. It contains all the farms and houses at this time.

There are also books with all farms, villages, estates and other properties listed. One of excellent quality is C.M. Rosenberg's *Geografiskt-Statistiskt Handlexikon Öfver Sverige*, a book that appeared in 1881–1883 in two volumes. It lists all places in Sweden down to the in dividual farms. It was reprinted in 1982 in four volumes, and can be bought through the regional archives in Gothenburg or the Swedish genealogical society. It is also available on microfilm through SVAR.

Another alternative is to use the search program GIDx in Genline FamilyFinder®. Put in the name of the farm, village or parish and get all the references in the database.

Above we see a list of farms named Hulan. Note that most of them are located in Skaraborgs län, the district we are studying. There seems to be a Hulan in almost every parish in this part of Sweden, so if all you know is that your ancestors came from a farm called Hulan it wouldn't do in this case. You would have to go through the church records for a large number of parishes. Once again we see how important the parish name is.

Finding Cottages and Other Small Places

It is usually more difficult to find smaller places. Often they have been abandoned, and today there are maybe only a few stones left or some lilacs or an old apple tree.

In the church records these small places were listed with the farm owning the land, *"en stuga"* (a cottage), *"ett torp"* (a crofter's holding). The location of the owner's farm will give a lead. The local historical societies have often made inventories of the locations of these houses and cottages. Sometimes they have made maps, and put up signs where houses once stood. Contact the local historical society (*hembygdsföreningen*) to enquire.

Gustaf Adolf's birth

In the church register in Zion Lutheran church we saw that Gustaf Adolf Rapp was born on 2 July 1858. The birth parish was given as Mölltorp. We know from the household examination roll in Mölltorp that this information was wrong and that Gustaf Adolf was born in Ransberg. But the date is probably accurate. Let's check his birth in the Ransberg parish birth and christening records for the year 1858. The number of the book is C:5, and the births are entered by dates. We just look up the date, July 2nd.

Ransberg Birth and Christening Record 1858 (C:5)

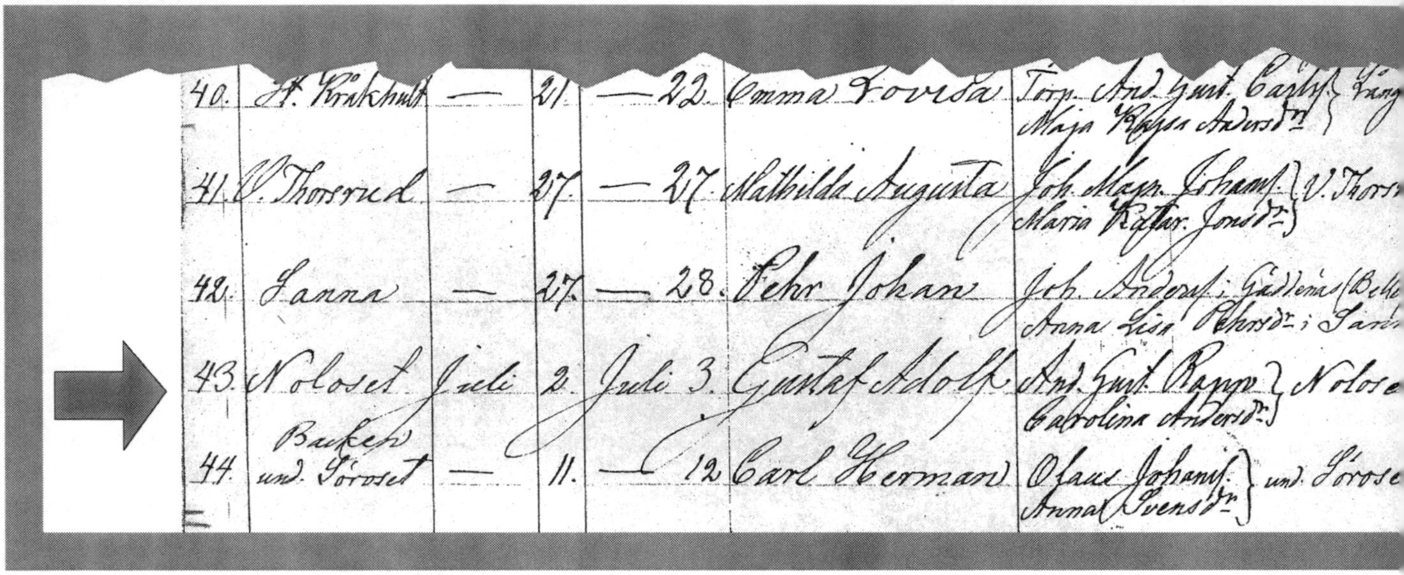

What Can We See in This Book?

Gustaf Adolf is the *43rd* child born this year in Ransberg. He is from *Noloset* (the place within the parish) and was born on *July 2nd* and baptized the day after, *July 3rd*. This was the common practice. The infant mortality rate was still relatively high, and the parents didn't want to risk that their child could die before being baptized.

Gustaf Adolf was given two names. In the list we can see that this practice was the most common, although some children also have just one name.

The parents' names are *And. Gust. Rapp* (Anders Gustaf) and *Carolina Andersd:r* (Andersdotter), and they also live at *Noloset*.

Godparents

On the second page there are columns for the age of the mother at the birth, the godparents, and the priest who baptized the child.

Carolina's age at the birth was *26* years. Note that most mothers were around 30, and very few much younger.

The godparents were usually neighbours or relatives. In this case *Joh*(an). *Aug*(ust). *Flodin* and *Maja Lisa Petersdr.* (dotter) *i St. Höghult*. (i =in).

The priests name was *J Lagerblom*.

Note 1:

Oäkta, which we often see noted in the birth register, means "out of wedlock". Sometimes the father's name is given, sometimes not. Read more about this on page 101.

Note 2:

The months in Swedish are easy, almost the same as in English:

Januari	January	Juli	July
Februari	February	Augusti	August
Mars	March	September	September
April	April	Oktober	October
Maj	May	November	November
Juni	June	December	December

Birth and Christening Records

The church law of 1686 stipulated that the priest should keep records of birth and christening dates, the parents' names, and godparents' names, both for children born in and out of wedlock. Originally these records were usually noted in the common church book, but eventually separate records were kept for births. It is not unusual that dates in the records are wrong. In the church archives you will find these records under the letter C.

Gustaf Adolf's Family in Ransberg

We now know that Gustaf Adolf's parents lived at Noloset in Ransberg at his birth, and that his mother's name was Carolina Andersdotter.

Now we can look in the household examination roll in Ransberg for this time period, and on page 122 in the roll we find the family (shown below).

Ransberg Household Examination Roll 1857 – 1868 (AI:9)
(Husförhörslängd)

122

Mosebo **Rote.**

	Personens Namn och Stånd.	Födelse- ort	Födelse- år	månad och dag.	Flyttningsort och flyttningstid. Inflyttning. från	Inflyttning. år.	Utflyttning. till	Utflyttning. år.
Nolosets	Husarboställe No 97							
Hus.	And. Gust. Rapp	L	1833	14/1				
	Hu Carolina Charl. Andreasdr	L. Höghult	1832	20/5	L. Höghult	1857		
	Son Gustaf Adolf	L	1858	2/7			149	65
	– Johan Herman	L	60	15/9				
Pig	Lovisa [illegible]	Mädtorp	1848	6/8	s 141		p. 124	60
	D. Emma Sofia — —	1	64	4/7				
	Dr. Lars Gustaf Pettersen	R	41	22/2	p 131	63	p 123	64
	Pig. Anna Beata [illegible]	R	35	1/9	[illegible]	64	[illegible]	65

The soldier stead where Gustaf Adolf Rapp was born.

What Can We See on This Page?

Mossebo Rote. Mossebo ward, the division of the parish where the place is located.

Nolosets Husarboställe N:o 97, Noloset's hussar residence. Each soldier stead had its own number within the regiment.

Hus. And Gust Rapp. The father was a hussar. His name has been shortened in the book, it was Anders Gustaf. He was born 14 January *(14/1) 1833* in *"l"* (loco = this place = the same parish, Ransberg).

Hu Carolina Charl. Andreasd:r, Hustru (wife) Carolina Charlotta Andreasdotter. Note that her last name is now given as Andreasdotter, and was given as Andersdotter in the birth and christening record. These two names were perceived as the same.

She was born in *L* (Lilla = little) *Höghult* on 25 May *(25/5) 1832*, and moved in from *L. Höghult* in *1857*. This is noted like a birth parish, but there is no such parish. Within Ransberg there is a village by name of Höghult, however. We can probably find more about Carolina and her parents there. 1857 is probably the parents' year of marriage. We can check in the marriage records.

We can see the three children born at the soldier stead, the sons *Gustaf Adolf* and *Johan Herman*, and the daughter *Emma Sofia*, born in *1858*, *1860* and *1864* respectively.

Pig. Louisa Larsdr. is not related. She is apparently a helper staying with the family for a while. The same goes for the other two people noted: *Dr. Lars Gustaf Pettersson* and *Pig. Anna Beata Pettersson*. Pig. (piga) is a woman farmhand, and Dr. (dräng) a male farmhand. Both titles were earlier used for young women and men in general, also for the sons and daughters in the families.

We can see that the family moved to page *149* (in the same parish) in 1865.

Note 1:

The soldier lived with his family in a small residence, soldier stead (small farmstead or cottage) located on the outskirts of the village, or close to the farms that were responsible for him. The soldier was contracted by a group of farmers, and was granted a small area of farmland, enough to keep a cow for milk, and some land for grazing and to grow potatoes and turnips. He could keep a pig, some chickens and so on. He could take firewood from the common forest. The farmers had to provide him with a uniform and other equipment. The farmers who kept a soldier for the cavalry regiment also had to furnish a horse with saddle, but were, in return, relieved of certain taxes.

Note 2:

Skaraborgs län had two regiments, an infantry and a cavalry regiment. Their soldiers lived in the parishes throughout the province. The soldiers would come together for practice at soldier's meetings at certain intervals, when their wives had to take responsibility for the soldier stead.

The number (in this case *97*) is both the number of the soldier and of the soldier stead, within the regiment.

Where Do We Go from Here?

We can follow the Rapp family to page 149 in the same book and see when the mother died. Then we can turn to the death and burial records to see if any cause of death is given. We can find notes about the father's remarriage and the move to Mölltorp when we look further in the household examination roll. We can check in marriage and moving records.

We can also go back in time and look at the birth and christening records from 1832 and 1833 and track the grandparents of Gustaf Adolf Rapp. This way we can zigzag our way back through history to find the ancestors. We will probably be able to get as far back as the early eighteenth century or the late seventeenth century at least.

The Marriage Between Gustaf Adolf Rapp's Parents

In the household examination roll we saw that Carolina Charlotta moved in at the soldier stead in 1857. Gustaf Adolf was born in 1858. From this we can presume that the marriage took place in 1857, and we look in the marriage records at the time. There we find the couple on page 27 (shown below), and see that the wedding took place on 12 April 1857.

Marriage Record for Ransberg and Mölltorp Parishes (E:2)

(Giftermålsbok för Ransbergs och Mölltorps församlingar)

År 1857 — Giftermålsbok för Ransbergs

Fästnings- numer.	Fästnings- år.	Fästnings- månad.	Fästnings- dag.	Fästehjonens namn, stånd och hemvist.	Födelse- ort.	Födelse- år.	Födelse- månad.	Födelse- dag.	möjligen föregångna äktenskap.	Fästnings-vittnen.
				Dräng Jakob Svensson i Anderstorp u. W. Thorsrud	Gothlunda	1823	Apr.	15		
				Piga Beata Svensdotter i Stugumossen.	Kyrkefalla	1806	Apr.	8		
				Statdräng Gustaf Andersson i Bengtstorp, Kyrkefalla	Grefbäck	1826	Juni	10		
				Piga Anna Stina Svensdotter i Anderstorp u. W. Thorsrud	Gothlunda	1828	Dec.	30		
				Husar No 97 Anders Gustaf Rapp vid Noloset	Noloset	1833	Jan	14		
				Hemmad: Carolina Charlotta Andreasd: i Lilla Höghult	L:a Höghult	1832	Maj	20		

Translations of Column Heads

Fästnings- nummer, år, månad, dag	Engagement, number, year, month, day
Fästehjonens	The engaged persons
namn, stånd och hemvist	names, class and residence
födelseort, år, månad, dag	Birthplace, year, month, day
möjligen föregångna äktenskap	Possible previous marriages
Fästningsvittnen	Witnesses to the engagement
Lysningens	The banns'
num(m)er, månad, dag	number, month, day
charta, R, sk	"charta," (money paid)
Vigsel-	Marriage
förrättarens namn, embete och hemvist	The officiating persons name, office and residence
år, månad, dag, vittnen	year, month, day, witnesses
Anteckningar om hinderslöshetsbevis, giftomans samtycke, afvittring	Notations about certificate of marriage, guardians consent, assignment
Öfrige anteckningar, enligt de i Kyrkolagen gifnaföreskrifter	Other notations, according to in the Church law given directions
Contrahenternas ålder, m.k. q.k.	Age of parties, male, female →

Mölltorps församlingar 27

Lysningens numer	månad	dag	charta R	charta sk	Bevillning enligt 2 Art. för chartber. R	sk	r.	Vigsel- förrättares namn, embete och hemvist	år	månad	dag	vittnen	Anteckningar om hinderslöshetsbevis, giftomans samtycke, afvittring	Öfrige anteckningar, enligt de i Kyrkolagen gifna föreskrifter	Contrahenternas ålder m.k.	q.k.
1	Jan	11 18 25		12				Th. a Theorell	1857	Febr	20	Olof Svensson i Stegmossen med Hu Katrina Pehrsd:r	Fästeqvinnans föräldrar döda; ende brodern Olof Svensson i Stegmossen närvarande		33	50.
2	Jan.	11 18 25		12				J. A. a Lindberg	1857	Jan	31	Lars Svensson med Hu i Anderstorp o. W. Thorsrud.	Fadren död; modren lemnat skriftligt samtycke; äldste brodern Lars Svensson i Anderstorp närv.	Hinderslöshetsbevis för fästmannen fr. Pastor i Kyrkefalla aflemnadt.	30	28.
3	Febr.	1 8 15		12				Th. a Theorell	1857	Apr.	12		Fadren närvarande	Skriftligt bifall af Sqvadrons befälhafvare aflemnadt.	24	24.

What Can We See in This Book?

Husar n:o 97 Anders Gustaf Rapp vid Noloset, the hussar number 97 Anders Gustaf Rapp, at Noloset, and *Hemmad:(dotter) Carolina Charlotta Andreasd.r (dotter) i Lilla Höghult*, are engaged to be married. *Hemmadotter* is a grown daughter still living at home with her parents.

The banns were announced in church three times, on the *1st*, *8th* and *15th* *Feb*ruary of *1857*. The priest conducting the marriage was *Th. A Theorell*, and the marriage took place on *April 12th*.

In the column of annotations it says: *Fadren närvarande* = the father was present. This means that the father of the bride was present as her guardian and giving her away.

In the column for other notations it says: *Skriftligt bifall af squadronsbefälhafvaren aflemnadt* = Written consent given by the squadron commander. Anders Gustaf, as a soldier, had to get the approval to marry from the commander of his hussar squadron.

Anders Gustaf and Carolina Charlotta are both noted as being *24* years old. Anders Gustaf's birth date is wrong, which we will see in a later document.

The records don't say where the marriage took place (in the church, the vestry, or at home), or if there was a wedding party.

Note 1:

Charta stands for *Charta Sigillata* (latin for stamp paper). During the years 1732–1860 there was a tax paid at each marriage, as a fee for the stamped paper used for the banns. In this case *12 skilling* (shillings), a sign that the family was relatively poor.

Note 2:

Afvittring stands for assignment. When a widower or widow remarried they had to present a written assignment to guarantee that the children of the first marriage were given their inheritance.

Note 3:

When the father was dead someone else had to "give the bride away". On this same page of the wedding book there are two such cases. In the first case the living mother has given her written consent to the marriage, and a brother is present at the marriage. In the second case both parents are dead and a brother is present. An unmarried woman was not legally competent, unless under the formal guardianship of her father or oldest brother, or other male relative. When she married this guardianship was transferred to her husband. Only as a widow did she have full legal competence. In Sweden unmarried women received their legal independence in 1884, and married women in 1920.

Records of Banns and Marriages
(Lysnings- och vigselbok)

According to the church law of 1686 the priest should keep records of marriages and the parents of the married couples. At first the records were usually kept in the same book as other records, in a common church book. But later on the records for marriages and banns were kept separate. Posting banns (*lysning*) is an old practice, dating back to medieval times. The couple's intention to get married was announced three Sundays in a row, to give an opportunity for anyone to present impediments to the marriage.

In the marriage records the couples are listed according to date, of the posting of banns, or of the marriages. The marriage records have the letter E.

Statistics Sweden (SCB, located in Örebro) maintains a Marriage Register. It includes information about marriage settlements, divorces, etc, starting in 1921. This picture is from 1924.

White bridal gowns didn't become common until in the nineteen-twenties. Before that the bride often had a black dress, which was practical since she could use it for other occasions. The picture is from 1899.

Gustaf Adolf's Mother's Death

Gustaf Adolf Rapp's mother died 1867, and his father remarried. We can find information about the death of Gustaf Adolf's mother in the death and burial records.

Death and Burial Record for Ransberg 1867 (F:1)

(Död- och begravningsbok för Ransberg)

Död- och Begrafningsbok för Rans=

År 1867.

Numer.	Personens namn, stånd och hemvist.	Ogift mankön.	Ogift qvinkön.	Gift mankön.	Gift qvinkön.	Enkling.	Enka.	Födelse- ort.	år.	månad.	dag.	Dödsfallets ort.	år.	månad.	dag.
6	Dräng Erik Gust. Svensson i W. Thorserud	1						Rbg	44	April	1.	W. Thorserud	67	Febr.	2
41	Enkan Anna Pehrs D:r Sandåsen						1	R.	92	Febr.	18	Sandåsen	–	Oct.	
42	Egf. Petter Eriksson i Skattegf.	–	–	1				R.	02	Jan.	18	Skattegf.	–	Oct.	
43	Hustr. Carolina Charl. Rapp i Höghult L:a				1			R.	32	Maj	20	Höghult L:a	–	Oct	
44	Fl. Anna Carls D:r i Fagerfanna Sergf.		1					R.	67	Jan.	11	Syanger		Nov.	

Translation of Table Column Heads

Nummer	Number
Personens namn, stånd och hemvist	Person's name, state, and residence
Ogift, mankön, qvinkön	Unmarried, male sex, female sex
Gift, mankön, qvinkön	Married, male sex, female sex
Enkling. Enka	Widower, widow
Födelse- ort, år, månad, dag	Birthplace, year, month, day

What Can We See on This Page?

The deceased person is: *Hustr Carolina Charl. Rapp i Höghult l:a. Hustrun* = the wife. L:a (Lilla = little) Höghult is the village closest to the Rapp family's little farm, given as the "address" instead of Noloset,
the village the soldier belonged to. Lilla Höghult is also Carolina Charlotta's home village before the marriage.

Carolina Charlotta was born in *"R"*, Ransberg, on *May 20*, 18*32*, in *L:a Höghult*.

The death occured at home, in *L:a Höghult*, on *Oct*ober *27*, 1867.

The burial took place in *R*ansberg on *Nov*ember *3*, about a week after the death.

The priest performing the burial ceremony was *And*(ers) *Hellström*.

Carolina Charlotta was *35* years, *5* months, and *7* days old at her death.

bergs församling.

Dödsorsak.	Begrafnings- ort.	år.	månad.	dag.	Den prestmans namn, embete och hemvist, som Begrafning förrättat.	Ålder År	m.	d.
	Ransberg	67	Mars	13	And. Hellström	22	10	–
			Oct.		D:o		2	25
	R.		Oct.	27	D:o	69	8	2
	R.		Nov	3	D:o	65	9	7
	R.		Nov.	3	D:o	35	5	7
	R.		Dec.	3	D:o	–	10	14

Translation of Table Column Heads continued

Dödsfallets ort, år, månad, dag — The death place, year, month, day

Dödsorsak — Cause of death

Begrafnings- ort, år, månad, dag — Burial place, year, month, day

Den prestmans namn, embete och hemvist, som Begrafning förrättat — The name, office and residence of the priest who performed the burial service

Ålder, År, m., d. (written by hand) — Age, year, month, day

Be sure to visit the graveyard at the parish church. The oldest graves are usually closest to the church. Swedish graves are in the summer decorated with flowers (never plastic!), and the graveyard often has hedges and trimmed trees, like the graveyard in Mölltorp. At All Saint's Day relatives put out candles.

Note 1:

To our disappointment the priest has not filled in the column for cause of death. This is often the most interesting column. A lot of children died at an early age and mothers commonly lost their lives in childbirth. Tuberculosis and other lung diseases were common during the nineteenth century. Since the names of diseases have changed a lot in the last 150 years the old names of diseases often require an explanation.

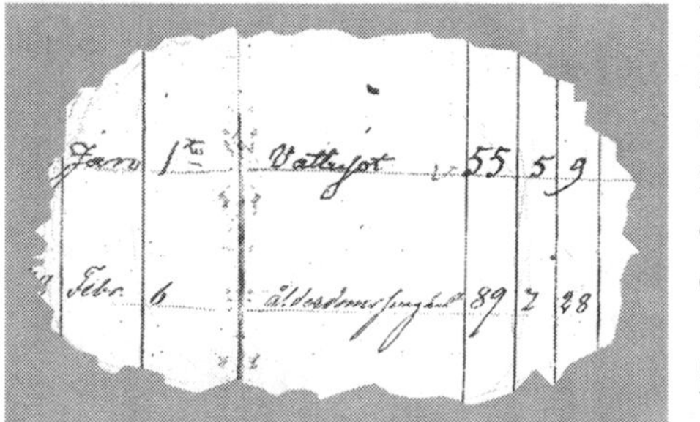

Jan	1ste	Vattusot	55	5	9
Febr	6	ålderdomssvaghet	89	2	28

In a later record (1877) we find notes of causes of death. *Vattusot* is edema and *ålderdomssvaghet* is "weakness of old age."

Note 2:

Grave records are unusual. Traditionally people have been buried in the graveyard at the parish church. The country churches have always been surrounded by their churchyards and that is where you first look for the graves of your relatives. Only in the cities and in the countryside during the last century have separate cemeteries been laid out, sometimes as "forest cemeteries." There are no "county cemeteries." Big cities may also have separate Jewish cemeteries.

Old graves have often been removed. The inscriptions on old gravestones are sometimes hard to interpret; some may use abbreviations instead of full names. Often wooden crosses were used to mark the graves. The Swedish Genealogical Society is conducting a nationwide gravestone inventory of Swedish churchyards and cemeteries, trying to register all stones before 1920. The results are published on the website as they are available.

Death and Burial Book
(Död- och begravningsbok)

According to the church law of 1686 the priest had to keep records of deaths and burials in the parish. These records are usually available from an early date. Sometimes the records are kept in a common church book together with records of births and marriages. Later on separate books were kept for the different records. Sometimes a single death book covers a very long period. The deceased are listed after their death or burial dates. Usually the cause of death is given. Death records are listed under the letter F.

Causes of Death

Beginning in 1749, the priest every year had to send in a report about the population in the parish. This statistical table was sent through the churchly channels to the diocese and finally to the national Statistical Board (*Tabellverket*) in Stockholm, where they were used for the production of the national statistics. One copy of the report was kept in the parish, and these statistical tables can still be found in the church archives. They are available on microfilm and can be found on the Internet through Genline. A couple of the pages were devoted to causes of death.

Below is a list of different diseases; there are several more mentioned in the statistical tables and in the death and burial records, but these are some of the most common.

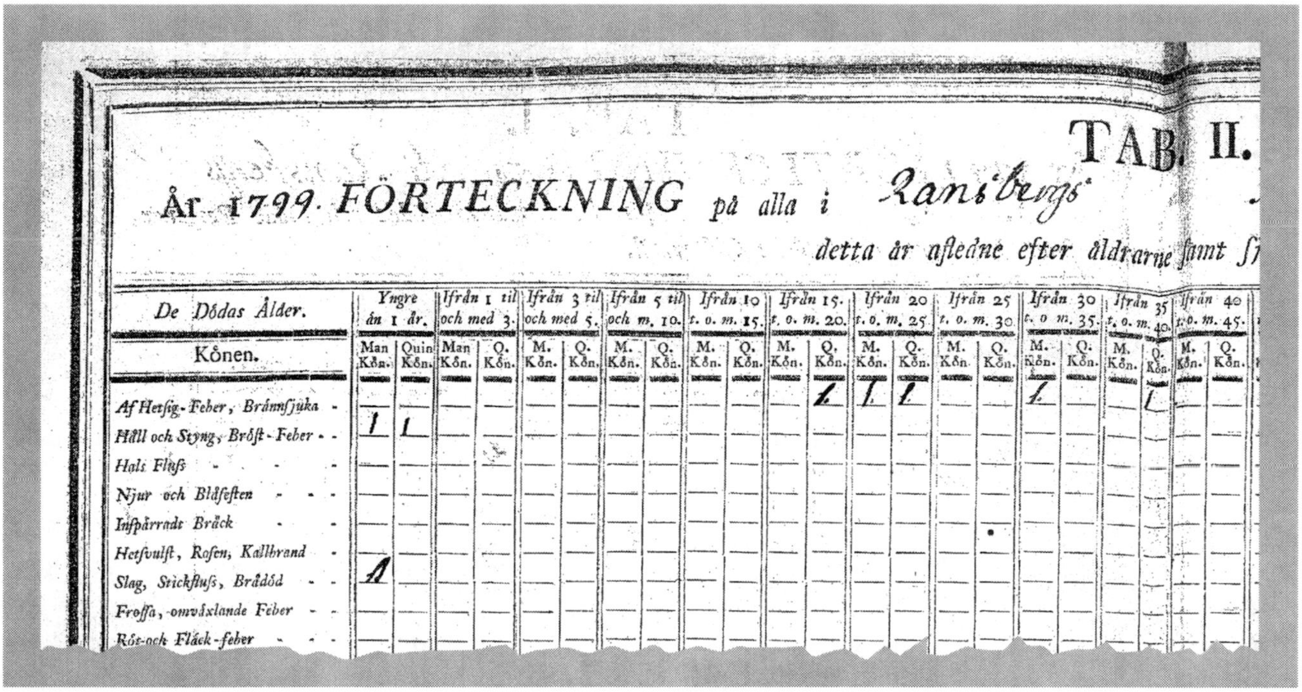
TAB. II.

År 1799. FÖRTECKNING på alla i Ransbergs ... detta år afledne efter åldrarne samt ...

De Dödas Ålder.	Yngre än 1 år.		Ifrån 1 til och med 3.		Ifrån 3 til och med 5.		Ifrån 5 til och m. 10.		Ifrån 10 t. o. m. 15.		Ifrån 15. t. o. m. 20.		Ifrån 20 t. o. m. 25		Ifrån 25 t. o. m. 30		Ifrån 30 t. o. m. 35.		Ifrån 35 t. o. m. 40		Ifrån 40 t. o. m. 45.	
Könen.	Man Kön.	Quin Kön.	Man Kön.	Q. Kön.	M. Kön.	Q. Kön.	M. Kön.	Q. Kön.	M. Kön.	Q. Kön.	M. Kön.	Q. Kön.	M. Kön.	Q. Kön.	M. Kön.	Q. Kön.	M. Kön.	Q. Kön.	M. Kön.	Q. Kön.	M. Kön.	Q. Kön.
Af Hetsig-Feber, Brännsjuka												1	1	1			1			1		
Håll och Styng, Bröst-Feber	1	1																				
Hals Fluss																						
Njur och Blåsesten																						
Inspärrade Bråck																						
Hetsvulst, Rosen, Kallbrand																						
Slag, Stickfluss, Brådöd	1																					
Frossa, omväxlande Feber																						
Röt- och Fläck-feber																						

Diseases

Old Swedish	Modern Swedish	English
Andtäppa	astma	asthma
Angina pectoris	bröstsmärtor	chest pain
Barnasjuka	engelska sjukan	rickets, rakitis
Barnkvävning	kvävning i moderns säng	child smothered by mother in the bed
Barnsbörd	barnsbörd	child birth
Barnsängsfeber	streptokockinfektion	childbed fever
Barnälta	engelska sjukan	rickets (vitamin D deficiency)
Benröta	inflammation i benvävnad	(bone) caries
Bleksot	blodbrist, anemi	anemia
Blodhostning		bloody cough
Blodsjuka, Blodsot	dysenteri	dysentery
Blodslag	hjärnblödning	cerebral hemmorhage
Brott	epilepsi	epilepsy
Bråck (inspärrat)	bråck	hernia (confined)
Brådöd	bråd död	sudden and violent death

Old Swedish	Modern Swedish	English
Brännsjuka	feber	fever
Bröstfeber	lunginflammation	pneumonia
Bukrev	magåkomma, t ex blindtarms-inflammation, gallsten, magsår	stomach condition, e.g. appendicitis biliary colic or gastric ulcer
Dragsjuka	ergotism, mjöldrygeförgiftning	ergotism, poisoning by ergot
Engelska sjukan	engelska sjukan	rickets (vitamin D deficiency)
Fallandesot	epilepsi	epilepsy
Fistlar	fistlar	fistula
Fluss	katarr	catarrh
Fläckfeber	tyfus	typhoid fever
Franska sjukan	syfilis	syphilis
Frossa	malaria	malaria
Förblödning	förblödning	bleeding to death
Gikt	gikt, reumatisk sjukdom	gout, rheumatic disease
Gulsot	gulsot, hepatit	jaundice, hepatitis
Hetsig sjukdom	feber	fever
Huvudsot	hjärnhinneinflammation	meningitis
Håll och styng	lunginflammation	pneumonia
Hård mage	förstoppning	constipation
Häfta	förstoppning	constipation
Kallbrand	kallbrand	gangrene
Kikhosta	kikhosta	whooping cough
Koppor	smittkoppor	smallpox
Kräfta	cancer	cancer
Lungsot	tuberkulos	tuberculosis
Magrev	kolik	colic
Magsot	magsjukdom	stomach disease
Maran	astma	asthma
Maskar	maskar, magparasiter	worms
Mjältsjuka	melankoli	melancholy
Mässling	mässling	measels
Nervfeber	tyfus	typhoid fever
Nässelfeber	nässelfeber	nettle rash, hives, urticaria
Obstruktion	förstoppning	constipation
Olyckshändelse	olyckshändelse	accident
Pleuresi	lunginflammation	pneumonia
Quinnors blodgång		womens bloodloss
Rosen	ros	erysipelas
Rödsot	dysenteri	dysentery
Rötfeber	kallbrand	gangrene
Scharlakansfeber	scharlakansfeber	scarlet fever
Skörbjugg	skörbjugg	scurvy
Slag	hjärnblödning, hjärtslag	cerebral hemmorhage or heart failure
Spanska sjukan	epidemisk influenca	Spanish (epidemic) flu
Spetälska	lepra	leprosy
Stenpassion	njursten, gallsten	kidney or gall stone
Stickfluss	astma	asthma
Strupsjuka	difteri	diphtheria
Svinnsot	tuberkulos	tuberculosis

Old Swedish	Modern Swedish	English
Trånsjuka	tuberkulos	tuberculosis
Tvinsot	Avtynande	gradual decline
Vattusot	vattensvullnad	edema
Vatnskräck, vattuskräck	rabies	rabies
Venerisk sjukdom	venerisk sjukdom	veneral disease
Ålderdomsbräcklighet	ålderdomssvagnet	weakness of old age
Älta	frossa	ague

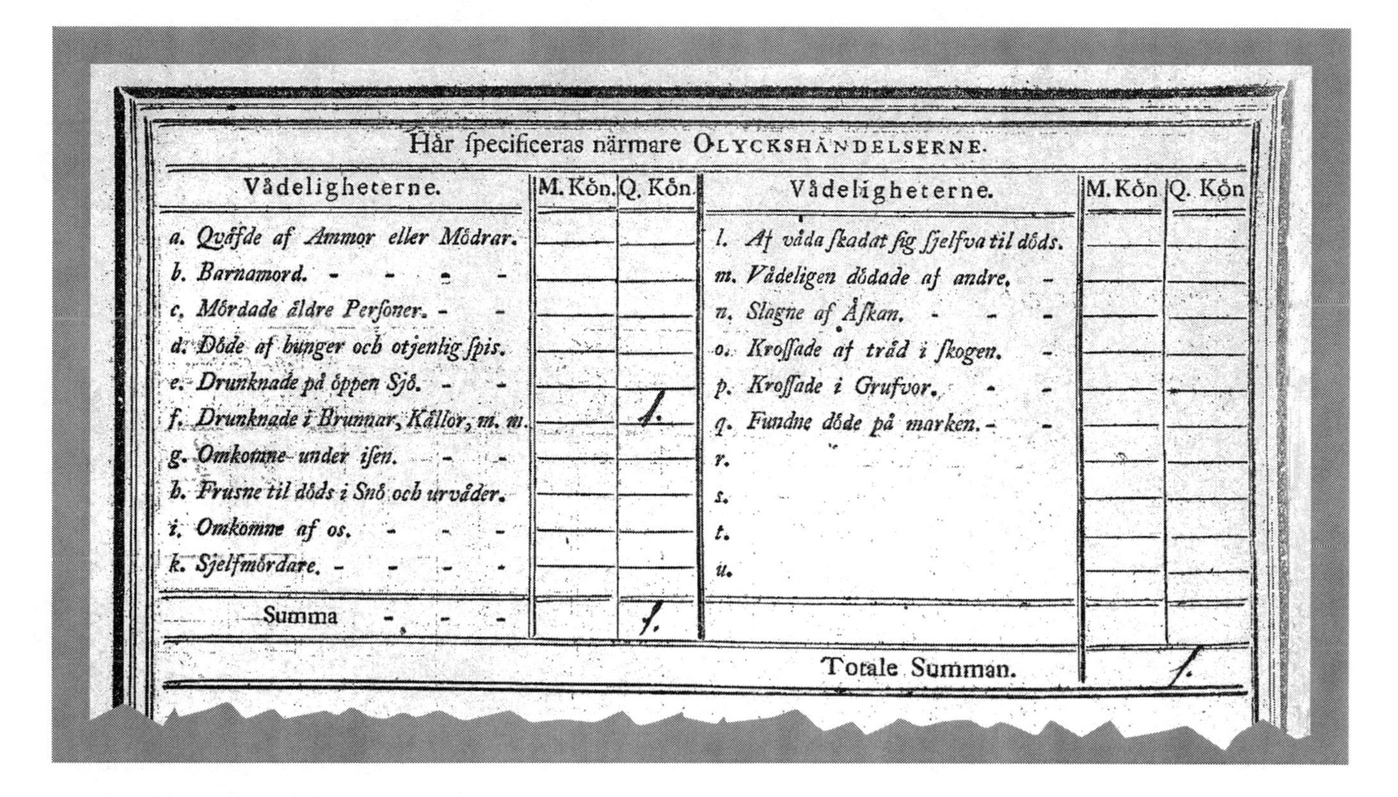

Hår ſpecificeras närmare Olyckshändelserne.

Vådeligheterne.	M. Kön.	Q. Kön.	Vådeligheterne.	M. Kön	Q. Kön
a. Qväfde af Ammor eller Mödrar.			l. Af våda ſkadat ſig ſjelfva til döds.		
b. Barnamord.			m. Vådeligen dödade af andre.		
c. Mördade äldre Perſoner.			n. Slagne af Åſkan.		
d. Döde af hunger och otjenlig ſpis.			o. Kroſſade af träd i ſkogen.		
e. Drunknade på öppen Sjö.			p. Kroſſade i Grufvor.		
f. Drunknade i Brunnar, Källor, m. m.		1.	q. Fundne döde på marken.		
g. Omkomne under iſen.			r.		
h. Fruſne til döds i Snö och urväder.			s.		
i. Omkomne af os.			t.		
k. Sjelfmördare.			u.		
Summa		1.			
			Totale Summan.		1.

Olyckshändelser

Quäfde af Ammor eller Mödrar.
Barnamord.
Mördade äldre Personer.
Döde av hunger och otjenlig spis.
Drunknade på öppen Sjö.
Drunknade i Brunnar, Källor, m.m.
Omkomne under isen.
Frusne till döds i Snö och urväder.
Omkomne av os.
Sjelfmördare.
Af våda skadat sig sjelfva til döds.
Vådeligen dödade af andre.
Slagne af Åskan.
Krossade af träd i skogen.
Krossade i grufvor.
Fundne döde på marken.

Accidents

Smothered by wet nurses or mothers.
Child murder.
Murdered older people.
Dead by hunger or unsuitable food.
Drowned on open sea.
Drowned in wells, springs, etc.
Perished under the ice.
Frozen to death in snow and storm.
Perished by fumes (carbon monoxide).
Suicide.
By accident inflicted death on themselves.
By accident killed by others.
Beaten by thunder and lightning.
Crushed by tree in the forest.
Crushed in mines.
Found dead on the ground.

Abbreviations of Names

On many an old gravestone you will find an abbreviation instead of a full name. The reason for this simplification was practicality or economy. To engrave a name on a stone was a tedious task. The same abbreviations can also be found in old church books, for example in birth records.

How do we know the meaning of these abbreviations? For the people in the parish at the time it was no big problem. "A N S" stood for "Anders Nils' son" and wife "J O D" stood for "Johanna Olof's dotter." The name of the farm and/or the birth and death dates helped with the identification.

But how can we today interpret these gravestones? We can be quite sure that the letters stand for the most common names. Otherwise the full name would have been written. The variety of names was in general very small. We mentioned this fact when we described the Swedish naming practice in chapter five.

These are the interpretations of the letters in abbreviations on gravestones. S as third letter of course always stands for "son" and D stands for "daughter." Here are the letters and names for the first two positions; female names can only be in the first position.

	Male	**Female**
A	Anders	Anna
B	Bengt	Brita (Birgitta)
C	Carl	Cajsa (Carin, Catharina)
D	Daniel (David)	
E	Erik	Elisabeth (Elsa, Lisa)
F	Fredrik	
G	Gustav	
H	Hans	
I	Isak	Inga (Ingrid)
J	Johan (Jan, Jon)	Johanna
K	Karl	Kristina (Kerstin, Stina)
L	Lars	
M	Martin (Mårten, Måns)	Margaretha (Maja)
N	Nils	
O	Olof (Olle, Olaus)	
P	Petter (Per, Peter)	
S	Sven	
U	Ulf	Ulrika

This beautiful marker is from the church yard at Ekshärad in Värmland. These kind of markers were made out of iron by blacksmiths in the area. MPD I HOLE stands for Maria Pers Dotter in Hole, which is a farm in the parish.

Note that many names have many different versions and forms. In some cases there are several possible names, and therefore we can expect the name to be written in full on the stone.

Abbreviations in a Birth Record

On next page are annotations for two children in an old birth record. The first one is a child in a peasant family, and all the names are abbreviated. The second one is a child to a priest, and the godparents are priest and nobility. All the names are written in full.

What Can We See on the Next Page?

The boy Jonas, a farmer's child (bondebarn) from Kahlabo, is the child of A:A:S and j:j:dr, Anders Andersson and Johanna Johansdotter. The godparents are Nils Svensson from Kahlabo, the married woman (Hustru) Margaretha (or Maja) Johansdotter from Gullered and the unmarried (pigan) Margareta (or Maja) Andersdotter from Gullered.

The girl Efva Ulrika's parents and godparents are given with full names except for three abbreviations: And. Stands for Anders, and G (Bieldal) for Gustaf, whereas N: (Warlund) is more uncertain (Nina? Nanna?).

Birth and Christening Record from Gullered Parish
(Utsnitt ur födelsebok från Gullered)

Septembri

15	*18*	*Jonas*	*A:A:S:* *J:J:dr.*	*Bondebarn* *utij* *Kahlabo*	*N:S:Son i Kahlabo* *Hust: M:J: dr. i Gullered* *dräng A:A:S: i Gulle-* *red pig: M:A:dr i* *Gullered*

Augustij

11	*14*	*Efva Ulrika*	*Sven: Heggren* *Catr. Timell*	*Coministers* *barn uti* *Tisered*	*Baron:Adam:Giermund* *Liljencrutz: Kyrkioherde* *Hr And. Warlund ähre-* *wyrd:e Hr G. Bieldal, Länds-* *man Torin Baronesa:* *Fru Marjana Liliecrutz* *Fröken Fridrika Liliecrutz* *Madame N: Warlund* *jungf. Margretta Warlund*

Gustaf Adolf's Father Becomes a Hussar in 1853

By going back through the household examination rolls we can see how the household developed. The Rapp family had lived at the Hussar stead for a long period. The roll kept for 1846 – 1857 (below) shows us that Gustaf Adolf's father, Anders Gustaf Rapp, took over the position as hussar in 1853, when he was only twenty years old. In reality, he was only nineteen, as we shall see in the birth records, shown on page 100.

Ransberg Household Examination Roll 1846 – 1857 (AI:8)

For Husar-Bostället No 97

Socken,

Köghults Rote.

Bostad och Personer.	Födelse. Ort.	Födelse. År och Dag.	Christend. kunskap. Innanläsning.	Utanläsning. Luth.	Utanläsning. Cath.	Förklaringen.	Försåtår.	Koppor.	Inflyttad År	Inflyttad ifrån	Utflyttad År	Utflyttad till	Anmärkningar.
Husar-Bostället No 97													
Hus. Johan Rapp	[illegible]	1797	x	x	/			k.					[illegible]
H. Stina Abramsd.	[illegible]	1804	x	x	x			k.			52	H. Köghult	
[illegible]	Här	1827	x	x	x	/		v.	48	[illegible]	47	[illegible]	
D. Christina Lovisa	do	1831	x	x	x	/		v.			52	Franemåla	[illegible]
S. Anders Gustaf Rapp	do	1833	x	x	x			v.			53	se nedan	[illegible]
D. Maria Sophia	do	1838	x	x	x			v.					Adm. 54.
S. Erik Johan	h. l.	1827	x	x	x			v.	54	H. Köghult	54	H. [illegible]	[illegible]
Husar And. Gust. Rapp	h. l.	1833	x	x	x			v.	53	se ofvan			[illegible] 57 N: 3

Translation

Socken Parish
Rote Ward

For other translations, see chapter eleven, page 120.

What Do We See on This Page?

When this record was first made the family consisted of the following people:

Hus. Johan Rapp, born in *Hasled* on 25 February *1797 (25/2)*. This is the old hussar Johan Rapp, Gustaf Adolf Rapp's grandfather. Hasled is old spelling for the parish of Hassle, north of Mariestad, the "capital" of Skaraborgs län.

H. Stina Abramsd.r, born on 10 June *1804 (10/6)*. His wife. Note that the name Abraham is often spelled Abram. Her birthplace *Hultet* is not a parish but a farm within Ransberg.

Their four children: the son *Erik Johan*, born on 14 September *1827 (14/9)*, *Här* (here, on this place), the daughter *Christina Lovisa*, born on 21 January *1831 (21/1)*, the son *Anders Gustaf*, born on 14 January *1833 (14/1)*, and the daughter *Maria Sophia*, born on 13 August *1838 (13/8)*. All children born at that place (Här = here).

The oldest son Erik Johan has moved back and forth, probably working as a farmhand at different farms. When he moves away to *St. Höghult* (a farm village very near) he is erased. When he comes back he is added further down on the page. In 1856 (hard to read) he moves to *St.holm* (probably Stockholm).

Anders Gustaf Becomes Hussar in 1853

Also Anders Gustaf is moved down on the page. In 1853, the moving out-column contains the notation *se nedan* = see below.

On the new line he has been given the new title *Husar. Se ofwan* in the in-moving column means see above.

In the column *anmärkningar* (annotations) is written: *Lyst 57 n:o 3*, meaning: banns (to get married) 1857, N:o 3 (in the marriage records of that year) See page 86.

The priest has also written. *F. d.* in front of the hussar Johan Rapp (f.d. = före detta = former). In the annotation column is written *Inhy.* (inhyses = dependant).

Gustaf Adolf has now, in 1853 at the age of twenty, taken over as hussar, and his parents have become dependants living on with him at the hussar stead. Four years later Anders Gustaf is ready to marry.

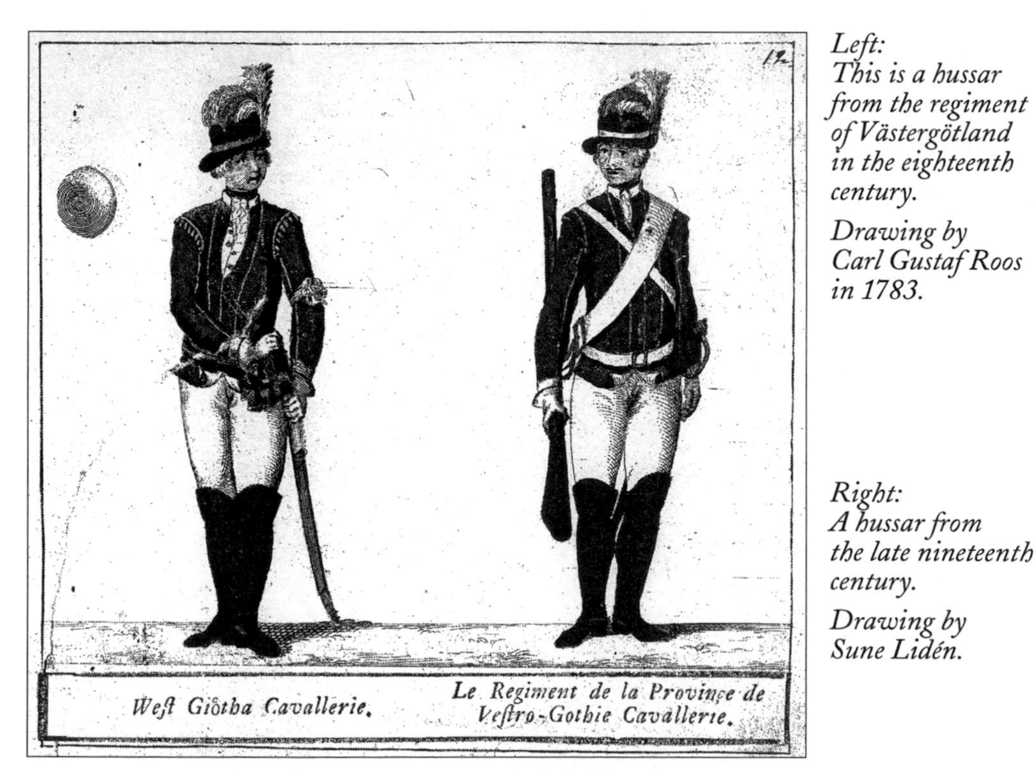

Left: This is a hussar from the regiment of Västergötland in the eighteenth century.

Drawing by Carl Gustaf Roos in 1783.

Right: A hussar from the late nineteenth century.

Drawing by Sune Lidén.

Wrong Birth Date for Anders Gustaf Rapp

Anders Gustaf's birth date has so far, in the books that we have seen, been given as 14 January, 1833. When we check in the birth records, shown below, we find that this is wrong. He was born a year later, in 1834. But the month and day are right.

Ransberg Birth Records 1834 (C:4)

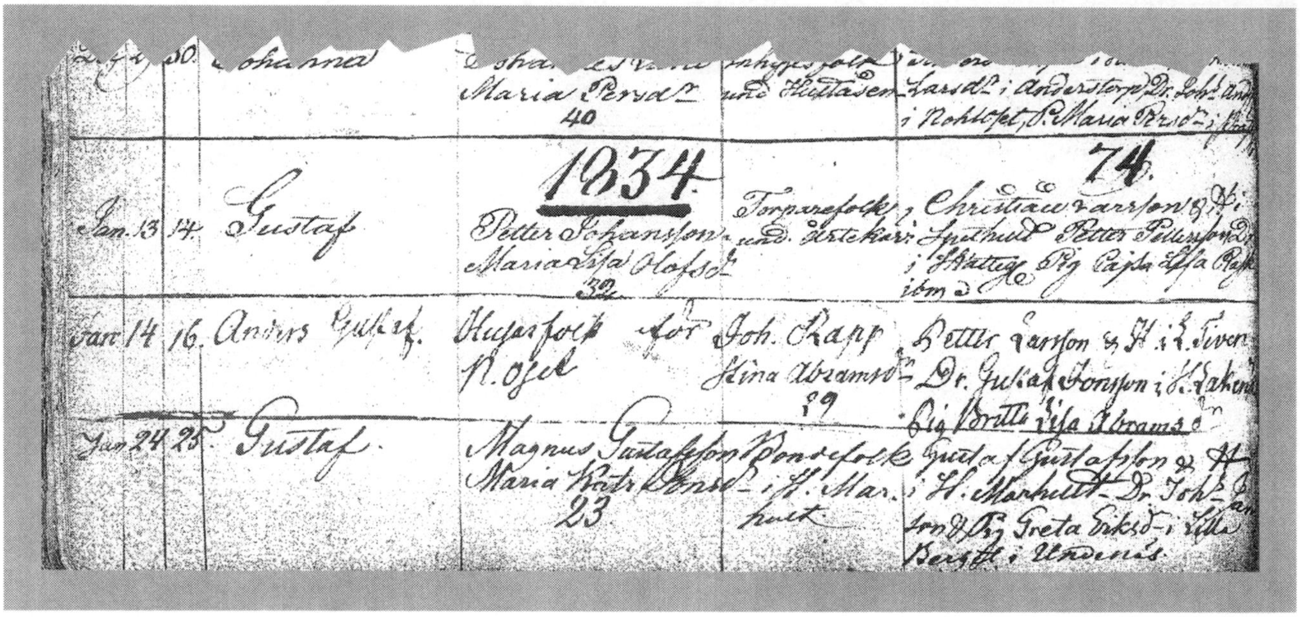

What Can We See in These Records?

The boy Anders Gustaf was born on *Jan*uary *14, 1834*, and baptized *Jan*uary *16*.

The priest has entered his annotations in the wrong order:

Husarfolk för N. Oset (Noloset, Nol is another word for Norr = North). Husarfolk = hussar people.

Joh. Rapp, Stina Abramsd:r 29, the parents, Stina was twenty-nine years old when she gave birth.

The godparents were: *Petter Larsson & H*(ustru = wife) *i L.*(Lilla) *Tiven*, *Dr.* (Drängen) *Gustaf Jonsson i St. Lakenäs*, *Pig* (Pigan) *Britta Lisa Abramsd:r.*

Why was Anders Gustaf's birth year wrong in the household examination rolls and other records? Did the priest just make a mistake or was there a reason why the parents pretended that he was a year older than his actual age? Did they want to make it possible for him to take over the position as hussar earlier?

How to Find the Father of a Child Born Out of Wedlock

The term "oäkta" in the church books stands for "out of wedlock" or illegitimate. Only the mother is noted in the birth and christening record. There is no name of the father in the records.

How can you find the father? There are several possibilities:

- The fact that the father isn't noted in the birth record doesn't mean that he wasn't known. It only means that the parents were not married. In many cases they married later and the child was considered legitimate. In such cases you can see this in the household examination records. Sometimes the marriage didn't occur until much later. Therefore you have to look through the records for the following time period.
- Having a child out of wedlock wasn't necessarily a shame. In Stockholm in the nineteenth century, for example, many couples lived together and had children without being married. These marriages were even called "Stockholm marriages." In the 1840s more than half of the children born in Stockholm were born out of wedlock. At the same time, about five percent of the children in the countryside were illegitimate.
- All extramarital sex was unlawful until 1864. When a child was born out of wedlock the mother and the father, if he was known, were taken to court. The man could free himself by taking his oath upon not being the father. After 1864 the case was taken to court only if the mother sued the man to get the paternity established and get custody. If you search in court records it is often possible to find the father. But this source is difficult to use, and you need help from a person who knows how to read old court records in Swedish.
- Later on, at the beginning of the 1900s, paternity became more of an administrative than a judicial matter. The unmarried father often signed a document submitted to the municipality, where he admitted the paternity and agreed to pay custody for the child. Such documents (*faderskapserkännande*) can be found in the archives of the local municipalities and cities.
- Before 1855 the person guilty of extramarital sex, usually only the woman, had to go through the process of schriving. Before 1741 this was public; she had to stand on a special stool in the church, to be shamed by the churchgoers, before she was taken up in the congregation. Names of fathers can therefore sometimes be found in the church protocols where schriving was noted.
- To avoid the shame and punishment some unwed mothers would try to hide their pregnancy, bear the child in secrecy, and then kill the newborn baby. To stop this practice the king, Gustaf III, in 1778 decided that a mother could bear her child, give it to foster care, and then remain unknown. She would, however, have to give a sealed letter to the priest, with her own and the father's name. This sealed letter was kept in the church archive together with the birth records, and can still be found in the archives to bear witness of unknown parents.
- Midwives kept diaries. Some of these have been saved and can be found in different archives and museums. The midwife might have noted a father in cases where his name wasn't noted by the priest in the church records. The same can be true for diaries kept by birth clinics.
- Names of fathers can also be found in archives of orphanages and in protocols and other documents about foster care in the municipal archives. An unmarried mother could leave her baby free of charge if she stayed at an orphanage as a wet nurse. Other mothers gave away their babies at birth, but had to pay for this.

In summary: If you have problems finding a father to one of your ancestors, and you meet the notes "oäkta" (out of wedlock) or "fader okänd" (father unknown): don't give up. There are several possibilities to find the father in the records; he has usually been known.

CHAPTER NINE

Anna Christina Carlsson's Family

We saw in the moving records (page 77) that Anna Christina Carlsdotter lived at Skäfverud. We also saw that we can find this place at page 188 in the household examination roll of this period. Here we find her family.

Mölltorp Household Examination Roll 1874–1887 (AI:8)
(Husförhörslängd)

188

Skäfverud

	Personernas namn, stånd, embete, yrke och näringsfång (backstugu-, inhyses- och fattighjon), nationalitet (om främmande), lyten (svagsinta, blinda, döfstumma).	Födelse- År.	mån. och dag.	Ort (socken i län, stad.)	Äktenskap. Gift.	Enkling eller Enka.	Koppor.	frå stad,
1	M. Carl Petter Andersson Eg 14/4 60	20	29/10	Dellefors				
2	H: Britta Lisa Jonsd:	25	27/3	Ransberg				
3	~~S. Johan Gustaf~~	~~52~~	~~23/9~~	~~Mölltorp~~				
4	~~D. Adina Sofia~~	~~54~~	~~16/2~~	d:o				
5	~~D. Anna Christina~~	~~55~~	~~29/12~~	d:o				
6	S. August	63	8/10	d:o				

For translation of the column heads in this roll, see page 78.

What Can We See on This Page?

Skäfverud is the name of the place (farm). The "fv" is an example of old spelling. This was later changed to "v," thus Skäverud.

M. Carl Petter Andersson. This is Anna Christina's father, from whom she gained her name Carlsdotter – which she at some point in the journey changed to Carlsson like her brothers' last names. At this time the system with patronymic names was still in use in the area. *M.* = "Mannen," the man.

Eg 13/3 60, means that her father has been the owner (Eg. = "egare," later spelt ägare) of the farm since 13 March 1860. He was born on 29 October (*29/10*) *1820* in the parish *Bellefors* (today spelt Bällefors). It is sometimes difficult to interpret the capital letters. Is this a "B" or an "H"? Look at the next line.

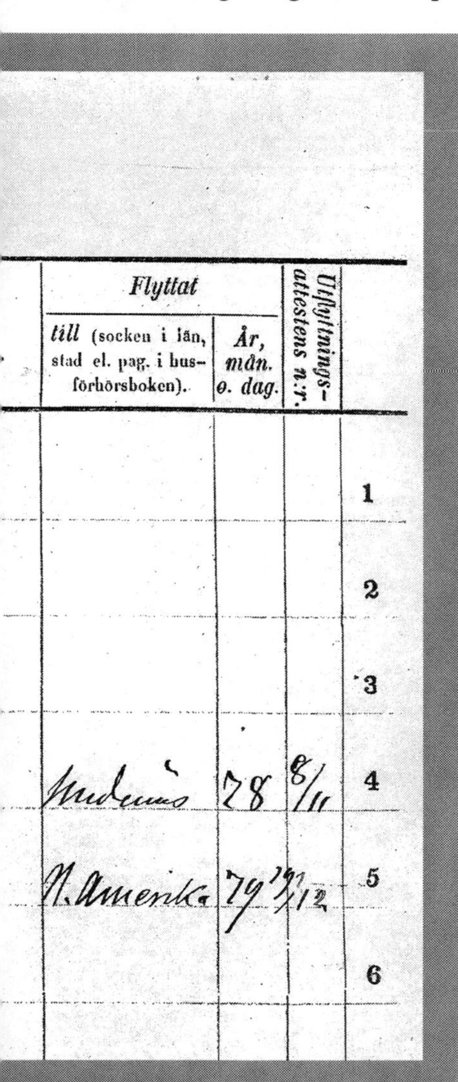

Flyttat		Utflyttnings-attestens n:r.	
till (socken i län, stad el. pag. i husförhörsboken).	År, mån. o. dag.		
			1
			2
			3
Undenäs	78 8/11		4
N. Amerika	79 7/12		5
			6

H. Britta Lisa Jonsd. We can see how this priest wrote H and B. H stands for "hustru" (wife). She is daughter of a Jon or Johan, and born on 27 March (*27/3*) *1825* in *Ransberg* parish.

Anna Christina has three siblings, a brother (*S.* = son) *Johan Gustaf*, born in *1852*, a sister (*D.* = daughter) *Adina Sofia*, born in *1854* and a younger brother *August*, born in *1863*. They were all born in *Mölltorp*.

In the notes we see that the sister Adina moved from the farm in *1878* to *Undenäs*, a year before Anna Christina emigrated – she moved to *N. Amerika* in *1879*. We should check if Adina stayed in Sweden or emigrated as well. We should also check if any of the brothers later emigrated.

Note 1:

Old and new spelling. The page shows several good examples of old spelling, before the spelling reforms around the turn of the century 1900: Skäfverud – Skäverud, egare – ägare, Bellefors – Bällefors.
See also page 45.

Note 2:

Names with different forms. Carl, Petter, Britta, Lisa, and Christina are all names with many different forms. See also page 43.

Where Do We Go from Here?

To further study Anna Christina's family we need to look in older household examination rolls, to see where the family lived before 1860 – on the farm or at some other place within the parish. We can also look in the marriage records to see when and where Carl Petter and Britta Lisa were married.

To find more about Carl Petter's and Britta Lisa's families we have to look in the birth records in Bällefors and Ransberg and the household examination rolls in these parishes.

Let's also look at her birth record.

Anna Carlsson in Mölltorp's Birth and Christening Records

If we don't have a reference to the right page in the household examination roll in the moving records, but we know the birth date, the best way to find the family is to look in the birth records. Remember, there may be several Anna Carlssons.

We learned from the church register in Portland, Connecticut, that her birth date was 29 December 1855, and the birth place was Mölltorp. This is actually enough information to find her without looking into ships registers and moving records. We can, through Genline or microfilm, find her directly in the birth records in Mölltorp.

Below is the entry:

Mölltorp's Parish Birth and Christening Records 1855 (C:4)

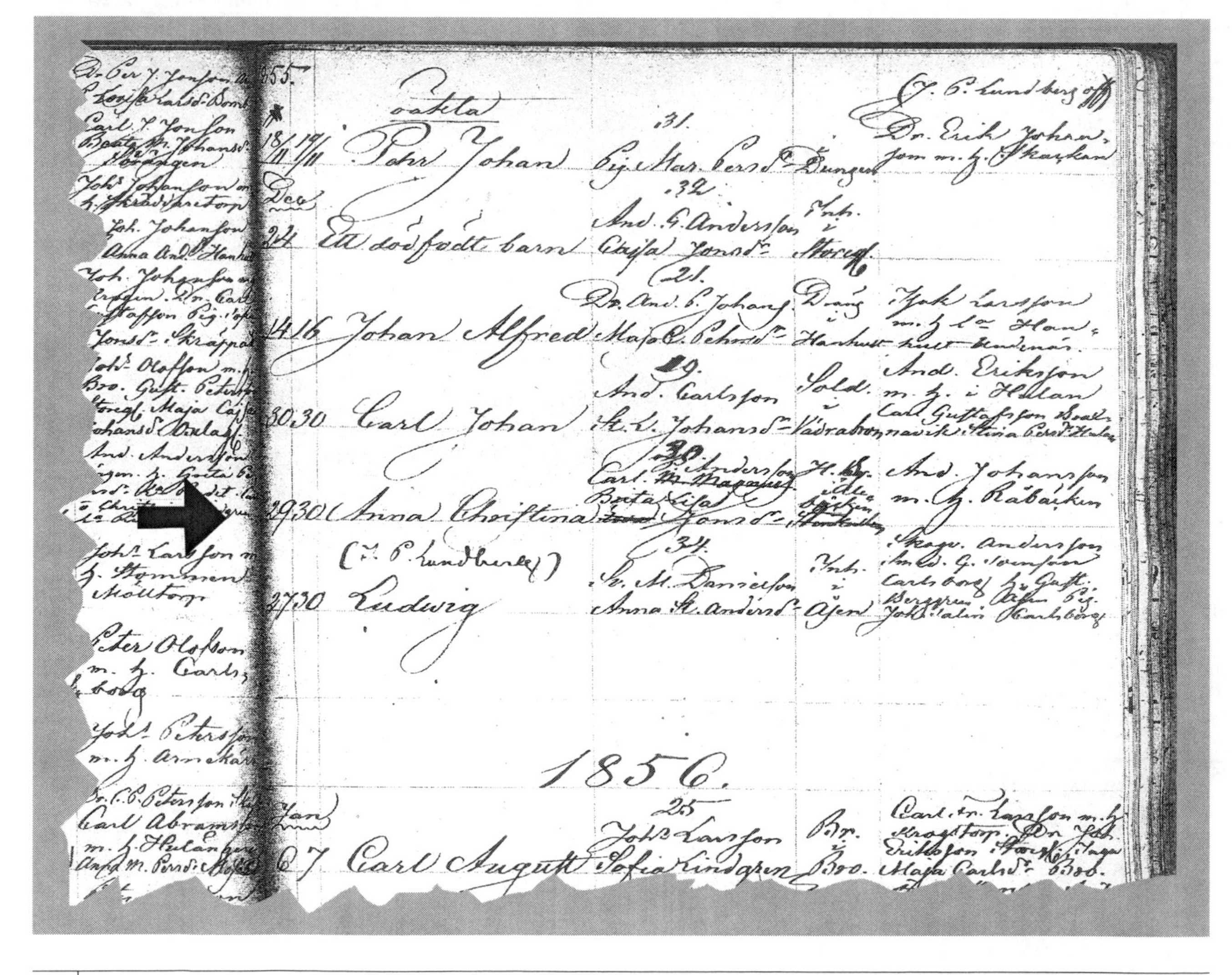

1855

oäkta

18/11 17/11 Petter Johan

Dec

24 Ett dödfödt barn

14 16 Johan Alfred

30 30 Carl Johan

29 30 Anna Christina

27 30 Ludwig

1856.

Jan

6 7 Carl August

What can We See in This Book?

The first two columns are birth date and christening date. Anna was born on December *29th* and christened on December *30th*. Her full name is *Anna Christina*.

The parents names are *Carl P. Andersson* and *Brita Lisa Jonsd:r.* It's partly hard to read, because the priest first has noted the wrong names and then crossed them out. Note that the first and the second s in Andersson are written in a different manner, and that Brita here is spelled with one t.

H. Br. i Ale-Bäcken This entry is about the parents' title and residence. *H.Br.* (hemmansbrukare) is another word for farmer, meaning "cultivator of an average farm." *Alebäcken* is the name of the farm.

And. (Anders) Johansson m. h. (med hustru = with wife), *Råbäcken* (their residence). These are the godparents to Anna Christina, and probably close neighbours, or near relatives or friends.

Where Do We Go from Here?

As we can see, the family has moved from Alebäcken to Skäfverud. If we had started our research in the birth records we would have had to first look up Alebäcken in the household examination roll, and from there on follow the family's whereabouts.

As long as they don't move out of the parish we can follow them from page to page in the same book, and they will never be noted in the moving records, which only list people moving in and out of the parish.

A mother and her baby around 1895.

CHAPTER TEN

Finding Your Ancestor in Swedish Passenger Lists

Almost all of the emigrants leaving Sweden between 1869 and 1930 were registered in passenger lists turned in to the police in the port cities. These police records are the main sources for information about emigrants from Sweden to North America. By far the largest number of emigrants left through Gothenburg.

It is possible to search for individual emigrants in a vast database containing 1.2 million Swedish emigrants who left Sweden between 1869 and 1930. In these lists we have found Gustaf Adolf Rapp and Anna Carlsson. Since we already had the name of their home parish in the American church register this search is not necessary, but we will show it as an example. We will also look at the passenger list for their departure from Gothenburg in 1879.

Sweden did not require citizens to have passports or visas in order to leave the country; the borders were open between 1860 and 1917. As a result no passport records for this period exist.

The Swedish passenger lists have been recorded and put into a database, and are accessible for gen-ealogical research. The work has been done at the regional archives in Gothenburg and the whole database is named "Emigranten" (the Swedish Emigrant) with the subtitle Emihamn for the reg-ister of passenger lists. The database is available on CD-ROM. The index can also be accessed on microfilm from SVAR and at the Emigrant Institute in Växjö.

The index gives all the vital information in the passenger list for each passenger. It is usually not necessary to look at the passenger list itself.

Anna Carlsson – A Search in the Database Emihamn/Emigranten

Adolf Rapp is a relatively unusual Swedish name. Anna Carlsson is an extremely common name. Carlsson is one of the three most common last names. Anna is probably the most common first name among women during this period.

We have the further complication that Carlsson could be spelt Karlsson, and that she might have used the patronymic Carlsdotter.

From 1864 to 1896 we find 177 entries in the database for *Anna Carlsson* (see facing page). If we know the year for certain, *1879*, there are only four possible Anna Carlssons. Had we only known that she left Sweden "around 1880," we would have been in bigger trouble. There was another Anna Carlsson leaving in *1878*, there were six leaving in *1880*, eight more leaving in *1881*, and another eight in *1882*.

In this case Anna's birth year would be sufficient to help us find her. Anna from *Vreta Klos* (ter) is *26*, thus probably born in 1853, Anna from Lungsund is *18*, born in 1861. We know that our Anna was born in 1855. As her birth date is 29 December she would be noted as *23* years old in *1879*. In *1881* and *1882* there are several Annas of the same age. In those cases an accurate birthdate would be needed.

One Anna Carlsson travelling from *1879* has the "home parish" noted as *Amerika*. She probably is leaving Sweden for the second time, after a visit in Sweden, and is already an American resident. The other three are from *Vreta Kloster*, *Mölltorp* and *Lungsund*. In our case we know that Anna was born in Mölltorp. If we hadn't had this information (or the birth year), we couldn't know for certain which one of these Annas was ours. In this case even vague clues

EMIHAMN / EMIGRANTEN / 2002-11-12
Namn: Carlsson Förnamn: Anna
Antal funna: 3091

Efternamn	Förnamn	Ålder	Församling	Län	Utvdrår	Destination
CARLSSON	ANNA	51	LINKÖPING	E	1873	RED OAK
CARLSSON	ANNA	16	ÖLMSTAD	F	1873	BOSTON
CARLSSON	ANNA	55	STRÅ	E	1875	WARREN
CARLSSON	ANNA	22	GÅSINGE	D	1876	NEW YORK
CARLSSON	ANNA	20	VEDDIGE	OA	1877	NEW YORK
CARLSSON	ANNA	27	HOF	E	1877	CHICAGO
CARLSSON	ANNA	56	FRILLESÅS	N	1878	DETROIT
CARLSSON	ANNA	26	VRETA KLOS	E	1879	NEW YORK
CARLSSON	ANNA	23	MÖLLTORP	R	1879	NEW YORK
CARLSSON	ANNA	29	AMERIKA		1879	NEW YORK
CARLSSON	ANNA	18	LUNGSUND	S	1879	ROCK ISLAND
CARLSSON	ANNA	26	LUDVIKA	W	1880	CHICAGO
CARLSSON	ANNA	41	AMERIKA		1880	NEW YORK
CARLSSON	ANNA	30	ARBOGA	U	1880	NEW YORK
CARLSSON	ANNA	1		G	1880	S:T PAUL
CARLSSON	ANNA	24	HALMSTAD	M	1880	NEW YORK
CARLSSON	ANNA	21	ÖREBRO	T	1880	NEW YORK
CARLSSON	ANNA	27		A	1881	NEW YORK
CARLSSON	ANNA	21	ALGUTSTORP	P	1881	BOSTON
CARLSSON	ANNA	18	HÖGSBY	H	1881	NEW YORK
CARLSSON	ANNA	24	MISTERHULT	H	1881	NEW YORK
CARLSSON	ANNA	19	LAXARBY	P	1881	FORT DODGE
CARLSSON	ANNA	18	SKOG	P	1881	NEW YORK
CARLSSON	ANNA	3	SVERIG		1881	NEW YORK
CARLSSON	ANNA	27		OA	1881	CHICAGO
CARLSSON	ANNA	22	LUNDBY	U	1881	VALPARAISO
CARLSSON	ANNA	36	SVERRIG		1882	GIBSON, ILL
CARLSSON	ANNA	20	ÖDESHÖG	E	1882	BROWNVILLE
CARLSSON	ANNA	22	GÖTLUNDA	T	1882	NEW YORK
CARLSSON	ANNA	22		A	1882	CHICAGO
CARLSSON	ANNA	3	MÖRLUNDA	H	1882	
CARLSSON	ANNA	25		OA	1882	NORWICH
CARLSSON	ANNA	23	SÖDERHAMN	X	1882	NEW YORK
CARLSSON	ANNA	1	ENKÖPING	C	1882	BOSTON

LAST NAME	FIRST NAME	AGE	PARISH	LÄN	EMIGRATION YEAR	DESTINATION

could be helpful. Maybe we knew that she came from a certain part of Sweden. The database gives the letter abbreviations for "län." Vreta Kloster is in Östergötlands län (*E*), Lungsund is in Värmlands län (*S*) and Mölltorp is in Skaraborgs län (*R*). If we knew she came from "Västergötland" or "not so far from Gothenburg" that would be good enough to make a guess. The town's name on a photo or a picture on a post card would also be helpful.

If we didn't have any specific lead, we could go to all three parishes and look in the different church books for other clues. The register doesn't give middle names, but we would find them in the church books. Maybe looking at the whole families would give some kind of lead. If Anna had children, could she have named them after her own parents?

In Summary

If you don't know the name of the parish from which the emigrant left, you need other specific facts, particularly if the emigrant has a common name. An accurate date of birth is very important since the possibility that two persons have the same birth date is very slim. If you don't have the exact emigration year you may have to check a number of persons by looking them up in their home parishes' church records. An indication of what part of Sweden they came from is helpful.

What Does the Database Say about Our Anna Carlsson?

EMIHAMN / EMIGRANTEN / 2002-11-12
Förnamn: ANNA
Efternamn: CARLSSON
Ålder: 23 Kön: K
Församling: MÖLLTORP Län: R
Utresehamn: GÖTEBORG
Utvandrdag: 1879 08 22
Destination: NEW YORK
Medåkande: NEJ
Källkod: 13:565:6566

First name: Anna
Last name: Carlsson
Age: 23 Sex: female (K = Kvinna = female)
Parish: Mölltorp Län: R
Port of departure: Göteborg (Gothenburg)
Date of emigration: 22 August 1879
Destination. New York
Companions: No
Code to source: 13:565:6566

Gothenburg harbour on a postcard. In the foreground is the custom's house (see also page 18–19). Over one million emigrants left by ship from Gothenburg.

Inloppet till Göteborg
Import Joh. Öl. Andreens Konstförlag, Göteborg.

Gustaf Adolf Rapp in Emihamn/Emigranten

Gustaf Adolf Rapp is an easier case than Anna Carlsson since Rapp is a relatively unusual last name. Even with very vague information, there are very few other possible persons.

In the whole period covered by the database (1859 to 1951) there were a total of 168 people with the name Rapp. Out of these there is one G A Rapp, one Gustaf Rapp, two Gust A Rapp and one Adolf Rapp. Of course there is always a possibility of error. But only one person fits our requirements for emigration year and part of Sweden.

This is how the entry looks for *G A Rapp*:

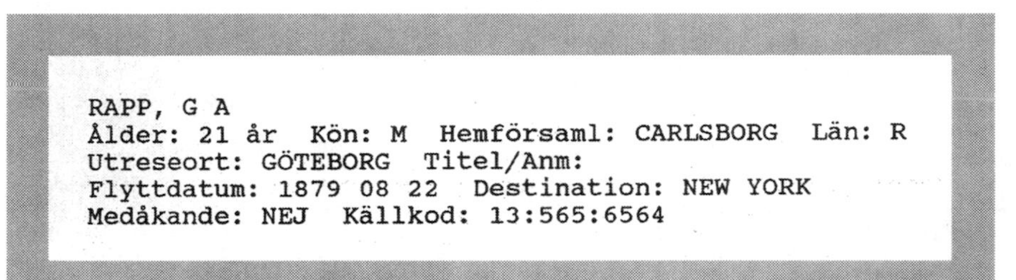

```
RAPP, G A
Ålder: 21 år  Kön: M  Hemförsaml: CARLSBORG  Län: R
Utreseort: GÖTEBORG  Titel/Anm:
Flyttdatum: 1879 08 22  Destination: NEW YORK
Medåkande: NEJ  Källkod: 13:565:6564
```

Note: The home parish is given as *Carlsborg*, not Mölltorp. Carlsborg is a town in the vicinity of Mölltorp and possibly the railway station Gustaf Adolf Rapp left from.

With this entry, if we hadn't known the parish, we would be misled to the wrong parish. In such a case the best measure would be to go through the records of the neighbouring parishes.

According to the source code (källkod) we now look for volume 13, page 565, and the passengers 6564 (Gustaf Adolf) and 6566 (Anna).

"Here You see the steamship Ariosto" – one of many emigrant ships leaving Gothenburg.

Her ser ni Ångaren Ariosta
Farväl från fosterjorden.
ETT SISTA AFSKED GE VI FOSTERJORDEN,
TILL LÄNGTANS DRÖMDA MÅL GÅR NU VÅR FÄRD.

Passenger List for the Steamship Orlando

Göteborgs poliskammare E IX: (Gothenburg Police Chamber)

With the information from the database Emihamn we can find the right passenger list. The lists are microfilmed and we can search for them according to date.

We know that the list we are looking for is in volume number 13, on page 565, and that the ship sailed on 22 August 1879. When we find the list (below) we see that the ship's name is Orlando.

C. W. Hällström.

Förteckning

öfver utvandrare, som af undertecknad befordras med Ångfartyget "Orlando", *som den* 22 augusti *härifrån afgår till* Hull

Göteborgs Handels-Tidnings Aktie-Bolag

Kontraktets No.	Utvandrarens yrke och namn.	Födelseort till län och socken.	Ålder.	Man.	Qvinna.	Summa.	Bestämmelseort.
6556.	Serafia Johnson	Stockholm	37		1		
–	systerson J. Bergström		16	1.		2.	Newyork.
6557.	C. W. Schmidt	Westerås, Odelsund	24	1.		1.	Moingona Ia
6558	A. Olsson	" Lungtorp	19	1.		1.	"
6559.	J. A. Larson	Göteborg	21	1.		1.	New york
6560.	M. Johansson	Stockholm	25	1.			
–	Bror Nils.		20	1.		2.	St Paul, Minn
6561.	Mari Jesperson	Skaraborg län, Ransberg	17		1.	1.	Newyork
6562.	Hilma Olausson	" "	24		1.	1.	Carbondale, Kan
6563.	C. J. Werner	Wermland, Carlskoga	24	1.			
–	cousin J. A. Herrmansson		22.	1.		2.	Newyork
6564.	G. A. Rapp	Skaraborg län Carlsborg	21	1.		1.	
6565.	Viktor Andersson	" "	20	1.		1.	"
6566.	Anna Carlsson	" Mölltorp	23		1.	1.	"
6567.	Lars Andersson	Elfsborg län Frändefors	37	1.			
–	dotter Hilma	" "	11 1/4		1.	2.	Danville, Ills
6568.	And. Larsson	Bohus län Södra Ryr	34	1.		1.	"
6569	C. [illegible]	Elfsborg län Skållerud	18	1.		1.	Minneapolis, Mi

Göteborg den 21 aug 1879.
C. W. Hällström

TRANSLATION OF SWEDISH TEXT AND COLUMN HEADS

Förteckning *öfver utvandrare, som af undertecknad befordras med Ångfartyget Orlando, som den 22 augusti härifrån afgår till Hull.*	**List** of emigrants, which by the underwriter are forwarded with the Steamship Orlando, which on 22 August from here departs to Hull.
Kontraktets N:o	Contract no.
Utvandrarens yrke och namn	Emigrant's trade and name
Födelseort till län och socken	Birthplace län and parish
Ålder. Man. Qvinna. Summa	Age. Man. Woman. Total
Bestämmelseort	Destination

WHAT CAN WE SEE ON THIS PAGE?

C W Hällström is the agent. The list was made at his office.

The contract is the same as the ticket

G. A. Rapp had contract number *6564* (also noted in the register). He has according to the list traveled without company (*1* man, *1* total).

His birth parish is given as *Carlsborg* in *Skaraborgs län*. This information is wrong, as we already have seen, and not in accordance with the note in the church book in Portland, Connecticut.

Carlsborg (usually spelled Karlsborg) is a town and a military fort near Mölltorp. It was probably the railway station from which Gustaf Adolf traveled. So why is the note of birthplace wrong? He was of course very much aware of his own birth parish, but maybe he didn't understand the question posed to him. Maybe he thought he was asked where he "came from," not where he was born.

Another reason for the mistake is that the information was all transmitted orally; a question asked and answered. The list was made by the emigrant agent who sold the ticket, and then turned the list in to the police. There was no other formal paper, certificate, or passport written by a priest or civil servant at this time.

The entry shows us how easily a mistake is made in the records.

If this were the only record of his birthplace we would at least be in the right area – his birth parish is quite close to Karlsborg. And we would have found him if we had gone through church books in the nearest parishes.

If he had been born somewhere far from Karlsborg or had had a very common name we would have great difficulty to find him. Remember: there are over 2,000 Swedish parishes!

Listed after G. A. Rapp are *Victor Andersson* and *Anna Carlsson*. They are also listed as travelling unaccompanied. But we know that Gustaf Adolf and Anna married when they came to the United States. Victor also gave *Carlsborg* as his birthplace and Anna gave *Mölltorp* as hers, which is correct, and in accordance with the entry in the church register in Zion Lutheran church.

It is probably safe to conclude that the three young people, Gustaf Adolf, Victor, and Anna, traveled together.

"The steam-ship Orlando, for passenger traffic to Sweden."

For more about how to find pictures and facts about emigrant ships, see page 117.

Swedish Passenger Lists

The passenger lists were handed in to the police authorities ("*Poliskammaren*," the Police Chamber) by the agents for the steamship companies. These agents sold the tickets to the emigrants, and are comparable to today's travel agents. They had their offices in the port city. The lists are also called ship's lists.

The document only shows that the people on the list had bought tickets for the sea fare. Sometimes they didn't actually depart, for various reasons. No identity papers were required.

The passenger lists have been kept in the archives of the police authorities and these archives are kept by the regional archives in Sweden. The lists have been microfilmed and extensive registers have been made to make it easier to search for people in the lists.

Passenger Lists in Different Ports

All the Swedish ports with emigrants and passenger lists are registered in the database. The other Swedish ports, besides Gothenburg, are Stockholm, Helsingborg, Malmö, Norrköping, and Kalmar. From the 1880s and 1890s passenger lists also exist for trains that took passengers from Gothenburg to ships in Oslo, Copenhagen, and Hamburg.

Some Swedish emigrants also traveled through Norwegian ports: Oslo (named Kristiania until 1925), Bergen, Trondheim, and others. These emigrants primarily came from western Sweden. Some Swedes boarded ships in Copenhagen, Hamburg, or Bremen; these were mainly people from southern Sweden. Databases are available also for the Norwegian and Danish ports. Most passenger lists in Bremen were destroyed by fire in World War II. Passenger Lists for Hamburg, 1850–1934, and for Bremen around 1920 are available on the Internet.

Passenger Lists for Swedish Ports are Available for the Following Time Periods

Göteborg	1869–1951	Stockholm	1869–1940	Helsingborg	1907–1964
Malmö	1874–1939	Kalmar	1880–1893	Norrköping	1861–1921

If You Don't Find Your Ancestors in the Passenger Lists

If you make a search in the register and don't find your relative there are a number of possible reasons:

1. He/she emigrated before 1869. See page 115.
2. He/she traveled through a harbour not included in the register, like a harbour in Norway, Denmark, or Germany.
3. He/she may have traveled with a direct boat to the United States instead of buying a ticket through an agent. In this case they are not in the lists.
4. He/she may have traveled under another name. No identity papers were required.
5. He/she may have changed his/her name, either in Sweden or upon arriving to the United States.
6. He/she may have spelled his/her name differently. See the chapter on Swedish names. Maybe a "Johansson" became a "Johnson." In some cases there is "old Swedish spelling," an e instead of an ä, fv instead of v (Öfverlund – Överlund).
7. He/she traveled in first or second class, not in "emigrant class." These passengers were not included in the lists and were mainly the more well-to-do people.
8. He/she may have been a sailor who jumped ship in an American port. In this case a special register of sailors leaving the ships is available in the Emigrant database.

CHAPTER ELEVEN

EARLY EMIGRATION

Between 1846 and 1850 about 4,000 Swedes emigrated to the United States and during the 1850s about 14,000 Swedes followed. But already in the late 1830s a few Swedes headed for the United States. This first wave of Swedish emigration was not big compared to the later mass emigration. The conditions were also different in several respects:

- The travel took place before the modern steam lines, and the trip by sail ships thus took much more time and was much more risky. Many perished during the trip.
- Emigrants from Sweden had to obtain a passport to leave their home country before 1860. After 1860 no passport was needed.
- There were no passenger lists in the Swedish embarkation ports submitted to the police authorities.

Research on early Swedish emigration, or early immigrants into the United States from Sweden, is very different from research on immigration at the end of the nineteenth century. The dividing line is the American Civil War. Emigrants arriving before the civil war follow the old order; emigrants after the Civil War the new order.

For early emigration the following sources are available:

- For the earliest time period, from 1820 until 1850, there is a printed source. The emigrants have been listed by the Swedish-American researcher Nils William Olsson. His books list more than 5,000 names.
- Nils William Olsson's research is based on verification lists found in the Military Archives in Sweden. Traveling passengers on merchant ships had to pay a fee to the Swedish Navy's pension fund until 1851. As a result there are lists covering all passengers before 1851 in the Navy's archives in the Swedish Military Archive (*Krigsarkivet*). These lists are also on microfilm. For a researcher it is of course easier to consult Nils William Olsson's books.
- As the emigrants had to obtain passports before 1860 there were records of all emigrants kept by the authorities issuing the passports in both cities and län. The län (*Länsstyrelsen*) had to send in lists with the names of all the emigrants year by year to the Central Statistic Bureau (*Statistiska Centralbyrån – SCB*) between 1851 and 1860. There are about 14,000 people recorded and there are indexes.
- From 1860 and the following years there are no such lists, as no passports were issued. Instead SCB obtained lists of emigrants from the parishes, year by year, as a basis for the statistics. These lists include all the emigrants from each län, and are therefore not so easy to work with. On the other hand, the number of emigrants was still quite small. These lists are available on microfilm.
- From 1869 on the passenger lists submitted to the police authorities in the port cities is the main source.

Thus, if you have the name of the emigrant and the year or approximate year of emigration you can go to Nils William Olsson's books or to the index of the SCB-lists and find the emigrant either in the early verifications or in the passport journals. One major obstacle is that you will often have problems finding the right parish, as this has not been noted. In the passport journals you will at least find the right län, and from there on you can start searching through parishes.

Old farmhouse from Enslöv parish in Halland on the West Coast.

An Early Example: Carl Freeman (Friman) and His Sons

Carl Freeman (Friman in Swedish) and his sons were the first Swedes to settle in Wisconsin. They came to America in the summer of 1838, and Mr. Freeman bought eighty acres of land in Racine County in the southeast corner of Wisconsin and started farming.

He left Sweden at the age of fifty-six with his five sons, ages eighteen, eleven, ten, eight, and six. His wife stayed behind, and Mr. Freeman returned to Sweden after a couple of years. The boys, however, stayed in Wisconsin.

Theirs is a truly remarkable story, and quite well documented by the Freeman Family Society (*Släktföreningen Friman*).

We will be looking at some of these documents. But first, let's examine Nils William Olsson's book.

Varnhem church.

The Freeman Family in Printed Literature

Nils William Olsson went through all the early passport records and looked the emigrants up in the ship's manifests in New York. So he's already done the job for us. At right is his information about the Friman (Freeman) family.

453. C. Frimann	50 M Farmer	9 July	ROSEN
454. Carl Johann Frimann	18 M Farmer	New York, NY	Göteborg
455. Otto Frimann	11 M Farmer		*Sweden*
456. Herrmann Frimann	10 M Farmer		
457. Adolp Frimann	8 M Farmer		
458. Wilhelm Frimann	6 M Farmer		

The name of Nils William Olsson's book is *Swedish Passenger Arrivals in the United States 1820 – 1850.* Nils William Olsson has gone through 33,000 ship's manifests looking for Swedes in New York alone! He has registered and given information on 5,012 early Swedish immigrants.

Note: Nils William Olsson has misread Carl Friman's age in the ship's manifest (see next page). He was *56* years old, not *50.*

Footnotes

The footnotes contain a lot of information about the individuals listed in the books. Below are footnotes about two of the Freeman brothers. Nils William Olsson gives information about their birth place in Sweden (Varnhem Parish in Skaraborg län), their birth dates, and for Otto also his death date and place. Nils William Olsson has collected a lot of very valuable genealogical facts.

454. Carl Johan Friman, b. in Varnhem Parish 26 March 1821, s. Carl Friman (see note 453). He settled in Wisconsin, was a grocer in Walworth County in 1860; m. and had seven children. In the 1870s he moved to York, NE, where descendants still live. - *GLA*; information courtesy Axel Friman, Göteborg.

455. Otto Friman, b. in Varnhem 11 Nov. 1831, s. Carl Friman (see note 453). He settled in Wisconsin but soon left for the goldfields in California. He returned to Wisconsin, but eventually went west and d. in Pasadena, CA 21 Sept. 1902. - *GLA*; information courtesy Axel Friman.

[illegible] Friman, b. in Varnhem 24 Feb. 1829, s. Carl Friman (see note 453). He accompanied his father

Freeman and His Sons in the Ship's Manifest in New York 1838

If we didn't know the origins of the Freeman family, the first place to look would be the ship's manifests in the American ports at the time of their arrival. We would have to look for ships arriving from Sweden. The most probable route is Gothenburg to New York, or Stockholm to New York, but other American ports are also possible, like Baltimore, Boston, and Philadelphia. There are also alternative Swedish ports, like Norrköping, Kalmar, Gävle, Karlshamn, Helsingborg, Malmö, and others.

The Freeman family came to the United States during the summer of 1838. They arrived in New York on the ship *Rosen* on *9 July 1838*. Here is the Ship's manifest, delivered to the Customs Office in New York.

Rosen ("The Rose") was a brig. It was a small cargo ship, a two-master. We have even found a picture of it.

The Ship's manifest doesn't give much information. It only lists the passengers: *C Frimann*, age *56*, *male*, *farmer* from *Sweden*, and his sons (no mention that they are sons), *Carl Johann, Otto, Herrmann, Adolf,* and *Wilhelm*. *Do* means "ditto", the same.

Note: There is no mention of a place in Sweden.

Sold by J. B. Jansen, 150 Nassau-street.

DISTRICT OF NEW-YORK—PORT OF NEW-YORK.

I, Z Kollenius do solemnly, sincerely, and truly swear that the following List or Manifest of Passengers, subscribed with my name, and now delivered by me to the Collector of the Customs for the District of New-York, contains, to the best of my knowledge and belief, a just and true account of all the Passengers received on board the Swed Brig Rosen whereof I am Master, from Gothenburg

Sworn to the 9 Jul 1838.

Before me,

LIST OR MANIFEST of all the PASSENGERS taken on board the Swed Brig Rosen whereof Z Kollenius is Master, from Gothenburg burthen tons.

NAMES.	AGE. Years.	Months.	SEX.	OCCUPATION.	The Country to which they severally belong.	The Country in which they intend to become inhabitants.	Died on the voyage.
C Frimann	56		male	farmer	Sweden	Sweden	
Carl Johann do	18				do	do	
Otto do	11		do	do	do	do	
Herrmann do	10			do	do	do	
Adolphe do	8			do	do	do	
Wilhelm do	6			do	do	do	

The picture of the ship Rosen is from Gothenburg Maritime Museum (Göteborgs Sjöfartsmuseum), which has a large collection of pictures of ships (paintings, photos, and copies of pictures).

The other two maritime museums in Sweden are located in Stockholm and Karlskrona. Contact these museums and inquire about pictures of your ancestors' ships.

The book Ships of our Ancestors *by Michael J. Anuta (Menominee 1983) also contains a large number of ships sailing on the immigrant route over the North Atlantic, mainly steamships.*

Freeman and his Sons in the Passport Journal in Gothenburg

The next place to look is the passport journals from the Swedish port. First Gothenburg, the main embarkation port for travellers to the United States.

We look in the passport journal for 1838, shown below, and find the Friman family registered on 5 May.

6275.

Förtekning öfver från Götheborgs Lands Canzlie År 1838. utfärdade Pass till Utrikes Orter –

Månad	dato	Namn och Caractaire	Banco Rd:r	s.	r.	Orten dit resan skett.
Januari	2.	Rob: Hancock Engl. Undersåte	–	16.	–	England –
	3.	Löwenliew Moritz, Skomak: Lärling –	–	8.	–	New York
	4.	Lindblom Ossian, Svensk undersåte	,	16.	–	d:o d:o
	,	F. A. Gyllenberg d:o	,	16.	–	New York
	,	Neumark, Fabian, Preussisk unders.	,	16.	–	d:o d:o
	5.	C. Friman, f: d: Mönsterskrifvare, med 5. mind: barn		16.	–	d:o d:o
	7.	J. L. Heyman, Hand: Bokh.	–	16.	–	Köpenhamn.
		Gust: Leonard Bergman, Sv. unders:	–	16.	–	America –

Translation:

Förtekning öfver från Götheborgs Lands Canzlie År 1838 utfärdade Pass till Utrikes Orter.

Listing of Passports issued by the Gothenburg province office the year of 1838 for foreign places.

Månad, dato, Namn och Caractaire, Banco (RD:r s. r.) Orten dit resan skett.

Month, date, Name and Title, (fees paid), Place of destination

C Friman, f:d: Mönsterskrifware,
med 5. mind: barn 16. – New York

The title *mönsterskrivare* is an old title for the enrollment clerck of a regiment. *f:d: = före detta* = former. *med 5 mind: (minderåriga) barn* = with five underaged children. The latter is hardly true, since the oldest one was eighteen years old.

Note: There is no mention of home parish or place within Sweden.

Freeman in the Navy's Pension Fund

The same notes have been made in the list submitted to the Navy's pension fund *(Flottans pensionskassa).* In this record, there is also a note of where the internal Swedish passport was issued.

Maj
5. C Friman f:d. Mönsterskrifvare med
5 mind: barn
hitk. med Pass från Sköfve af d. 28 april
1838

The last text means: Came here with Passport from Sköfde of 28 April 1838.

At this time a passport was also required for internal travel within Sweden. To go to the port city of Gothenburg the Friman family also had to have this internal passport. We now know this passport was issued in the town of Sköfde (today spelled Skövde). We can go to the passport journal in Skövde and see what is recorded there.

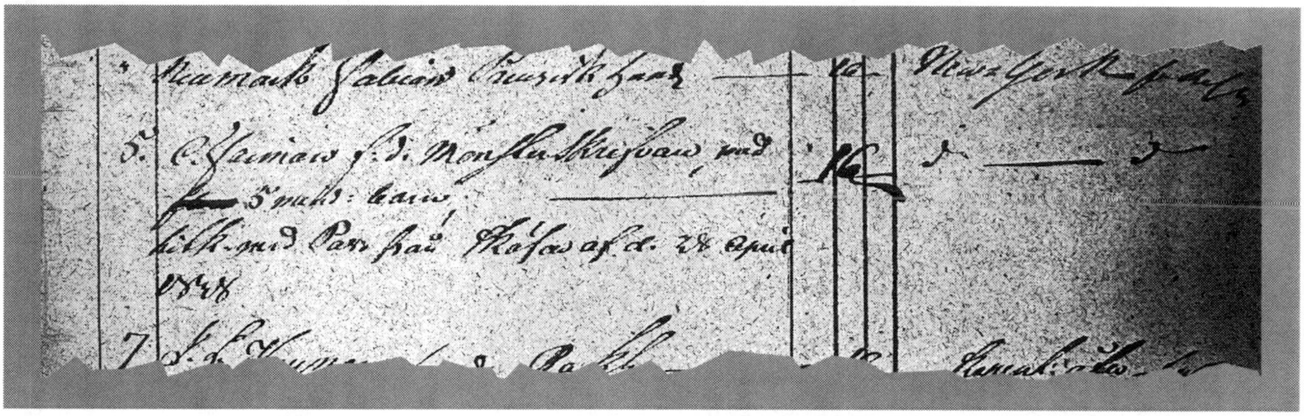

Freeman and his Sons in the Passport Journal in Skövde

The record in Skövde magistrate's passport journal does not give us any further information. The record reads:

F.d. munsterskrifvare
C. Friman med fem söner Götheborg

Friman and his five sons have obtained a passport for a trip to Gothenburg, and the passport was valid for the duration of the trip.

This list is a copy that has been submitted to the province office in Skaraborgs län. The original list in the Skövde city archive gives no further information.

Note: In none of these lists is there a note of the place of origin or home parish. The only way to proceed is to look through all the parishes in and around Skövde at this time, using moving records and/or household examination rolls of them. In this case another alternative would be to go to the military records of the regiments in Skaraborgs län (there are only two) to try to find Mr. Friman.

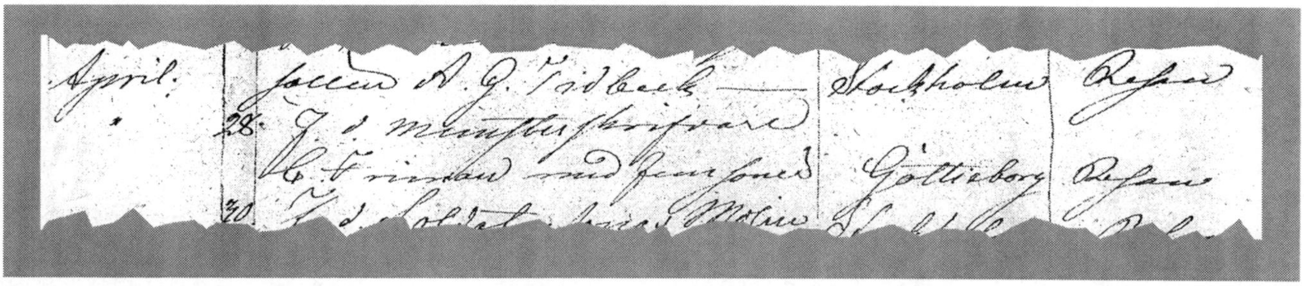

Freeman and His Family in Varnhem

We find the Friman family in one of the area's parishes, Varnhem west of the city of Skövde. The Friman family lived at a place called Stenhammaren. We can look the family up in the household examination roll in Varnhem, where we find it on page 59, shown below. The whole family is listed and we can see that the mother didn't follow her husband and sons to America but moved to a neighboring parish.

Varnhem Parish Household Examination Roll 1838

Socken, Varnhem — 59
Rote.

Bostad och Personer.	Födelse. Ort.	Födelse. År och Dag.	Christend. kunskap. Innanläsning.	Christend. kunskap. Utanläsning. Luth. Cath.	Christend. kunskap. Utanläsning. Förklaringen.	Förstår.	Koppor.	Inflyttad År	Inflyttad ifrån	Utflyttad År	Utflyttad till	Anmärkningar.

Translation:

Socken	Parish
Rote	Ward

Column titles

Bostad och Personer	Dwelling place and persons
Födelse	Birth
Ort	Place (of birth)
År och dag	Year and day (of birth)
Christend.(oms)kunskap	Knowledge of Christianity
Innanläsning	Reading in book
Utanläsning	Reading by heart
Luth. Cath.	Luther's catechism
Förklaringen	The explanation
Förstår	Understands
Koppor	Smallpox (vaccination)
Inflyttad	Moved in
År	Year
ifrån	from
Utflyttad	Moved out
År	Year
till	to
Anmärkningar	Notes

What Can We See on This Page?

Stenhammaren is the name of the farm or house where the family lived.

Äg. Expeditions Munster Skrifvaren
H. C Friman   Björsäter   1781 2/10   America

Äg. Ägaren = the owner. *Expeditions Munster Skrifvaren* is the military title. *H.* = Herr = Mr. Born in the parish of *Björsäter*, on *2 Oct 1781*. He was 56 years old at the time of emigration.

Fru Christ. Fröding   Dahla   1785 5/5   38
Eric Olofsg. Lundby

Fru = Wife, *Christ.* = Christina, born in the parish of *Dahla* on *5 May 1785*, moved to *Eric Olofsgård* in *Lundby* 18*38*.

In Carl Johan   här   1821 26/3   38   America
v adm.

In = *Infant* (here infant is the latin word for child, in Swedish *barn*). Carl Johan is born *här* = here, in Varnhem on *26 March 1821*. He moved to *America* in 18*38*.

v = vaccination (same word in Swedish as in English). Note that the vaccinations have been noted in the column for general annotations, although there is a special column for smallpox (koppor).

All the younger brothers are born in *D:o* = *ditto*, the same place, Varnhem, and all of them went to America with their father. The mother moved to a neighboring parish of Lundby (Norra Lundby). *Eric Olofsgård* is the name of a farm, named after a person.

For young Otto, there is no birth date noted.

It's hard to imagine a mother letting all her five sons leave for a trip to the other side of the earth. What could have motivated this man to take his five sons on such an adventurous journey?

Carl Friman and His Son William Freeman

Carl Friman returned to Sweden already the following year, 1839, because of failing health. He took his son Herman with him back to Sweden. Carl Friman died in Sweden in 1862. He had a vast corr-espondance with his sons in America, and several of these letters were printed in Swedish newspapers, like *Aftonbladet* and *Skara Tidning*. Herman returned to the United States, participated in the War with Mexico and died in Pasadena, California in 1913. Wilhelm Friman, alias William Freeman, was the youngest emigrating brother, and lived with his brothers in Racine county, Wisconsin. He left for California during the gold rush in 1849, and returned to Wisconsin with $4,000. He died in Pasadena as well.

Carl Friman.

William Friman.

An Emigrant in the 1850s: Ivar Alexis Hall

Nils William Olsson's book and records only cover the period until the end of 1850. That year the fee to the Navy's pension fund expired and through the 1850s there are only the passport journals in the different län. Fortunately every län had to send a report each year listing all its emigrants to Statistics Sweden *(Statistiska Centralbyrån, SCB)* in Stock-holm. These records list names from the passport journals and are available on microfilm. There is an index with some 14,000 names. To find a certain emigrant in the 1850s, start with the index to find the right microfilm (available from SVAR, the Swedish National Archives). Below we see one of these lists, for Skaraborgs län in 1851. There are still relatively few emigrants. In this list several young men are listed. This was around the time of the California gold rush, and many left home to seek adventure.

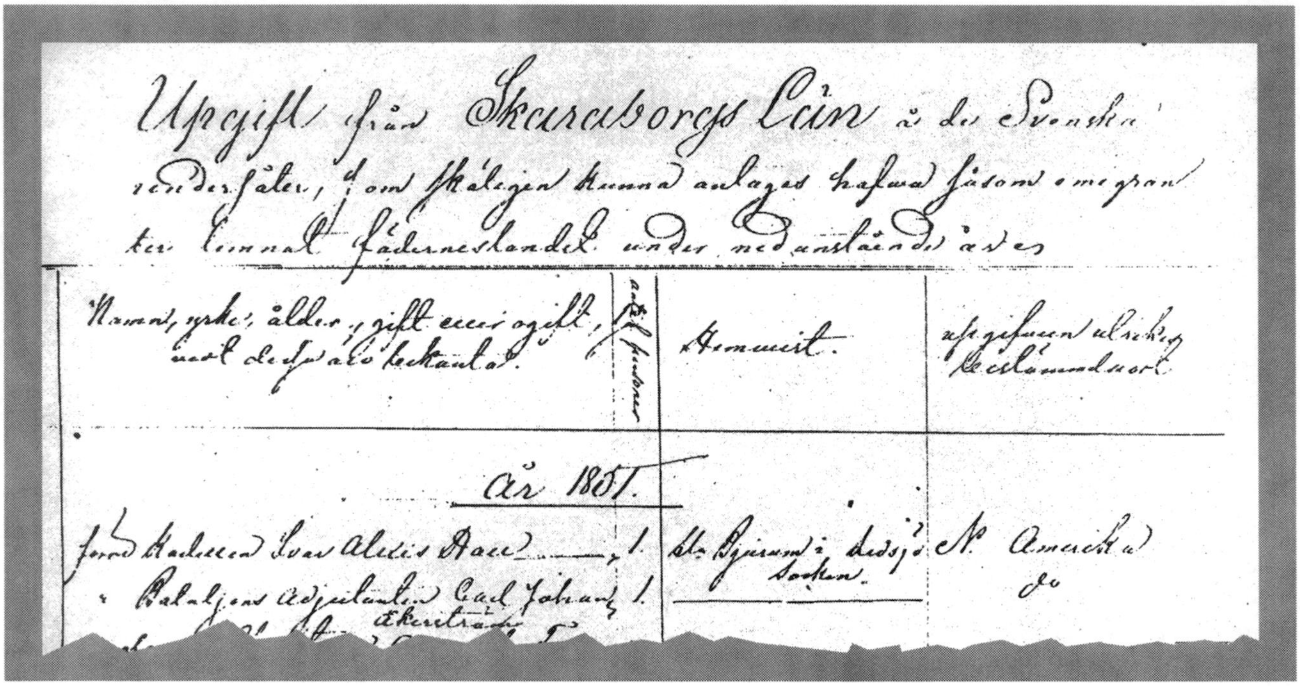

Translation:

Upgift från Skaraborgs Län å de Svenska undersåtar, som skäligen kunna antagas hafwa såsom emigranter lemnat fäderneslandet under nedanstående år.	Statement from Skaraborgs län about the Swedish subjects, who we have reason to believe have as emigrants left their native country during the year stated below.
Namn, yrke, ålder, gift eller ogift, mest dessa äro bekanta	Name, occupation, age, married or unmarried, as these are known
antal personer	number of persons
Hemvist	Residence
upgifven utrikes bestämmelseort	given foreign destination
År 1851	Year 1851
förre kadetten Ivar Alexis Hall	the former cadet Ivar Alexis Hall
Lla. Bjurum i Ledsjö socken *N. Amerika*	Little Bjurum in Ledsjö parish North America

Ivar Alexis Hall's Family

When we look for Lilla Bjurum in Ledsjö parish we cannot find it. It turns out the farm (estate in this case) is located in the neighbouring parish Vättlösa. Below we show the family of Ivar Alexis Hall.

110. 2 Lilla Bjurum.

4 Rote.		Födelse–			Flyttningsort och flyttningstid.			
					Inflyttning		Utflyttning	
	Personens Namn och Stånd.	ort.	år.	månad och dag.	från.	år.	till.	år.
Arrendator.	Löjtnant Albert Ossian Hall	Säfvared	1828	10/9	fr. nedan			
Inhyses	Öfversten och Ridr. Birger Hall	Västerås	1788	/9			Ogstunda	60
pag. 113	Fru Jeanna Carlsson	Vinköl	1800	31/8				
	D:r Emma Adelina	Säfvared	1823	27/6				
	– Ida Hildegard	ib	1825	4/4			Warnhem	56
Löjtnant	Son Birger Hjalmar	ib	1827	28/1			Warnhem	60
Arrendator	– Albert Ossian	ib	1828	10/9				
d:o	– Victor Danica	ib	1830	2/4			Åsaka	60
	– Ivar Alexis	Lidköping	1842	19/2			America	61

Vättlösa household examination roll.

Translation:

Personens Namn och Stånd	The person's name and state (rank)
Öfversten och Ridr. (Riddaren) Birger Hall	The colonel and knight Birger Hall

What Can We See in This Document?

The father was a nobleman and military man. Thus Ivar Alexis also was of Swedish nobility, which of course, but unfortunately for him, was of no importance when he arrived in the United States.

Ivar Alexis was one of six siblings. One older brother, Albert Ossian, has taken over the estate from the aging father. He is leasing the estate (*arrendator* = lease holder). Another brother, Birger Hjalmar, has followed in the father's footsteps and become an officer (*löjtnant* = leutenant). Maybe Ivar Alexis had a conflict with his father, or with his older brothers. Maybe he didn't feel there was any future for him at the family farm. Maybe he had been unsuccessful in his military career ("former cadet"). Maybe he was just an adventurous youth.

We can only speculate why a nineteen-year-old man would leave his upper class noble family to seek his fortune in America.

Swedish Nobility

If you have an ancestor belonging to the Swedish nobility you are fortunate. There is extensive printed information about the noble families, and you can find the whole genealogy in print. Let's use Ivar Alexis Hall and his family as an example.

From the household examination roll (on the previous page) we know that his father's name was Birger Hall. He was born in 1788 in Västerås (a city in middle Sweden). He was a colonel.

We can look him up in the book *Den introducerade svenska adelns ättartavlor* (Genealogies of the Introduced Swedish Nobility) by Gustaf Elgenstierna. The book was published in 1925–1936 (several volumes). It is in Swedish and is available on microfilm through the Family History Library, but so far not on the Internet.

For noble people who were not yet born when Elgenstierna wrote this book, we can look in the book *Adelskalendern*, which is a calendar about the nobility published yearly or, lately, every other or every third year.

In Elgenstierna's book we find the noble family "von Hall" as family number 2328, and we find Birger Hall, born 1788, on the first page (see next page).

It turns out that Birger Hall was knighted (*adlad*) in 1858. The family is listed with all the children; Ivar Alexis is the youngest one. He moved to North America in 1850, and died there in 1892. Apparently the family had contact with him and knew about his whereabouts.

This book is full of abbreviations: *f.* means *född* (born). The cross stands for "died." *Sn* means *socken* (parish).

How to Recognize Nobility

How do we know a family is nobility? There is often some kind of reference to nobility in the church books. The Swedish word for nobility is *adel*. In this case the father has a title, *"Riddaren"* (the knight). Other noble titles are *greve* (*grefve*), which means count, and *friherre* or *baron* which means baron. In old times the titles *Herr* for the husband and *Fru* for the wife could imply nobility. The peasants, for comparison, were called *Man* and *Hustru*. To a Swede the noble family name usually rings a bell. Many noble families are well known. It is more difficult for an American to spot a noble family name. In many cases the noble names have a prefix, like "von" or "af" (von Hall, von Essen, af Trolle), but often this is not the case.

Estates

Not all noble people were wealthy. But many had estates, some with large areas of land. These estates are listed in the church records just like all other dwellings.

Few emigrated

Altogether less than one percent of the Swedish population was nobility. Fewer emigrated from the nobility than from other groups.

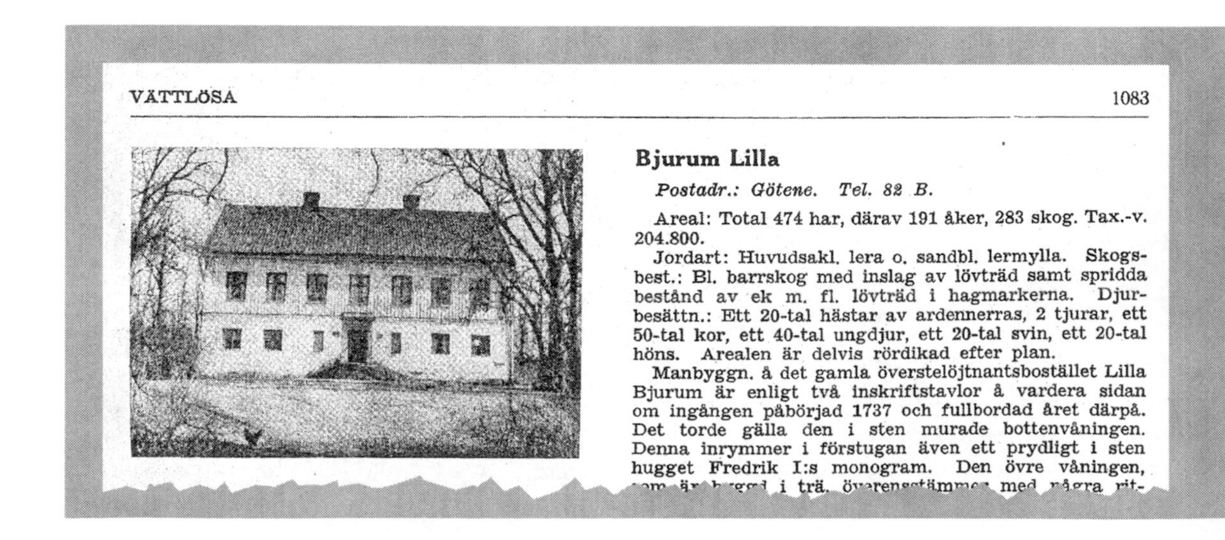

VÄTTLÖSA 1083

Bjurum Lilla

Postadr.: Götene. Tel. 82 B.

Areal: Total 474 har, därav 191 åker, 283 skog. Tax.-v. 204.800.

Jordart: Huvudsakl. lera o. sandbl. lermylla. Skogsbest.: Bl. barrskog med inslag av lövträd samt spridda bestånd av ek m. fl. lövträd i hagmarkerna. Djurbesättn.: Ett 20-tal hästar av ardennerras, 2 tjurar, ett 50-tal kor, ett 40-tal ungdjur, ett 20-tal svin, ett 20-tal höns. Arealen är delvis rördikad efter plan.

Manbyggn. å det gamla överstelöjtnantsbostället Lilla Bjurum är enligt två inskriftstavlor å vardera sidan om ingången påbörjad 1737 och fullbordad året därpå. Det torde gälla den i sten murade bottenvåningen. Denna inrymmer i förstugan även ett prydligt i sten hugget Fredrik I:s monogram. Den övre våningen,

Adliga ätten VON HALL, nr 2328.

Adlad 1858 $^{13}/_{4}$ enl. 37 § R.F., introd. s. å.

TAB. 1.

Börje Petersson Hall, f. 1667; borgare i Borås; † där 1739. [1]

S o n :

Peter Hall, f. 1707[1]; handlande och rådman i Borås; riksdagsman 1751—52; † 1776.[1] — G. 1736 $^{31}/_{8}$ i Uppsala m. *Eva Margareta Wargentin*, f. 1714 $^{26}/_{3}$, † före 1754, dotter av[2] råd- och handelsmannen i Uppsala Adolf Wargentin och hans 1:a fru Anna Ubman.

S o n :

Birger Martin Hall, f. 1741 $^{26}/_{8}$ i Borås; student i Uppsala 1753 och i Greifswald 1755; disp. i Uppsala 1759; underfältskär vid serafimerordenslasarettet 1764; kir. exam. 1766; promov. med. doktor i Uppsala 1768 $^{11}/_{11}$; praktiserande läkare i Stockholm s. å.; provinsialläkare i Västmanlands län 1773 $^{22}/_{4}$; avsked 1793; † 1815 $^{10}/_{8}$ i Västerås [SB]. — G. där 1777 $^{13}/_{3}$ m. *Anna Engel Schenström*, f. 1749 $^{2}/_{10}$ i nämnda stad, † där 1801, dotter av handlanden, rådmannen och kämnärspreses i Västerås Jonas Schenström och Anna Engel Dragman.[3]

S o n :

Birger Hall, adlad von Hall, f. 1788 $^{6}/_{9}$ i Västerås; kadett vid Karlberg 1803 $^{9}/_{9}$; avgången 1808 $^{3}/_{1}$; fanjunkare vid Västgöta dragonreg. s. å. $^{29}/_{1}$; kornett därst. s. å. $^{8}/_{12}$; 1. adjutant 1809 $^{10}/_{10}$; löjtnant vid norra skånska infanterireg:t 1811 $^{20}/_{12}$; transp. till Västgöta reg. 1812 $^{25}/_{2}$; kapten i armén 1813 $^{23}/_{2}$; kapten vid reg:t 1818 $^{19}/_{12}$; major 1824 $^{4}/_{5}$; RSO 1826 $^{11}/_{5}$; överstelöjtnant 1829 $^{22}/_{5}$; överste i reg:t 1840 $^{13}/_{4}$; chef för reg:t 1842 $^{30}/_{8}$; RDDO 1848 $^{23}/_{9}$; KSO 1854 $^{18}/_{12}$; CXIVJoh:s medalj 1855; generalmajor i armén 1857 $^{2}/_{11}$; adlad 1858 $^{13}/_{4}$ enl. 37 § R.F. (introd. s. å. $^{9}/_{10}$ under nr 2328); avsked s. å. $^{4}/_{5}$; † 1865 $^{1}/_{3}$ på sin egendom Flämslätt i Äggby sn (Skarab.). Han bevistade kriget i Tyskland och Belgien 1813—1814 och i Norge 1814. — G. 1822 $^{31}/_{8}$ på Blombacka i Vinköls sn (Skarab.) m. *Jeanna Carlsson*, f. 1800 $^{31}/_{8}$ på nämnda egendom, † 1867 $^{16}/_{7}$ på Flämslätt, dotter av proviantmästaren Carl Carlsson och Christina Maria Simberg.

B a r n :

Emma Adeline, f. 1823 $^{27}/_{6}$ på Alebäck i Sävare sn (Skarab.), † ogift 1884 $^{4}/_{12}$ i Stockholm.

Ida Hildegard, f. 1825 $^{4}/_{4}$ på Alebäck, † 1897 $^{29}/_{1}$ i Skövde. G. 1855 $^{13}/_{9}$ på Lilla Bjurum i Vättlösa sn (Skarab.) m. överstelöjtnanten vid Västgöta reg., RSO, RVO m. m., *Bror Mörcke*, f. 1821 $^{8}/_{10}$ på Svansö i Bottnaryds sn (Älvsb.), † 1892 $^{19}/_{9}$ i Stockholm.

Birger Hjalmar, adelsman vid faderns död 1865; f. 1827; överstelöjtnant; † 1907. Se Tab. 2.

Albert Ossian, f. 1828; major; † 1891. Se Tab. 4.

Viktor Zaméo, f. 1830; kapten; † 1869. Se Tab. 5.

Ivar Alexis, f. 1832 $^{19}/_{2}$ i Lidköping; kadett vid Karlberg 1849 $^{9}/_{8}$; avgången 1850 $^{4}/_{12}$; överflyttade till Nordamerika; † där 1892.

In the opening paragraphs of the genealogy for the family von Hall in "Den introducerade svenska adelns ättartavlor" by Gustaf Elgenstierna, we can find Birger von Hall and his son Ivar Alexis.

DESCRIPTIONS OF FARMS AND ESTATES

During the early twentieth century several books were published with the intention to describe all farms and country estates in the provinces. In the book *Svenska gods och gårdar* (Swedish estates and farms), published in 1939, we found this entry about Lilla Bjurum, the place of Alexis von Hall's family. It describes in detail the property, its acreage, the soil and farming, the buildings, and so on. Finally the people living at the farm in 1939 are listed. From this description we can see that this estate was used as the residence for the leutenant colonel of the regiment and that the manor house was built in 1737. The von Hall family is not mentioned in the text.

Direct passenger traffic between Sweden and the United States was started by Swedish American Line (Svenska Amerika Linjen), SAL, in 1915. With SAL the most common way to travel to the United States was to take the "America-boat" from Gothenburg to New York. To the right: SAL ships in Gothenburg harbour in the 1930s.

BREVKORT
SVENSKA AMERIKA-LINIEN
GÖTEBORG - DIREKT - NEWYORK
Ångaren STOCKHOLM
framkom till Halifax
11 FEB 1925
Allt väl!
SVENSKA AMERIKA LINIEN

On this postcard the Swedish American Line has helped the traveler with a stamped greeting. Not all emigrants could read or write very well and especially not in their new language. The stamped text in Swedish tells: "The steamer Stockholm came to Halifax 11 February 1925. All is well! Arrival to New York around 36 hours later."

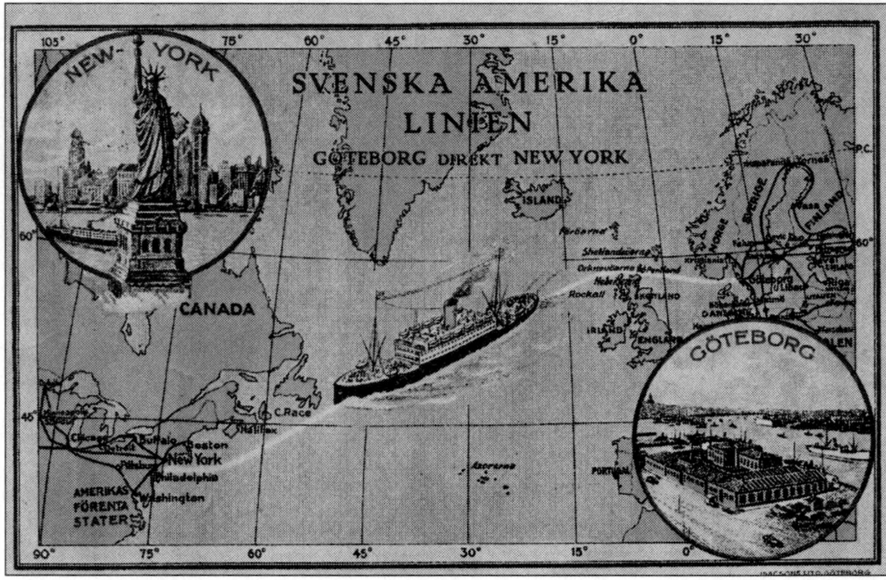

A postcard showing the Swedish "M/S Gripsholm" in New York harbour, probably in the 1930s.

CHAPTER TWELVE

Traveling with the Swedish American Line

When you are looking for emigrants who left Sweden after World War I, there are alternatives to the regular passenger lists from the Swedish ports.

Direct passenger traffic between Sweden and the United States was started by the Swedish American Line (*Svenska Amerika Linjen*), SAL, in 1915. Earlier the emigrants had to travel through other European ports, usually Liverpool, but also ports like Bremen, Hamburg, le Havre, and Glasgow. With SAL the most common way to travel to the United States was to take the "America-boat" from Gothenburg to New York. These boats had names like Stockholm, Drottningholm, Kungsholm, and Gripsholm.

The SAL archives are kept by the Regional Archives in Gothenburg, and there are 109 volumes of printed passenger lists for the period 1916 to 1971. A register has been made to the printed passenger lists and is available on the Emigranten CD. The name of the database is EMISAL, and it contains about 242,000 names.

The printed lists always include the names of first- and second-class passengers. They sometimes include third-class and even, though rarely, tourist-class passengers. This of course limits the value of these passenger lists. Many emigrants were poor and traveled in the least expensive tourist class. The database consists of travel in both directions, to and from the United States.

The information given in the lists is rather meager, but can be enough to trace a relative.

You can search on name, residence, and traveling date. We made a search on "Mölltorp" and found twelve names for the period 1921 to 1932. Below we also show a printout for Oscar Kjellberg. Of course, not that many Swedes by the name Oscar Kjellberg were emigrating or traveling to the United States in the mid-1920s. This database would quickly locate Oscar's home parish in Sweden. Mölltorp is probably the post address – the parish could be Mölltorp, Brevik, or Ransberg.

Twelve names from Mölltorp were found in EMISAL, for the period 1921 to 1932 (below). The mentioned printout for Oscar Kjellberg can be seen on the next page.

EMISAL / EMIGRANTEN / 2003-05-31
Hemort: Mölltorp
Antal funna: 12

Efternamn	Förnamn	Hemort	Resdatum	Fartyg
BOSTRÖM	AUGUSTA	MÖLLTORP	1932-10-22	GRIPSHOLM
CARLSON	AUGUSTA	MÖLLTORP	1921-10-22	STOCKHOLM
CARLSON	C A	MÖLLTORP	1921-09-24	DROTTNINGHOLM
CARLSON	CARL	MÖLLTORP	1924-03-15	DROTTNINGHOLM
JOHANSSON	INGRID	MÖLLTORP	1929-02-09	DROTTNINGHOLM
→ KJELLBERG	OSCAR	MÖLLTORP	1926-02-13	GRIPSHOLM
LUNDBERG	HANNA	MÖLLTORP	1922-09-26	STOCKHOLM
LUNDGREN	KARIN	MÖLLTORP	1929-02-09	DROTTNINGHOLM
LUNDGREN	OSKAR	MÖLLTORP	1927-05-28	GRIPSHOLM
NILLSON	HARRY	MÖLLTORP	1927-05-28	GRIPSHOLM
NILSSON	DORIS	MÖLLTORP	1928-04-20	STOCKHOLM
OLSON	LYDIA	MÖLLTORP	1923-02-24	DROTTNINGHOLM
LAST NAME	FIRST NAME	RESIDENCE	TRAVEL DATE	SHIP

EMISAL / EMIGRANTEN / 2003-05-31

Namn: OSCAR KJELLBERG
Kön: M
Hemort: MÖLLTORP
Land: SVERIGE Län/Stat: P/R
Resdatum: 1926-02-13
Fartyg: GRIPSHOLM Klass: 2
Från: GÖTEBORG Till: NEW YORK

The printout for Oscar Kjellberg.

Name: Oscar Kjellberg
Sex: male (*M* = *Man* = male)
Residence: Mölltorp
Country: Sweden Län/state: P/R
Travel date: 13 February 1926
Ship: Gripsholm Class: 2
From: Göteborg (Gothenburg) To: New York

Oscar Kjellberg can of course also be found in the passenger lists in Gothenburg. We look in Emihamn, the register for the passenger lists (also on the CD "The Swedish Emigrant"). Here his first name is spelled Oskar, and his age is given – 24 years. The parish is given as Mölltorp (below).

LAST NAME	FIRST NAME	AGE	PARISH	LÄN	EMIGRATION YEAR	DESTINATION
KARLSSON	VALBORG E.	15	MÖLLTORP	R	1907	WILLMAR MN
KJELLBERG	GUNHILD	17	MÖLLTORP	R	1914	NEW YORK
KJELLBERG	HJALMAR M	19	MÖLLTORP	R	1928	NEW YORK
→ KJELLBERG	OSKAR	24	MÖLLTORP	R	1926	NEW YORK
KÄLLMAN	EMMA	28	MÖLLTORP	R	1902	BOSTON
LANDIN	BERTA CH	19	MÖLLTORP	R	1908	CHICAGO IL
LARSSON	ANNA M	29	MÖLLTORP	R	1902	CONCORD
LARSSON	CARL VALEN	19	MÖLLTORP	R	1905	BOSTON

Often Swedish-Americans made at least one trip back to their native Sweden. If they had been able to earn a little money they traveled in a more expensive class on the boats. Consequently they turn up in the passenger lists.

The Swedish Emigrant CD

The Swedish Emigrant CD is a valuable source for searching for emigrants from Sweden to the United States; it can also be used to search for people going in the other direction – Swedish-American immigrants visiting or returning to Sweden for good, or other Americans traveling to Sweden.

These are the different databases on the CD:

• Emihamn

The database listing all the registered Swedish emigrants in the passenger lists in the Swedish and other North European ports. The database contains 1.4 million names from the following ports:

Port	Years	Names
Gothenburg	1869 – 1951	1,135,888 names
Malmö	1874 – 1928	159,903
Stockholm	1869 – 1940	34,887
Norrköping	1859 – 1922	8,545
Kalmar	1881 – 1893	3,338
Helsingborg	1929 – 1950	413
Copenhagen	1868 – 1898	56,127
Hamburg	1850 – 1891	21,708

• Emibas Gothenburg

The database contains information about approximately 53,000 emigrants who were registered in Gothenburg at the time of their emigration. It covers a number of parishes in Gothenburg from the oldest existing church books until 1950.

• Emisjö

This database includes information on 17,000 seamen, registered with the merchant marine offices in Gothenburg and other ports in western Sweden, who are listed in the rolls as being either discharged, deceased, or having jumped ship outside Europe. Many of these sailors are believed to have emigrated.

EMISJÖ / EMIGRANTEN / 2003-05-31

Namn: GUSTAF BJÖRK
Födelsetid: 1897
Föddförsaml: MÖLLTORP Län: R
Hemförsaml: MÖLLTORP Län: R
Yrke/Titel: JUNGMAN Sjömanshus: GÖTEBORG
Fartyg: CARLSHOLM Typ:
Hamn: NEWPORT NEWS Land: Landskod:
Datum: 1924-03-25 Orsak: RYMD
Källa: GÖTEBORG DIC:174 År/nr: 1925:00199

Name: Gustaf Björk
Birth year: 1897
Birth parish: Mölltorp Län: R
Home parish: Mölltorp Län: R
Profession/title: Ordinary seaman, deck-hand
Merchant marine office: Göteborg (Gothenburg)
Ship: Carlsholm Type:
Port: Newport News Country: Country code:
Date: 25 March 1925 Reason: Escaped
Source: Göteborg (Gothenburg) DIC:174
Year/number: 1925:00199

• Emipass

This database includes more than 16,000 records of early emigrants, up to 1860. The excerpts have been taken from the Naval Pension Fund's lists of passengers (for passenger's fees) 1817 to 1850, from Statistics Sweden's copies of passport registers 1851 to 1860, and from passport registers in Gothenburg 1783 to 1850.

(See chapter 11 about early emigrants, page 119)

• Emisal

This is the database for the Swedish American Line, including 242,000 names (many travelers crossed the ocean in both directions) for the period 1915 to 1950.

• Emivasa

This database lists more than 43,000 persons who are or have been members of the Vasa Order of America from 1896 and on.

• Saka

The index to the 2,000 Swedish-American church archives, 1842 to 1867, which have been microfilmed by the Swedish Emigrant Institute in Växjö.

• The Ships

Many descendants of Swedish emigrants are interested in the ships their ancestors used to cross the ocean and want to obtain pictures of these ships. Between Gothenburg and England transportation was run by the Wilson Line and its steamers. The Swedish Emigrant CD includes a database of the Wilson Line's vessels. There are also special websites with images of ships (see the list of websites at the end of the book). The Maritime Museum in Gothenburg (*Göteborgs Sjöfartsmuseum*) has many pictures of emigrant ships.

• Emiweb

For more, and updated information, go to www.emiweb.se.

Postcards show the countryside in old times:

RYGGÅSSTUGA I BRODDETORP. I de minnesrika trakterna kring Horn-
borgasjön finnas ännu några gamla ryggåsstugor. De förtjäna att bevaras som intressanta byggnads-
minnen från en gången tid.
VÄSTERGÖTLAND 47
STF
FOTO C. G. ROSENBERG
LADUGÅRDSLÄNGA I SÄTUNA. Falbygden vilar på kalkstensgrund och
är även i kulturellt avseende ett område för sig. Bebyggelsen är delvis ålderdomlig, och de talrika
gamla kalkstenslängorna giva gårdarna en annan prägel än på slätterna runt omkring.
VÄSTERGÖTLAND 46
STF
FOTO C. G. ROSENBERG

Old cottage at Broddetorp, between Falköping and Skara. The cottage shows a very old style.

Old barn and cows at Sätuna close to the city of Falköping. The barn is built out of limestone.

CHAPTER THIRTEEN

Old Records

The Oldest Church Book in Ransberg

How far back do church records go? Many parishes have at least some records from around 1700, shortly after the new Church law in 1686. In some cases earlier records exist.

In Ransberg the oldest records are from 1689, listing children born during the year. The oldest church book is a Church accounts' book dating back to 1638. This *Ransberghz Kyrkios Rekenskaps-book* (Ransberg's church's accounting book) has a beautifully printed title page.

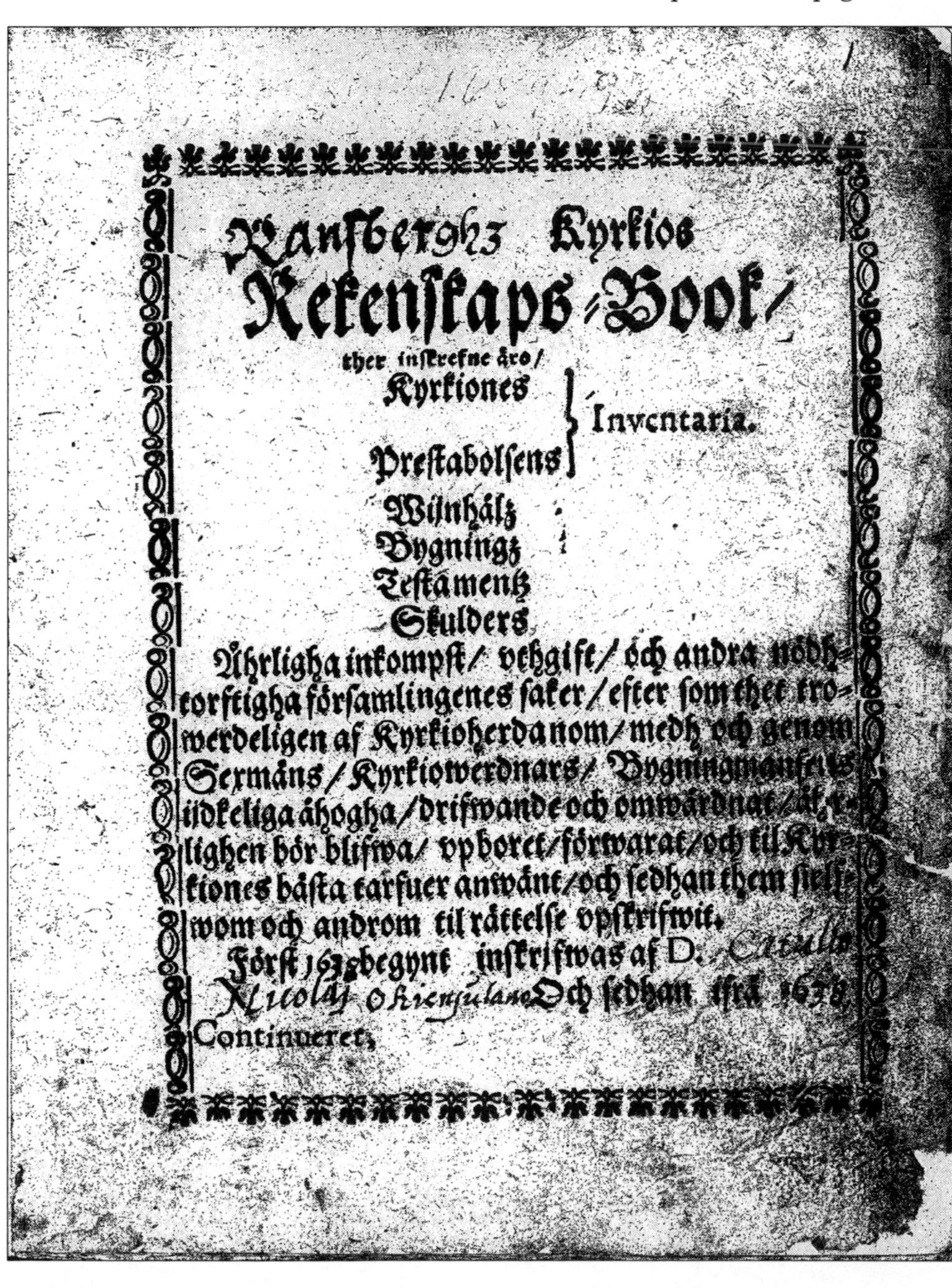

Ransberghz Kyrkios
Rekenskaps-Book/
ther inskrefne åro/
Kyrkiones
Prestabolsens } Inventaria.
Wijnhålz
Bygningz
Testamentz
Skulders
Åhrligha inkompst/ vthgift/ och andra nödh-
torftigha församlingenes saker/ efter som thet tro-
werdeligen af Kyrkioherdanom/ medh och genom
Sexmåns/ Kyrkiowerdnars/ Bygningmans [illegible]
tidkeliga åhogha/ drifwande och omwårdnat/ [illegible]
lighen bör blifwa/ vpboret/ förwarat/ och til Kyr-
kiones båsta tarfuer anwånt/ och sedhan them siel-
wom och androm til råttelse vpskrifwit.
Först 1638 begynt inskrifwas af D. Catullo
Nicolai Oriensulano Och sedhan ifrå 1638
Continueret.

Translation:

The bottom paragraph reads:

Först 1638 begynt inskrifwas af D(omino) Catullo Nicolai Oriensulano Och sedhan ifrå 1638, Continuerer

In 1638 started to be recorded by D(omino) Catullo Nicolai Oriensulano and thereafter from 1638 continues.

What Can We See on This Page?

Catullus Nicolai Oriensulanus was pastor in Flistad parish and rural dean for the area. His brother Jonas Nicolai Oriensulanus was superintendent (bishop) in the city Mariestad.

The Earliest Birth Records in Ransberg

The birth register starts in 1689 with this annotation:

Anno 1689

En antekning i Ransbergs Sochn
uppå

1. Barn

Den 3 Januarij föddes Anders Swens dotter
i Kåhlbäck, den 6 döptes wid N Elisabeth
faddrar: Anders Håkonsson i Kylfvanäs
Lars Olsson i TåresRud, Jon Swenss i Kals
hage. Hustru Ingrin Swensd. ibid
h Margreta Svensd i Kålbäck, pijga Elisa-
bet Swensdotter i Mobohl

den 23 Jan. föddes…

What Can We See on This Page?

Anno is Latin for year.

Barn means children.

The first note is a bit difficult to understand. A girl is born on 3 January 1689. She is daughter to Anders Svens(son). The family is from Kåhlbäck, and five godparents are listed.

Note 1:

If you find a priest in your family's history you are fortunate. You will have extensive printed literature to consult. Every diocese has published its own books about their priests, with biographical data about each priest: where the priest was born, who his parents were, where he went to school and university, and in which parish he served. In addition, other facts about the family are often noted. These books are called *Herdaminnen* (Pastoral memorials) and are of course written in Swedish, and are available in most Swedish libraries.

Note 2:

Do you have difficulty reading old handwriting? Many books have been published about paleography (the science of handwriting), with alphabets from different periods. There is also a CD to help you practice reading Swedish handwriting. The directions for use and the explanations on the CD are so far available only in Swedish.

A remarkable priest

The priest was an important person in the community. Many priests had portraits painted, which can often be found in the churches. This amazing painting of the priest Gustaf Fredrik Hjortberg and his family can be seen in the church Släp south of Gothenburg.

Reverend Hjortberg was a versatile man. Besides being a priest he was also an inventor; a builder of organs, instruments, and machines; an amateur doctor administering "electric therapy"; and an experimenting farmer. And, as a ship's priest, he made three trips to China with the Swedish East India Company.

In this painting we can see his large family. The painter has included both the living and the dead children. The dead children are partly hidden in the background or turn away their heads. The animal is a lemur, brought back from Madagascar. The painting was made by Johan Dürck around 1770.

Other Old Records

In addition to church records, genealogists can also make use of other records to find information about the early family background. There are different kinds of tax records, military records, and land records (also used for taxation) which sometimes cover the time period prior to the oldest church records.

These kinds of records are, in general, less detailed than the church records. They usually list only the owners or the holders of the farms. Sometimes all adults or at least all adult men are listed. Though limited, this is still highly useful information. By comparing the oldest church records and such records it is usually possible to verify whether you have found the right family or not. But be aware – people moved frequently also in these times.

Älvsborgs lösen
(Special tax records)

The oldest tax records are called *Älvsborgs lösen*. Before Sweden took the western and southern provinces of Skåne, Halland, and Bohuslän from Denmark in the mid-seventeenth century, the only Swedish access to the western sea was a small stretch of coast around Gothenburg. This was also the lo-cation of a fortress named Älvsborg. Sweden lost this strategic fortress to Denmark twice and was forced to pay very heavy ransoms to get it back from the Danes.

To raise money for these ransoms, the Swedish government levied a special tax on all Swedish farms and households. To that end special tax records were created in every parish, listing all the tax paying households. The first Älvsborgs lösen tax was imposed in 1571, and the second in 1613. These tax records are available on microfilm through SVAR.

Mantalslängder
(Population registers for taxation)

These registers have been kept since the middle of the seventeenth century. In 1625 the parliament agreed to a tax on all grain that was milled to flour. At first the tax was levied at the mills, but many farmers milled at home, and the tax was soon changed to a general tax paid by every adult.

In 1652 it was decided that the tax (*mantalspenning*) should be paid by every person between the ages of fifteen and sixty-three. Many were excused from paying, such as soldiers and sick or destitute persons. The nobility were exempted altogether. The records are therefore incomplete as population records; you will only find the taxpayers in these lists, and at times half of the population was excluded. But these lists are the best alternative when no other records are available. That goes for the seventeenth and early eighteenth century before household examination rolls were established, or where parishes have no church books or where church records have been lost.

The original *Mantalslängder* are kept in the National Archives and the regional archives. They have been microfilmed and are available through SVAR.

Jordeböcker
(Land records for taxation)

Taxation was usually based on the farms, both the value of the farm and its production. The taxes were delivered in produce and in money, and the farm had to pay a large number of different taxes each year. When Sweden participated in the big wars during the seventeenth and early eighteenth century the tax burden was very heavy on the farm community.

The records give detailed information about what the farms had to pay and deliver. The name information is often incomplete and also unreliable. The government in this case had little interest in the names of the people on the farms as long as it got the maximum amount of taxes. The major advantage with these records is that in some cases they date back as far as to the mid-sixteenth century, which make them the very earliest records.

The original *Jordeböcker* are kept in the National Archives and in the regional archives, and are available on microfilm through SVAR.

CHAPTER FOURTEEN

Finding Your Family in Sweden Today

If you have lost track of the Swedish side of the family, finding them is probably a primary goal for your research. In this chapter we will give advice on how to go about "researching forward" into the present time.

The technique is the same as we have already presented. The households are always listed in the household examination roll, or as the record is called after 1896, the Parish Book or *Församlingsboken*. As long as the family stays at the same place we just need to look for it in the parish books, one book after another. Each parish book covers a time period of about ten years. If the family moved out of the parish, we need to look in the moving records. The parish they move to is usually noted in the parish book. Therefore we only need to look in the moving-IN records of the new parish, its *Inflyttningslängd*. There we find the place where the family settled, and we can look at the right page in the parish book in the new parish. If the family moved a lot the process of following them can be quite tedious.

Around the turn of the nineteenth century the industrial revolution took a strong grip on Sweden. Not only did people emigrate, many people also migrated within the country to the cities and other industrial places.

Church Books after 1895

Greetings from Mölltorp – a postcard from the 1960s.

The church books from before 1895 were delivered to the regional archives early on. These old church books were later microfilmed by The Church of Jesus Christ of Latter-day Saints. These microfilms are the basis for all the microfiche covering this period used by genealogists today. These microfilms are also used for scanning and publication of church records on the Internet (Genline).

The church books from 1895 until 1991 are a different matter.

In 1991 the official Swedish population records were taken over by the National Tax Board (*Skattemyndigheten,* from 2004 *Skatteverket*). All the church records with the population records kept for the period 1895–1991 were delivered to the regional archives. These records are now also being microfilmed for the future benefit of researchers.

Records up to 1920 were already available on microfilm through SVAR. Certain records have also been available through Statistics Sweden (SCB).

In times past, the general genealogical advice was to visit the parish office, or *Pastorsexpeditionen*, and ask to look at the church records (e.g., parish books, moving records, etc.). This is still a possibility as many of these offices also keep copies or microfilm of all the records after 1895. It is practical if you only need to visit one or a few parishes. It becomes time-consuming if you have to travel to a large number of places.

In the future all the records for this period (1895–1991) will be available on microfilm, through SVAR and different archives and libraries, and possibly published on the Internet. They will of course also be available at the regional archives, where the original books will be stored.

Privacy during Seventy Years

The Swedish privacy law (*Sekretesslagen*) provides a time limit of seventy years for matters of importance to personal privacy. The seventy years are counted from the time the record was made, not the person's death. The decision about what records can be opened to the genealogist is in each case made by the keeper of the records, that is the archivist or the local priest. In general, the legislation favors openness. A negative decision can be appealed and overruled.

Records of marriage and divorce, children, moves and addresses, birth and death dates, and taxed income are open to the public. Medical information, cause of death, and mental illness are examples of information that is covered by the privacy law.

Special Sources

There are a number of special sources that can be used in addition to the church books and population records and that can lead to faster results. One such source is the death book (*dödboken*). Another is the marriage register (*äktenskapsregistret*). Both of these are specific databases. A third source is the national telephone directory.

We will show some examples of how these sources can be used.

But first, we will start with the family left behind in Sweden when Gustaf Adolf Rapp left the farm Hulan in Mölltorp in 1879.

What Happened to the Rapp Family in Sweden?

Let's start with Gustaf Adolf Rapp's family at Hulan. We return to the Mölltorp household examination roll, see page 78.

There were five children in the family. Gustaf Adolf's two years younger brother Johan Herman had died in 1876 when he was only fifteen years old. His sister Emma Sofia had emigrated the year after Gustaf Adolf in 1880, and joined him in Connecticut. This left two younger half sisters at the farm Hulan: Alida Josefina and Agda Maria, eleven and sixteen years younger than Gustaf Adolf. And of course also his parents.

Looking at the household examination roll for the following period, we find that the family moved several times. First they moved to Oxlagården, a farm in Mölltorp parish. But from there they moved to Ransberg, 5 November 1888. The parents returned to the parish where they both had grown up.

We find them in the moving records, when they moved into Ransberg. See next page.

Tre Rapp family lived at Hulan in Mölltorp before they moved to Ransberg. Above right is Mölltorp church.

What Can We See in This Book? (next page)

We see that the whole family moved to the place *St. Lakenäs* on *Nov 5, 1888*. The priest has used the preprinted list in a very free manner. The notes are not always written in the columns indicated by the column titles.

We translate all the column titles even if many of the columns have not been used by the priest as intended.

73 – 76, the members of the family are the 73rd to 76th individuals to move into the parish this year.

Herr Anders Gustaf Rapp
H.(Hustru) Charlotta Eriksdotter
Dotter Agda Maria
Hemmadotter Alida Josefina Rapp

These four people moved on 5 November 1888 (*5/11*) to *St. Lakenäs*, which is a place (a farm village) within the parish of Ransberg. There is no such column ("moving to"), but the priest has used the record book in his own way. The family has come from *Mölltorp*, as noted in the right column.

We will find more about the family on page *376* in the household examination roll.

We see that Alida Josefina Rapp is now staying with her parents. In earlier records we saw that she had moved to the parish Undenäs. Possibly she went away to work in a household or on another farm. Her title is now *hemmadotter* (daughter living at home), and she is noted as having the last name Rapp, as a family name. Her mother still has her "last name" Eriksdotter, not her husband's last name.

The note *34 19/1* in pencil is Anders Gustaf Rapp's birth date.

Ransberg Moving Records 1888 (B:3)
(Inflyttningslängd)

År 1888

Inflyttningslängd för

Inkommen attests numer.	Utskrifningsår, månad och dag.	Den attesterades namn och stånd.	Födelse- ort.	år.	månad och dag.	Dop. ort.	månad och dag.	Den attesterades föräldrars namn och stånd samt den Församling, de vid hans födelse tillhörde.	Ort, hvarifrån inflyttning skett.	Christend. kunskap: Innanläsning.	Utanläsning: lilla katechesen.	stora katechesen.
72	3/11	Pig. Sofia Gustafsdotter						St. Lakenäs	Mölltorp			
73	5/11	Hem. Anders Gustaf Rapp						St. Lakenäs	"			
74	"	H. Charlotta Eriksdotter						"	"			
75	"	Dotter Agda Maria						"	"			
76	"	Hemmadotter Maria Josefina Rapp						"	"			

Translation of Column Titles

Inkommen attests numer	Arrived certificate number
Utskrifningsår, månad och dag	Year of notice, month, and day
Den attesterades namn och stånd	Name and state of the person with certificate
Födelse-, ort, år, månad och dag	Birth, place, year, month, and day
Dop, ort, månad och dag	Christening, place, month, and day
Den attesterades föräldrars namn och stånd samt den Församling, de vid hans födelse tillhörde	The certified persons name and state and the parish they belonged to at his birth
Ort, hvarifrån inflyttning skett	Place (parish) from which the move occurred
Christend. kunskap	Knowledge of Christianity
Innanläsning	Reading in book
Utanläsning	Reading by heart
lilla katechesen	the shorter Catechism
stora katechesen	the longer Catechism
Begrepp	Sense

Where Do We Go from Here?

We look at page *376* in the household examination roll (see next page).

församling. 159

61 1Å

Bevistande	Senaste nattvardsgång, år.	Senaste nattvardsgång, månad och dag.	Frejd.	Anteckning om giftermål, fästning eller annat äktenskapshinder.	Koppor.	Sidan, der första anteckning skett i husförhörslängden.	Mankön.	Qvinkön.	Attestutgifvarens namn och embete.
						377		/	
				34 19/1		376	/		
						-		/	
						″		/	
						″		/	

Translation of Column Titles (continued)

Bevistande af husförhör	Presence at household examination
Senaste nattvardsgång, år, månad och dag	Latest communion, year, month, and day
Frejd	Character
Anteckning om giftermål, fästning eller annat äktenskapshinder	Annotation about marriage, engagement to be married, or other impediment to marriage
Koppor	Smallpox
Sidan där första anteckning skett i husförhörslängden	Page where the first annotation has been done in the household examination roll
Attestutgifvarens namn och embete	The certificate writer's name and office

Note: We can conclude from the column titles that the movers had to bring an "attest," or a certificate, from the old parish to the new. The priest in the new parish was also to note if the moving persons had attended the most recent household examination and knew their basic Christianity, and if they had attended communion. As we see in this record the priest hasn't bothered to record this information.

The Rapp Family at Stora Lakenäs

On page *376*, shown below, we find the family listed. *St. (Stora) Lakenäs* is a farm village.

Ransberg Household Examination Roll 1877–1894 (AI:11)

Page 376

376 Lakenäs rote St. Lakenäs

	Personernas namn, stånd, embete, yrke och näringsfång, nationalitet, lyten, (svagsinta, blinda, döfstumma).	Födelse-			Äktenskap.		Koppor.	Flyttat		Inflyttnings-attestens nummer.	Död
		År.	Mån. och dag.	Ort, (Socken i Län, Stad).	Gift.	Enkling eller Enka.		från (Socken i Län, Stad eller pag. i Husförhörs-Boken).	År, månad och dag.		
14											
15	67/1344.9. Anders Gustaf Rapp	34	19/1	Ransberg			v.	Mölltorp	88 5/11		
16	H. Charlotta Eriksdotter	39	25/2	d:o			v.	"			
	~~Alida Josefina~~	69	18/11	d:o			v.				
17	Barn: Agda Maria	74	8/10	Mölltorp			v.				

What Can We See on This Page?

Anders Gustaf Rapp, his wife *Charlotta Eriksdotter* and their two daughters now live at Stora Lakenäs. *Alida Josefina* emigrates in *1891*.

The numbers *67/1344* in front of Anders Gustaf Rapp indicate that they own a house and a small piece of land – but not a farm. Anders Gustaf has no title indicating that he is still a farmer. They are vaccinated for smallpox.

They have also attended a household examination. *Försvarl.* (*Försvarlig* = defensible) means that they have shown passable knowledge of the catechism. This "grade" is given to Charlotta and to Alida Josefina. The father has the grade *godk* (*godkänd*) which is a step better. For Agda Maria the priest has noted *godkänd adm 89*, which means that she has had her confirmation in 1889. *Godkänd* = approved, *adm* = *admonitus* (latin) = confirmed. We can find more about her confirmation in the special confirmation record.

Alida Josefina has moved away in 1891, to *Amerika*. Even if the priest knew that she had moved to join her brother and sister in Connecticut, this has not been noted. For a Swede researching his or her emigrating relatives this is a problem. Very few official records have been made about the destination within the United States.

For translation of most of the column heads, see page 78.

Läser			Förstår.	Bevistat Förhör och begått H. H. Nattvard. 18	Frägd och enskilda anteckningar.	Flyttat		Utflyttnings-attestens nummer.
Innantill.	Luthers Kateches.	Förklaringen.		79 … 87		till Socken i Län, Stad m. m.	År, månad och dag.	
								14
godk	försvarl.							15
	försvarl.	försvarl.						16
	godkänd			adm. 89.		Amerika	91 5/[illegible]	17

This is the house where Anders Gustaf Rapp and Charlotta Eriksdotter lived in Stora Lakenäs.

Agda Maria Marries in 1894

When we look in the next household examination roll (below) we find that Agda Maria married in 1894. She has moved, but only a few pages in the book, still within the same limited area within Ransberg. Her husband is also from Stora Lakenäs, which is a farming village north of the lake Örlen in Ransberg. We can look at the couple on page *365* (shown on page 144).

Ransberg Household Examination Roll 1894–1899 (AI:13)

Page 376

376 Stora Lakenäs

	Personernas namn, stånd, embete, yrke och näringsfång, (backstugu-, inhyses- och fattighjon), nationalitet (om främmande), lyten (svagsinta, blinda, döfstumma).	Födelse- år.	mån. och dag.	ort, (socken i län, stad).	Äktenskap. Gift.	Enkl. eller enka.	Koppor.	Hitflyttad från (socken i län, stad eller pagina i husförhörsboken).	år, månad o. dag.	Inflyttningsattestens nummer	Dö
	75 ~~27~~/1344 ej.										
1.	Anders Gustaf Rapp	34	19/1	Ödeg			v				
2.	H. Charlotta Eriksdotter	39	25/2	"			v				
3.	d. ~~Agda Maria~~	74	8/10	Mölltorp			v				

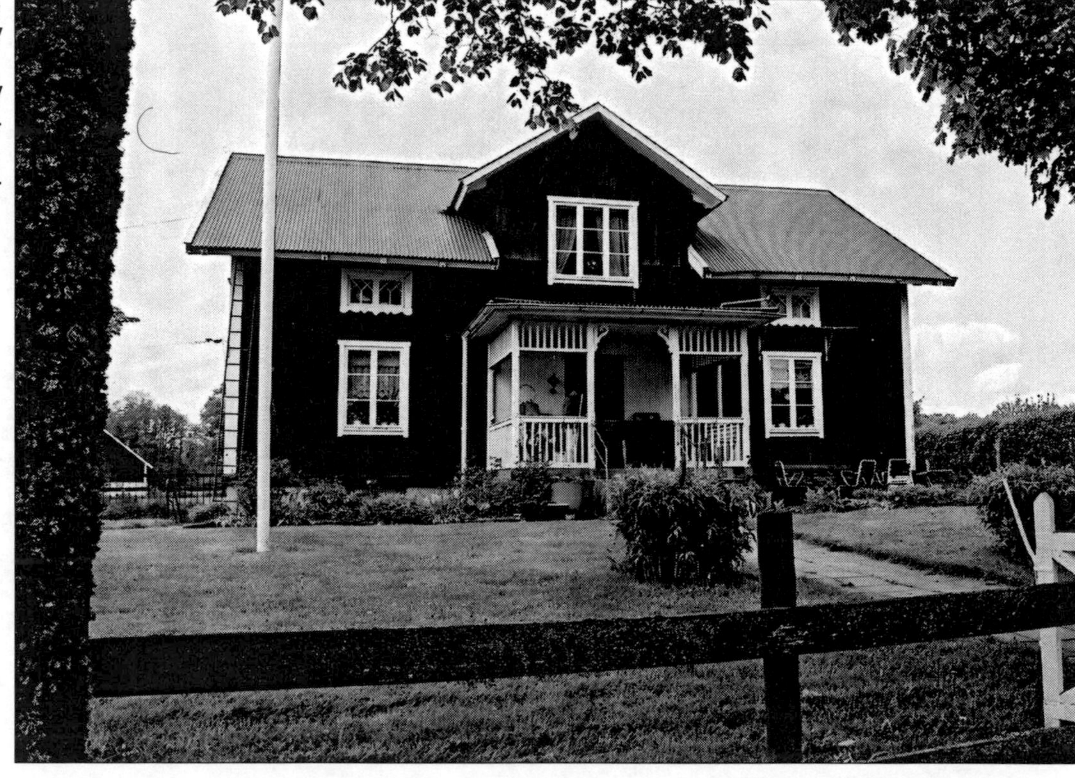

When Agda Maria married she moved into this house, built for her and her husband by her father-in-law, as we will see later (see page 161).

What Can We See on This Page?

The family now only consists of *Anders Gustaf Rapp* and his wife *Charlotta Eriksdotter* and their daughter *Agda Maria*. The daughter is crossed-out *94* (1894) with the note *Lysn.* (*lysning* = banns) *94*, and moved to *p 365* (pagina 365 = page 365). She is getting married in 1894.

Innanläsning.	Kristendoms-kunskap.	Bevistat förhör och begått H. H. nattvard. 1895 F.	1895 N.	1896 F.	1896 N.	1897 F.	1897 N.	1898 F.	1898 N.	1899 F.	1899 N.	Värn-pligt.	Fräjd och särskilda anteckningar.	Bortflyttad: till (socken i län, stad eller pagina i husförhörsboken).	år, månad o. dag.	Utflyttnings-attestens nummer	
13																	1.
ba																	2.
13													Lysn. 94	p. 365	94		3.

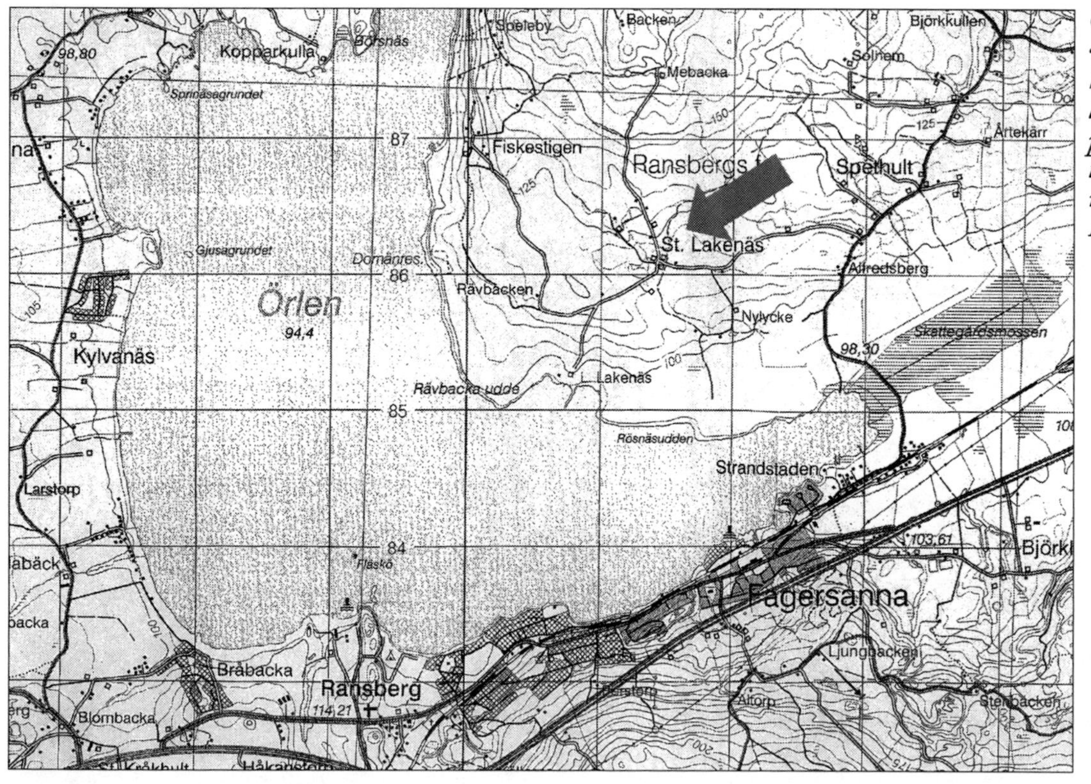

On a modern map we can see that Stora Lakenäs is located in Ransberg parish north of the lake Örlen and north of the town Fagersanna.

Ransberg Household Examination Roll 1894–1899 (AI:13)

Page 365

365 Stora Lakenäs

	Personernas namn, stånd, embete, yrke och näringsfång, (backstugu-, inhyses- och fattighjon), nationalitet (om främmande), lyten (svagsinta, blinda, döfstumma).	Födelse- år	mån. och dag.	ort, (socken i län, stad).	Äktenskap. Gift.	Enkl. eller enka.	Koppor.	Hitflyttad från (socken i län, stad eller pagina i husförhörsboken).	år, månad o. dag.	Inflyttnings-attestens nummer	Död.
	[illegible] ägare 32/1/1920										
1.	Per Adam Lagerin	36	17/2	Rby	38		v				
2.	H. Maria Lovisa Johansdr	38	26/6	"			v				
3.	d. Augusta Paulina	59	7/10	"			v				
4.	~~Karl Ludvig~~	70	8/10	"			v				
5.	s. ~~August Valfrid~~	73	10/9	"			v				
6.	s. Adolf Fritiof	76	17/8	"			v				
7.	Karl Ludvig Lagerin	70	8/10	"	94		v	Segervan	94		
8.	H. Agda Maria Rapp	74	8/10	Mällby	13/10		v	p. 376	"		
9.	s. Paul Natanael 94	94	11/12	Rby			v.				

What Can We See on This Page?

Agda Maria was married to *Karl Ludvig Lagerin* on 13 October 1894 (*94 13/10*). She had a son, *Paul Natanael*, on 11 December (*94 11/12*), that same year.

We can see several interesting things on this page, for example, Karl Ludvig and Agda Maria have the same birthday. She is four years younger than he is.

Karl Ludvig's younger brother, August Valfrid, leaves for *Kongo* (Congo) in *Afrika* (Africa) in 1897.

Where Do We Go from Here?

We have not followed the family any further in the church books.

What possibilities do we have to proceed from here?

- We can continue our search in the church books. Genline has published church books only until 1895. SVAR has microfilm until 1920, which is not available on the Internet. We can order it as microfiche directly from SVAR or through the Swenson Institute in Rock Island (or look at it at a library, archive or re-search center in Sweden). This microfilm is also available at the Family History Library and through the Family History Cen-

Kristendoms-kunskap.	Bevistat förhör och begått H. H. nattvard. 1895 F.	1895 N.	189.. F.	189.. N.	189.. F.	189.. N.	189.. F.	189.. N.	189.. F.	189.. N.	Värn-pligt.	Fräjd och särskilda anteckningar.	Bortflyttad till (socken i län, stad eller pagina i husförhörsboken).	år, månad o. dag.	Utflyttnings-attestens nummer	
[illegible]																1.
[illegible]																2.
[illegible]	abs															3.
3c	dis										6 81/91	Lysn. 91.				4.
3	abs										120 81/94.		Kongo i Afrika	97 2/4	7.	5.
3	abs	12/5									Fri					6.
3c		12/5									6 81/91					7.
3.		12/5														8.
																9.

ters.

- If we want to track the family's movements any further using church records we will need to visit the local church office in the Swedish parish (or contact the office by mail or telephone). Within a few years these later records will be available on microfilm – but there will always be limitations because of the need for privacy

- We can also look in the records collected by Statistics Sweden. These records have been used to compile statistics, and they were sent in from the parishes. They are not as detailed as the church books, but they are good enough as they include the basic facts about individuals. They are kept at the National Archives' branch in Arninge, a suburb north of Stockholm.

- We can also go to the death book (*Dödboken*) which is a CD containing information on all the people who died in Sweden between 1968 and 1996.

- Agda Maria was married to Karl Ludvig Lagerin. Lagerin is an unusual last name. We can look in the current telephone book to see if the family is still in the area around Ransberg and Mölltorp.

Searching in databases can be tedious, and looking for a certain Andersson is like looking for a needle in a haystack. With an unusual family name, a search can be much easier and faster.

The Death Book
(Dödboken)

The death book is a database listing all Swedes who died from 1950 until 2003. We will first look for Agda Maria and Karl Ludvig Lagerin, to see what year they died and where they lived, although is likely that they passed away before the time covered by the death book. We will then try to find their son, Paul Natanael Lagerin, born in 1894.

A search in the death book tells us that eighteen people with the family name Lagerin died during the period (see list below). Three of these died in Ransberg and four in the neighbour parish Tibro. To know if any of these are children or grandchildren of Adga Maria, we will have to look further in the church records.

Sveriges Dödbok II **Sida 1**

Tabell, i namnordning, 2003-06-01. Sveriges Släktforskarförbund & DIGDATA 2000.

Personnr	Namn	Dödsår	Dödsförsamling
19000418-3208	Lagerin, Anna Kristina	12/4 1997	Rone, Gotlands kn, Gotlands län
19060106-5915	Lagerin, August Bertil Esaias	18/3 1994	Beateberg, Töreboda kn, Skaraborgs län
18850507-6151	Lagerin, Axel Rickard	8/3 1976	Ransberg, Tibro kn, Skaraborgs län
19030109-6426	Lagerin, Berta Sofia	15/12 1974	Visnum, Kristinehamns kn, Värmlands län
19071220-6135	Lagerin, Ejnar Axel Isidor	3/3 1994	Tibro, Tibro kn, Skaraborgs län
19140129-6221	Lagerin, Elisif Maria Viktoria	25/10 1993	Degerfors, Degerfors kn, Örebro län
18930410-6108	Lagerin, Ellen Matilda	14/1 1980	Ransberg, Tibro kn, Skaraborgs län
18990524-5743	Lagerin, Ester Konkordia	17/11 1983	Caroli Borås, Borås kn, Älvsborgs län
18950616-3238	Lagerin, Gustaf Adolf	7/1 1980	Rone, Gotlands kn, Gotlands län
19090116-6470	Lagerin, Karl Ivan	20/12 1987	Visnum, Kristinehamns kn, Värmlands län
19040203-5992	Lagerin, Karl Johan Valdemar	13/9 1984	Tibro, Tibro kn, Skaraborgs län
19101024-6104	Lagerin, Lilly Elsa Hillevi	16/5 1991	Tibro, Tibro kn, Skaraborgs län
19180412-6140	Lagerin, Margit Viktoria	23/11 1995	Tibro, Tibro kn, Skaraborgs län
→ 19020826-6130	Lagerin, Martin Joakim Esaias	5/12 1987	Ransberg, Tibro kn, Skaraborgs län
19091207-5900	Lagerin, Märta Charlotta	19/8 1995	Beateberg, Töreboda kn, Skaraborgs län
19240324-0506	Lagerin, Rut Ingeborg	29/6 1998	Essinge, Stockholms stad, Stockholms län
19161228-6110	Lagerin, Torsten Elof Valdemar	19/7 1987	Skövde, Skövde kn, Skaraborgs län
18940320-5751	Lagerin, Wolrat Natanael	25/4 1975	Caroli Borås, Borås kn, Älvsborgs län

(Martin Joakim Esaias Lagerin, born in 1902, is a son of Karl Ludvig and Agda Maria. He died in 1987.)

If we find the right person in the death book we can get the following information: personal number, full name, address at death, death date, parish registration at death, birth parish and birth date, married or unmarried, and date of marriage if married.

Sweden's Population 1970

(Sveriges befolkning 1970)

This database lists the whole Swedish population in 1970, residents, not just citizens. We search the name Lagerin and get a list of 62 people, young and old. Many of them live in the area around Ransberg and Tibro. There is no Paul Natanael. But there is a Martin Joakim Esaias born in 1902, and a Karl Gunnar Natanael born in 1926. These are son and grandson to Agda Maria, but we still don't have this connection. A printout from this register gives us the following: birth date, full name, address, parish of residence, number of property (residence), birth place – parish, län, and province/landskap.

Sveriges befolkning 1970 **Sida 2**

Tabell, i namnordning, 2003-06-01. Sveriges Släktforskarförbund & DIGDATA 2002.

Född	Namn	Boendeförsamling	Födelseförsamling
→ 1926-08-14	Lagerin, Karl Gunnar Natanael	Ransberg (Tibro kn, Skaraborgs län, Västergötland)	Ransberg (Skaraborgs län, Västergötland)
1921-06-09	Lagerin, Karl Gösta	Rone (Gotlands kn, Gotlands län, Gotland)	Rone (Gotlands län, Gotland)
1909-01-16	Lagerin, Karl Ivan	Visnum (Kristinehamns kn, Värmlands län, Värmland)	Visnum (Värmlands län, Värmland)

A Search in the Telephone Book

We go to the website for the Yellow pages in Sweden (www.gulasidorna.se).

We then choose *privatpersoner*, or private persons. We make a search for the name Lagerin, and get a list with 41 names.

Three of the people on the list still live at Lakenäs or Stora Lakenäs! Many of the others live in the vicinity, in Tibro, Karlsborg, Fagersanna, Hjo, and Skövde.

We are on the right track. Now we can start making phone calls.

In this case we were lucky. Agda Maria married into a family with an unusual last name. The family had a farm and kept that farm, staying in the area.

After a couple of telephone calls we've reached our goal. Gunnar Lagerin in the village of Fagersanna, in Ransberg parish and just south of Stora Lakenäs, is a grandson of Agda Maria Lagerin, born Rapp. He tells us she was called Maria. In the village she was known as "Rappens Maria," or Rapp's Maria.

We are now ready to plan our trip to Sweden. In chapter sixteen we make a visit to Gunnar Lagerin and the places where Gustaf Adolf Rapp and Anna Kristina Carlsson lived.

Claes-Göran Lagerin
Tel. 0504-24027
Lakenäs 4213, 543 94 TIBRO
Gunnar Lagerin, Skogsarb.
Tel. 0504-20070
Fageråsv. 3, 543 95 FAGERSANNA
Tore Lagerin, Lantbr.
Tel. 0504-24060
St. Lakenäs, 543 94 TIBRO

Useful Databases

When researching current family, and the developments within the last hundred years, there are a number of useful databases. We have given examples from a couple of them on the previous pages. Some of the main resources for immigrant research are also available in databases, either on the Internet, or on CD-ROM. Some databases are free, others cost money. We will list some of the most useful databases and how you can get hold of them.

One general problem is language. Most of the Swedish databases are only in Swedish. Some have directions and information in English.

Swedish

Sveriges befolkning 1970
(Sweden's population 1970)

Sveriges befolkning 1980
(Sweden's population 1980)

Available on a CD-ROM from *Svenska Släktforskarförbundet* in Stockholm (easiest to find through the web-site *Rötter* (www.genealogi.se). The database includes information on all residents in Sweden in 1970 and 1980. The information has been compiled from different public records. There are a number of search possibilities, e.g. name, birth place, birth date, and living place. Instructions are in Swedish but will be translated into English.

Sveriges befolkning 1880, 1890, 1900
(Sweden's population 1880, 1890, 1900)

The population records, or census, from 1880, 1890 and 1900 are available on CD-ROM and on the Internet. The records from 1880 are incomplete. The Swedish census is not a result of a separate population count. Instead, each congregation listed its population, as it appeared in the parish book, and submitted this to Statistics Sweden. It was then used for the national population statistics. All these lists of individuals and families have been put together in a "household examination roll for all of Sweden." The records are in digitalized form (not the scanned documents), and the CD-ROM is published by Arkion/SVAR (within the Swedish National Archives) in cooperation with *Sveriges Släktforskarförbund*. (more information through www.ra.se/arkion or www.arkion.se, or www.genealogi.se). The census is also available on the website of SVAR, by subscription (www.svar.ra.se).

Sveriges dödbok
(The Swedish Death Book)

All deaths in Sweden from 1950 until 2003 are registered in this database, available on a CD-ROM, published by *Sveriges Släktforskarförbund*. For information, go to the website *Rötter* (www.genealogi.se). For the period 1950–1972 the records give the personal ID-numbers, but not the names. Volunteers are extracting the names out of the church records, to complete the records. This database is available on the Internet at the website of SVAR. To get access You need a subscription. As with the records from 1970 and 1980 (above) this is a compilation of data from parish records.

Sveriges Befolking 1930
(Sweden's population 1930)

This database is available on the Internet at the website of SVAR. To get access, you need a subscription. As with the records from 1970 and 1980 (above) this is a compilation of data from parish records.

Folkräkningen 1890
(Sweden's population 1890 – certain provinces)

Certain parts of the 1890 Swedish census are available on the Internet free of charge. The database has been made available by the university of Umeå (www.foark.umu.se/folk). The university has a department called the demographic database (*Demo-*

grafiska databasen), which is specialized in preparing population records for computerized research. The districts available in digital form on the Internet are: Norrbottens län, Västerbottens län, Jämtlands län, Västernorrlands län, and Värmlands län. This database provides good search possibilities.

Indiko

This is another database (www.ddb.umu.se) connected to the university in Umeå and the demographic database. A number of parishes have been thoroughly indexed, for the purpose of demographic research. They are located around the cities of Umeå, Sundsvall, and Linköping.

Söderskivan, Klaraskivan, Gamla Stan-skivan
(Population Records from Stockholm)

These CDs include lists of all people in three parts of Stockholm. The basis is the city population records kept between 1878 and 1926, a period when Stockholm grew fast. A lot of Swedes moved to Stockholm. Many moved on, and emigrated. *Söderskivan* (*skiva* = disc) contains some 520,000 names of persons who lived in the southern part of Stockholm during these years. *Klaraskivan* includes all persons who lived in the inner city Klara congregation. *Gamla Stan-skivan* is somewhat different. It tells about the Old Town through 750 years, and also has population records. The CDs can be obtained from Stockholm City Archives (www.ssa.stockholm.se).

Regional Population Records and Registers

There are a number of other digitized, scanned, or indexed records from different parts of Sweden. The work has usually been done by a local genealogical society by volunteers. The genealogical society in Halland has, for example, made ninety-three CDs with the tax records (mantalslängder) for each of the ninety-three parishes in the province. The best way to find these kinds of records is to consult *Rötter* (www.genealogi.se).

Begravda I Sverige
(Buried in Sweden)

This database is based on grave records in the parishes, and includes more than 5.3 million buried Swedes on 2,250 cemeteries, as well as maps of cemeteries. The database does not yet include all parishes. It is available Sveriges Släktforskarförbund on CD-ROM (www.genealogi.se). On the Internet you can also find grave records for Stockholm (www.hittagraven.se), and Gothenburg (www.svenskakyrkan.se/goteborg/kgf).

Sveriges Ortnamn
(Swedish Geographic Names)

This is a CD-ROM produced by the Swedish Genealogical Society that lists names of places: towns, parishes, villages, farms, estates, cottages, etc. It has excellent search properties. You can, for example, search on a part of a name. If you are uncertain of the interpretation of a handwritten name, this can be very valuable. You will find information about this CD on *Rötter* (www.genealogi.se).

The Telephone Directory

It is possible to buy the Swedish telephone directory on CD-ROM. Today this seems redundant as the phone books are also available on the Internet. The Swedish phone book can be reached either at Eniro (www.eniro.se) or at the Yellow Pages (www.gulasidorna.se).

Föreningen Släktdata
(Swedish Parish Files)

This organization collects and publishes parish files from all over Sweden. In these files amateur researchers have compiled data out of different records. For example, you can get lists with references to all deaths, births, and marriages in a certain parish. All the available files are listed on the homepage (www.slaktdata.org). The whole database can be purchased on CD-ROM.

Emigranten
(The Swedish Emigrant)

This CD has been thoroughly presented in an earlier chapter (see page 128). It contains a number of databases related to the Swedish emigration between 1820 and 1950. The most important is Emihamn, the index to the ship's lists. The CD-ROM is a joint project between the Swedish Emigrant Institute in Växjö, the Swedish American Center in Karlstad and "The Gothenburg Emigrant" (*Göteborgs-Emigranten*). There is an English version. The CD can be purchased from Göteborgs-Emigranten (www.goteborgs-emigranten.com).

Emibas

This emigrant database lists emigrants in moving records and household examination rolls between 1860 and 1930 from parishes around Sweden. Some regions have been indexed completely, others are incomplete. The indexing has been done by volunteers. The database is kept at the Swedish Emigrant Institute in Växjö, at the Swedish American Center in Karlstad, and at the Regional Archives in Gothenburg. It is not yet available on CD. To access the database you have to contact one of these institutions and ask for the information you need. There is a fee.

SAKA
– Svenskamerikanska kyrkoarkiv
(Swedish-American Church Archives)

The microfilm is kept in Växjö, at the Swedish Emigrant Institute. There is also a database with search indexes that are very helpful to find certain names. The database is handled the same way as Emibas. It is not available except at these three institutions.

Other Scandinavian

The Norwegian and Danish archives have records about Swedes who passed through these countries and their ports. Norway has a lot of records available on the Internet (www.hist.uib.no/arkivverket). The Danish records can be found through the Danish Emigrant Archives (www.emiarch.dk). You can, for example, find the Copenhagen passenger lists.

American

Ancestry.com

This large genealogical website is excellent. Most databases and records cost, and you get access to them by paying a monthly or annual fee. But there are also a lot of sources that are free of charge. Through Ancestry.com (www.ancestry.com) you can search for a certain person or persons across the site's databases, which include a complete set of U.S. Census records and a growing collection of historical newspapers, immigration records and passenger lists, family and local histories, and vital records.

Ellis Island

The ships manifests at Ellis Island can be studied as scanned pictures on the web-site of Ellis Island (www.ellisislandrecords.org), without cost. From 1892 to 1924 more than 22 million immigrants and crew-members passed through Ellis Island. The manifests have been scanned and transcribed. You can search for an individual and look at the manifests where that individual is listed. You can also order the manifest for a small fee. And you can read the transcription. The indexing of Swedish geographical names is sometimes not quite accurate. The handwriting in the manifests can be difficult to interpret.

FamilySearch

This website (www.familysearch.org), owned and operated by The Church of Jesus Christ of Latter-day Saints, provides access to the enormous collection of genealogical material collected by the church, as listed in the Family History Library Catalog, and many other databases and indexes. FamilySearch has indexed Swedes and other Scandinavians and published CD-ROMs through which it is possible to search for individuals. These indexes are far from complete and sometimes names and spelling have been misinterpreted.

Social Security Death Index

This index covers American deaths from as early as the 1930s. The database contains information provided by the Social Security Administration, SSA. In 2003 the database lists some 71 million names. The index can be reached through Ancestry.com and other websites, and can also be purchased as a CD-ROM.

Vital Records

To find vital records in the different U.S. states can be a challenge, since states handle records at either the state or the county level. There is a Vital Records Information website (www.vitalrec.com) that specializes in information about these kinds of records (birth, death, marriage, etc.).

CHAPTER FIFTEEN

Prepare for a Trip to Sweden

At some point in most family historian's research, there is a time when a visit to the country of origin becomes desirable or necessary. As a Swedish researcher, once you have found Swedish relatives, the planning is relatively easy. You will probably get their help to plan a trip to visit other relatives, the old farmstead, the old parish church, etc.

If you haven't yet found the Swedish family, you need to plan a trip to one or more of the research centers mentioned earlier in the book: one of the regional archives, the Swedish Emigrant Research Center in Växjö (*Utvandrarnas hus* = House of Emigrants), the Emigrant institute in Karlstad, SVAR's research center in Ramsele, the "House of Genealogy" in Leksand, the genealogical center in Kyrkhult or one of the Family History Centers associated with the Family History Library.

Before you leave for Sweden, be sure that the institutions you plan to visit in Sweden will be open on the days you will be visiting and that they can give you the kind of service and help you need. All of them have home pages on the Web. Visit these sites to get as much information before your trip as possible. Check opening and visiting hours, and ask about the research possibilities (e.g. if you have to sign up beforehand, if there is a waiting line, and so on). Some of the facilities have rooms to rent, or their personnel can recommend nearby hotels or cottages to rent. Inquire and book beforehand so you don't get stranded in the middle of the busy Swedish summer vacation period.

Places to Visit Locally

In addition to these larger national or regional institutions there are local places to visit. Every city and municipality has a library, often of excellent quality. In some cases the libraries have special sections or rooms for local history.

There are usually local museums and local historical societies (*hembygdsmuseum, hembygdsföreningar*). Be sure to visit them after you have found your emigrant's home parish. Quite often there is an open air museum with old farm houses and cottages, where old household items, old farm tools, and handicrafts are on display.

The large outdoor museum in Stockholm, *Skansen*, served as a model for these museums. Be sure to visit Skansen if you come to Stockholm on your trip. At Skansen you can see examples of traditional farms from different parts of Sweden, as well as houses from towns, an old school, an old wooden church, an old market place, and a number of other traditional buildings and environments. Other cities have similar outdoor museums, for example, in Lund (*Kulturen*), Östersund (*Jamtli*), Örebro (*Wadköping*), Linköping (*Gamla Linköping*), and in many small places like *Julita* in Södermanland and *Bunge* on the island Gotland.

At these "ethnological museums" you can get a good picture of how life was lived in Sweden before the Industrial Revolution, and what your ancestors' lives might have been like.

In almost every parish around the country you will find a hembygdsgård, *a local historical museum where old farm houses and cottages have been saved and where midsummer celebrations and other gatherings take place. This is Finnerödja hembygdsgård in northern Västergötland.*

The Local Church and Churchyard

A visit to the old parish church and the graveyard is a must on a trip to Sweden. The church will usually be open during the daytime hours. If it is locked, there will often be a vicarage or a church office (*pastorsexpedition*) nearby, although in the smallest parishes this will not be the case. Ask someone living nearby or look in the local phone book (listing under *Svenska Kyrkan* = the Swedish church) for further information. There may be a caretaker or churchwarden living close to the church.

As noted earlier, in the countryside the graveyard is usually located around the church. In the cities and larger places there are often separate cemeteries. At times you will find "forest cemeteries" located on the outskirts of the city. Most people are buried in their own parish graveyard. Sometimes many members of the same family are buried in a "family grave." Beside names, and dates of birth and death you will often find the names of farms or villages on the stones. But remember the Swedish naming practices. You will find all the Anderssons, Karlssons, and Johanssons also in the graveyards! It's easy to get mixed up.

The Swedish Genealogical Society is conducting an inventory of old gravestones nationwide, and the results are being published on the Web. You will find links on the genealogical websites.

If you don't find graves that you had expected there are several possible reasons. Maybe the relatives are buried in a neighbouring parish or town. Maybe their graves have already been removed to make room for new graves. Ask for information at the church office. If they don't have records, try the undertaker firms in the nearest town; they have often kept records of where their clients have been buried. Look for obituaries or death notices in the local paper at the time of the death. There will probably be an invitation to the funeral service. The papers are often kept at the local library, at least on microfilm.

Get a Good Road Map

Once you get to Sweden, we suggest you get a good map. We recommend *KAK bilatlas* ("Sweden's AAA road map") or *Motormännens (M:s) Sverige Vägatlas.* They both have all the parish churches clearly marked on the maps, and also most of the smaller country roads. A good road map is well worth its cost (around 250 – 300 Swedish kronor).

Sweden is a relatively large country, larger than California, and there are fewer expressways than in the United States. So allow time for travel inside Sweden in your itinerary.

Get a Good Local Map

To find a specific farm, a cottage or a street address, you need a more detailed map. There are a number of good maps available. Go to the local bookstore and buy the maps you need. Or visit the library to look at the maps beforehand to be sure that you get the right kind of map. You need a map where all the farms and houses in the countryside are shown and named. The topographic map ("the green map" scale 1:50,000) gives a good overview and includes all farms, cottages, and roads in the countryside. The economic map ("the yellow map" scale 1:20,000 or 1:10,000) shows all the buildings on farms as well as all the boundaries between individual farms. This map is not kept in stock but has to be ordered from the Land Survey Office (*Lantmäteriet*). They will produce and print out your individual map from a digital database. See also page 154.

People Know English

An old steamboat of a type used on the lakes or canals. Many of them are still in use.

Where to Go in Western Sweden

We have identified a number of places connected to the Rapp family and others. Adolf Rapp's and Anna Carlsson's families lived in a limited area in Mölltorp and Ransberg parishes. When family members moved and found their spouses this took place within these two, and the neighboring, parishes. To make our travel itinerary we can plot the places we want to visit on a map.

In this case we have several alternatives:

1. Flying into Gothenburg and renting a car.
2. Flying into Stockholm and renting a car.
3. Taking the train to Skövde and rent a car, or be met by relatives.

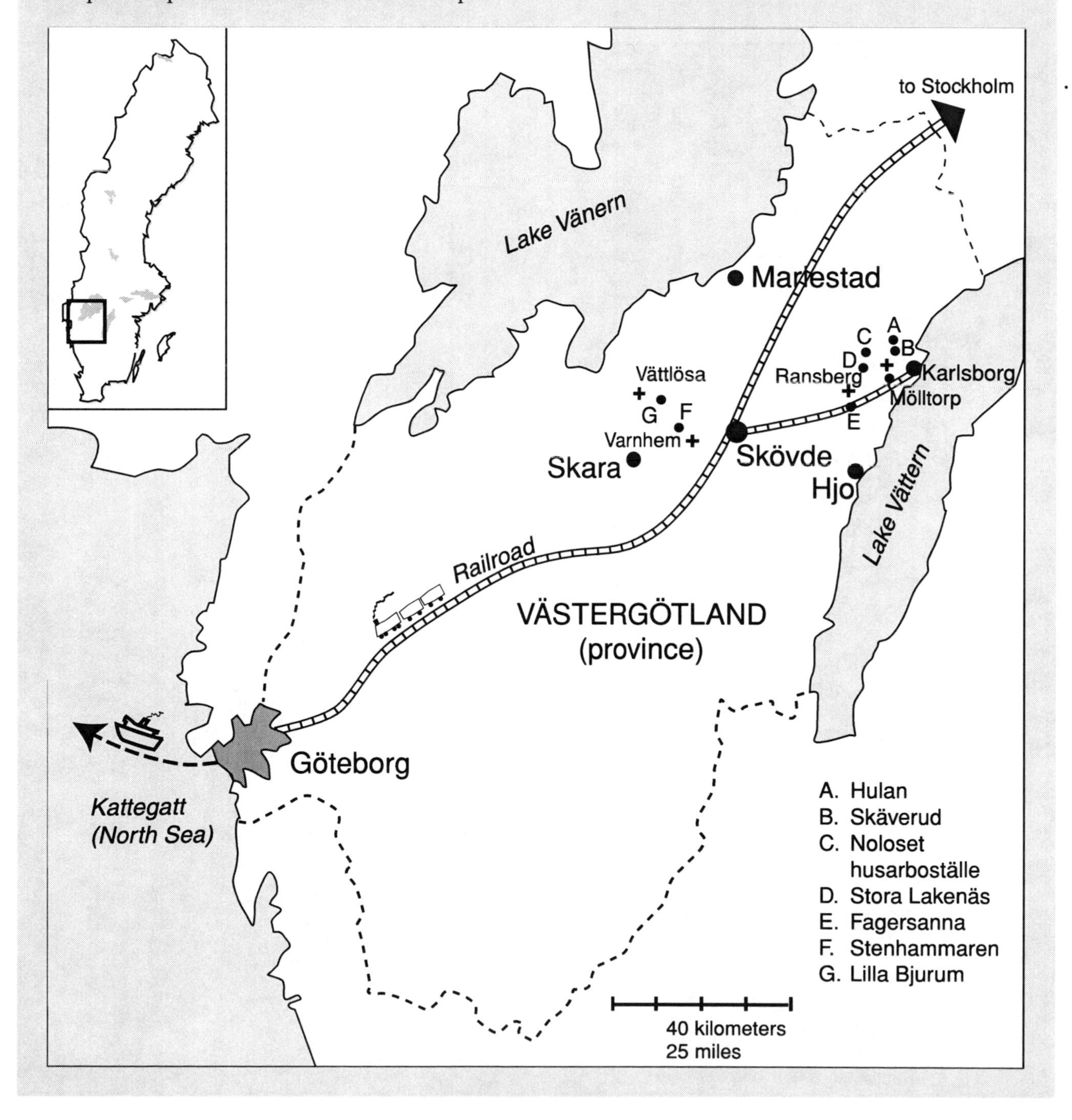

Maps Available on the Internet

If you want a good Swedish map, a fast and simple way is to buy one on the Internet from the national Swedish land survey – *Lantmäteriet.* You can either have the map delivered in digital form, and print it on your own printer, or have it delivered by mail. You make your own map of the area you need. Just place "your" parish church or village in the middle of the map. The service is easy to use, and has directions in English. Go to www.lantmateriet.se, choose English text, and go to "Your map – Map search." You can pay for the map with your credit card.

We show three different examples on these two pages.

Vägkartan, or the road map, gives a good overview over the area, but also includes most smaller roads, farms and villages. We can see the parish churches, Ransberg and Mölltorp, the towns, Fagersanna and Mölltorp, and also farm villages like Stora Lakenäs

Vägkartan

and Höghult. But most single houses and smaller places are not named. Valuable information is also the boundaries between parishes. There is also a map named *översiktskartan*, or the overview map, that is even less detailed, and is a good map to use while driving around a wider area.

Terrängkartan, or the terrain map, is more detailed, and here we can find the cottage Sjöhagen northwest of Höghult. This is the place where Gustaf Adolf Rapp was born – Nolosets Husarboställe. It has since then been renamed.

Fastighetskartan, the property map, is the most detailed map you can purchase. It even gives property boundaries. We can also see the individual buildings on the farmsteads, like the barn and other small buildings at Sjöhagen. We also see some names of places in the middle of the forest with no houses at all, like Fredriksberg west of Sjöhagen, and Blombygget to the south. These are probably names of cottages, which have been abandoned and torn down.

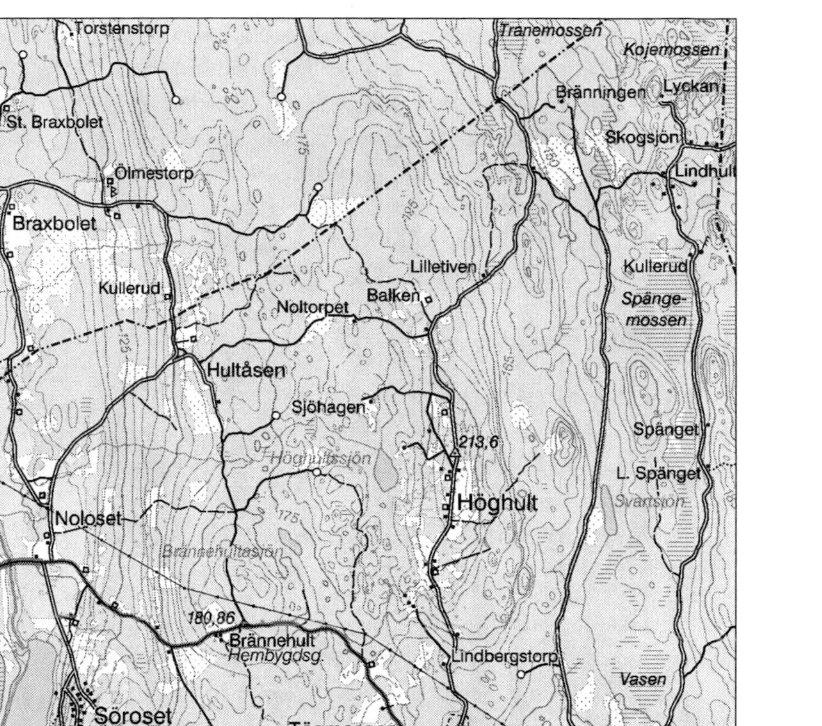

Terrängkartan

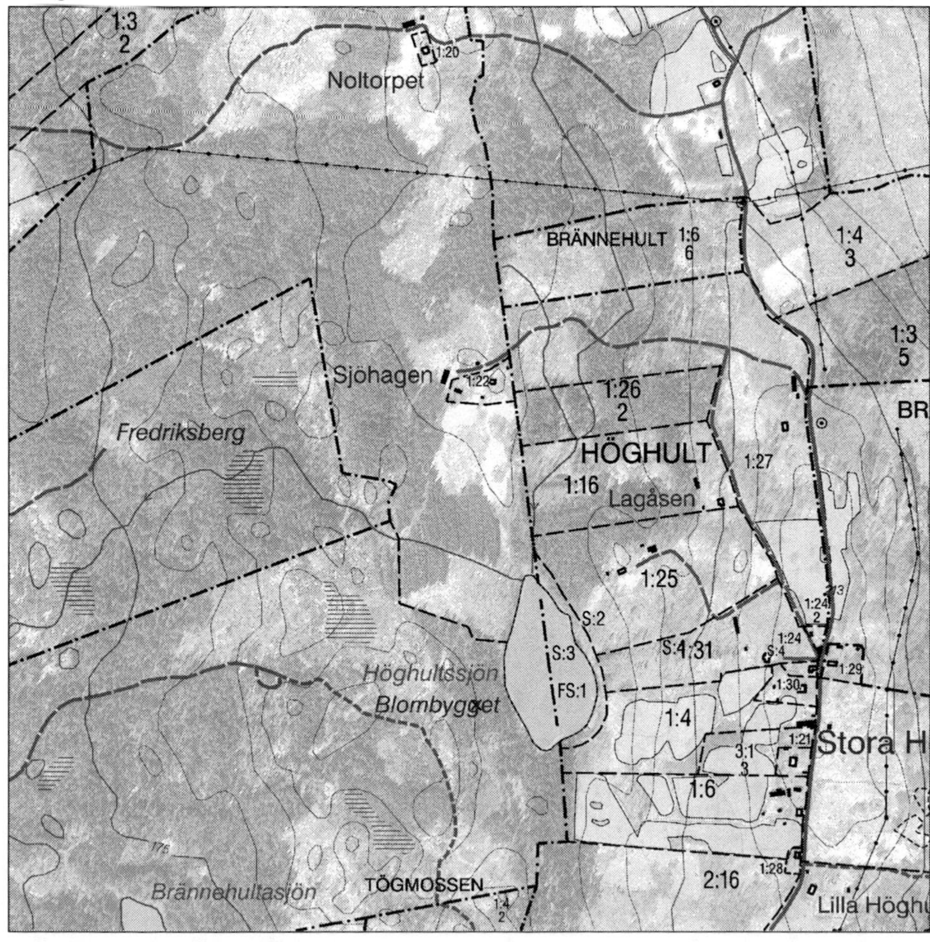

Fastighetskartan

Historical Maps

All these maps are current maps, useful when you travel to Sweden today. They are also useful when you plan the trip, even if you don't buy the maps. On Lantmäteriet's website you can also view and purchase historical maps, from the seventeenth century until today. More than 45,000 maps are available.

Don't worry that you don't know Swedish. All young people (under the age of fifty-five) have had English in school, and most of them know the language well. The younger, the better their knowledge of English. Many older people also speak English, but others, and possibly many of your older Swedish relatives, will not know English. But you will find plenty of people around who will be happy to help interpreting.

Travel in the Summer

Sweden is located quite far to the north, about the latitude of Alaska – the northernmost part is even north of the polar circle. The winter isn't always very cold, due to the influence of the Gulf Stream, but it is always very dark, because of the high latitude. The winter days are very short.

In contrast the summer days are long, with midnight sun in the north. If you are able to visit in the summer you will find that you get a lot done in a day. You can make a number of visits to different relatives in a single day. You can also travel around the countryside late in the evening and still see a lot of the landscape and the buildings. The climate is usually perfect in summer and is seldom uncomfortably hot.

If you cannot take advantage of the Swedish summer, go in late spring (late April, May) or early autumn (September, early October).

Almost every Swede takes an extended vacation in the summer. July is the peak vacation time, but many people also take time off in late June or early August. A lot of people leave the cities for summer homes in the countryside, on the coast, by the lakes, or in the mountains. Be aware that during the vacation month of July opening hours can be shorter in offices and private companies sometimes close down completely.

When Visiting Swedes

Swedes are easygoing and hospitable. If you visit someone's home you will always get something to drink and munch on, usually coffee (and don't ask for decaf, since most Swedes have never heard of it), often strong black coffee and some sweet bread or cookies. Swedes think of themselves as quiet and dull, but you will probably find most people very friendly and open.

It's always good to call before a visit, so people can prepare. But don't hesitate to drive up to a farm or a house and knock on the door without a prior appointment.

Free Access to Land

Visit the local country store when you travel.

The free access to all private land gives you an opportunity to explore the forests. You can also pick flowers, berries, and mushrooms wherever you want.

Sweden has an old law of free access to all land (*Allemansrätt*). Everyone has a right to walk freely on everyone's land, except around the houses (a small area of privacy). All forests, woods, and meadows are always open, as well as all farmland where there is not growing plants. The seashores are always accessible, and it's forbidden to build along shores.

This old legislation goes back to medieval times and there are several reasons for it. In a sparsely populated country with few roads people traveled by horse or on foot. Boundaries had little meaning. In addition, poor people have always had the right to pick berries and other products in the forests, both on private and common lands.

One even has a right to put up a tent for a night without the landowner's permission. You will find no signs of "private property" or "no trespassing." To keep people out of your private property is simply illegal! Also as a visiting foreign tourist you have the freedom to hike wherever you like as long as you don't disturb people or their animals around their houses and as long as you don't harm growing farm plants. But remember — you are still a guest on someone's land. Don't litter and be careful with fire. Driving is only allowed on roads and private roads can be closed to traffic.

Plan the Trip

Remember that Sweden is a sparsely populated country. It can be quite a distance between hotels, restaurants and food stores, especially in inner and northern Sweden. So plan your travel accordingly.

It is easy to rent a car, and you can find good offers at reasonable prices. But driving is expensive because gas is expensive. Don't be surprised if the gas price is twice or three times what you are used to back home. Try to use a small and compact car with good mileage if you have a choice.

Taking the train is a good alternative, except when you need to visit smaller communities. Some of them can be reached by train, but they are few.

About lodging:

• The hotels are rather few and relatively expensive,

In many Swedish cities you can find old wooden houses. These are from a hilly part of southern Stockholm (Södermalm) where laborers lived. Take your time, put on your hiking shoes and discover the back streets!

Midsummer is as important to Swedes as Thanksgiving is to Americans. Dancing around the midsummer pole is part of the celebration.

although some have discounts in the summer. In tourist areas, however, they are more expensive in the summer. In the big cities staying in a hotel is the main alternative.

- Motels are relatively uncommon. The typical American-style inexpensive roadside motel is nonexistent.
- Youth hostels (*vandrarhem*) are a good inexpensive alternative, and they are for all ages, despite their name in English. They are much cheaper than regular hotels, and they are generally clean. But the beds are often rather simple bunk beds. You usually have to bring your own sheets, make your own breakfast in a common kitchen and clean the room before you leave.
- Especially in tourist areas you will find cottages for rent. They are often located at a camping ground and are comparable to youth hostels in standard and price. As with youth hostels you have to bring your own sheets.
- Bed & Breakfasts are not as common in Sweden as in England or Scotland. Local inns are also not common, as in Germany, although both do exist.
- A good alternative, if you want to experience the countryside, is to stay at a farm (*Bo på Lantgård*).

When the tourist season ends a lot of hotels, youth hostels, and campgrounds close, especially in the tourist regions, for example on the islands of Gotland and Öland and along the coast.

In general, Sweden is an easy country to travel in and you will, as a genealogist, meet a lot of hospitable and interested Swedes, eager to be of help. You will find that most Swedes have a great interest in their family history as well as in the local history. Hundreds of thousands of Swedes are members of local historical societies and genealogy is a very popular activity. Swedes take great pride in preserving their cultural treasures and love to learn more about the local history. And the Swedes are very eager to share their interest with visiting Americans.

Connecting with unknown American family is as much a thrill to Swedes as it is to Americans who try to find their Swedish roots and Swedish relatives. So, just go and connect! You have everything to win, and nothing to lose!

Stockholm is a city on the water. The ferry lines connect Sweden with Finland and Estonia.

CHAPTER SIXTEEN

Meeting the Swedish Family

Gunnar Lagerin – Agda Maria's Grandson

When we visit Gunnar Lagerin and his wife Ingrid, they show us a picture of Maria. She died in 1912, long before Gunnar was born in 1926.

Gunnar also has in his possession a couple of invitation cards to the funerals for Charlotta Rapp in 1902 and for Anders Gustaf Rapp in 1913 (shown below).

The printed invitation card to the funeral service for Charlotta Rapp is typical for the time. The text reads: *(Per and Lovisa Lagerin) are invited to honor, with their presence, my ardently loved wife Charlotta Rapp's funeral service Tuesday 8 of this month. Gathering at the house of sorrow at 8.30 AM. Stora Lakenäs 1 April, 1902. A.G. Rapp.*

Note that she is now called Charlotta Rapp, not Charlotta Eriksdotter, as in most church records, The habit of family names instead of patronymic names had finally taken over.

The handwritten card for Anders Gustaf Rapp's funeral is much simpler, but also more personal, signed by his son-in-law, Karl Ludvig Lagerin, Maria's husband. The old soldier was seventy-nine. He had survived both his second wife and his daughter Maria. He had two grandsons in Sweden but most of his family was living in the United States – children, grandchildren, and great-grandchildren.

Gunnar Lagerin Shows Us Around

Gunnar Lagerin grew up in the little farm village Stora Lakenäs. His father's name was Martin, and he was the younger brother to Paul, the firstborn we see

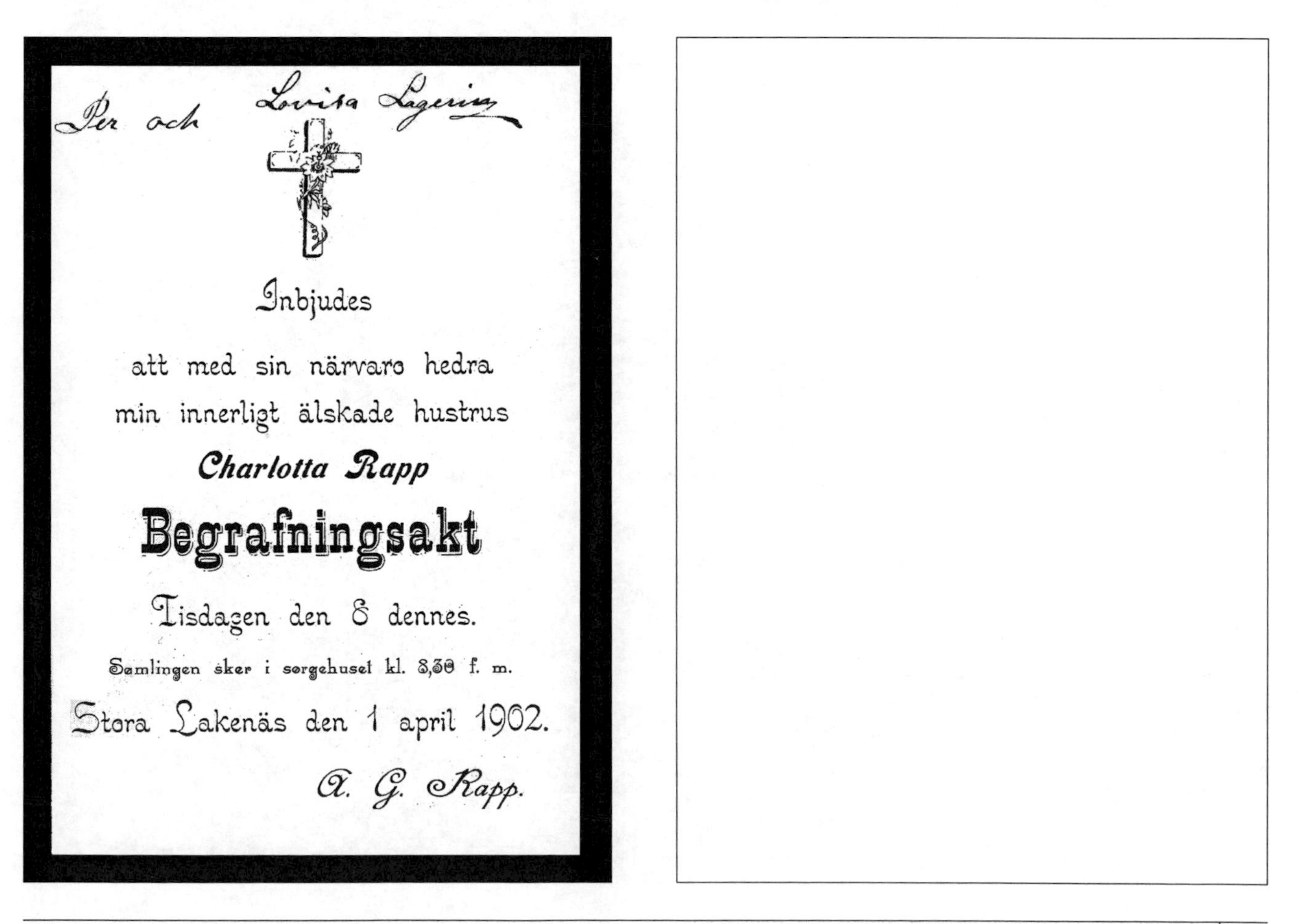

Per och Lovisa Lagerin

Inbjudes

att med sin närvaro hedra
min innerligt älskade hustrus

Charlotta Rapp

Begrafningsakt

Tisdagen den 8 dennes.

Samlingen sker i sorgehuset kl. 8,30 f. m.

Stora Lakenäs den 1 april 1902.

A. G. Rapp.

Gunnar Lagerin in front of the house that was built for his grandparents, Maria Rapp and her husband Karl Lagerin around 1895.

This framed picture of Maria Rapp is a treasure for Gunnar Lagerin, her grandson.

in the page of the household examination roll on page 144. Martin was born in 1902, and the two brothers were the only children in the family.

Gunnar takes us around to some of the farms and places where the family has lived and tells us about the family:

– I know that my grandmother gave birth to her boy shortly after the marriage. The story is that my grandfather would visit her secretly. Maria lived with her parents in a small house in the outskirts of the village.

– When they were married, Karl's father built a new house for the newlyweds.

This house, probably built in 1894 or 1895, still stands in the middle of the village, and Gunnar's second cousin Tore Lagerin, a retired farmer, lives in the house. It doesn't seem like the Lagerin family was unhappy about the marriage.

To Gunnar's knowledge there hasn't been much contact between the Swedish side of the family and their American relatives. One reason for this could simply be that Maria was the only sibling left in Sweden, and that she died at a rather young age. Another could be that the emigrating siblings were only her half-siblings and quite a lot older.

Gunnar shows us the house where Maria lived with her parents, Anders Gustaf Rapp and Charlotta Eriksdotter. The house has been rebuilt since those days, and doesn't much resemble their old cottage. But parts of it are still the same structure, which stands on the same location on a hillside overlooking the village, a nice pasture on one side, and a farm across the road on the other side.

The old soldier and his wife spent their last years in this little house of their own, growing their own potatoes, maybe keeping a pig and a few hens. Of Anders Gustaf Rapp's five children, three emigrated to the United States, one boy died at age 15, and the youngest daughter stayed in Sweden and married a local boy from the village. Perhaps she stayed because she was loyal to her parents. More likely she stayed in Sweden because she found love at a young age. Otherwise she might have joined her sisters and older brother in Connecticut.

This is where Maria Rapp lived with her parents. The house has been rebuilt since then.

Gustaf Adolf Rapp's Birthplace

With the help of Gunnar we also managed to find the old hussar stead, Nolosets husartorp. When we came to the village Noloset we found a farmer who remembered that the soldier's cottage up in the forest was sometimes referred to as "Rapp's place." Today the place is owned by a German family and used as a summer home. On the map it is called Sjöhagen.

As was so often the case, the soldier was given a small piece of land on the outskirts of the village. The small soldier stead seems almost untouched since the late nineteenth century: a small house, covered with a modern metal roof, but otherwise kept in the old style; a small barn with room for a cow, a horse and a few small animals; a wood shed and a couple of other small buildings; a few small pastures in the clearing in the forest; and a couple of small fields, probably for potatoes and turnips, for oats for the horse and some hay for the cow. The place is an idyllic spot in early summer. But it was a poor place to live at, with small fields with meager soil. Remote and cold in the winter, it is lonely for a soldier's wife when her husband went away to military exercises.

The old hussar stead, Nolosets husartorp, where Gustaf Adolf Rapp was born. The place is now called Sjöhagen.

Hulan and Skäverud

We also try to find the place Hulan, where the Rapp family lived in 1879, when Gustaf Adolf emigrated. Hulan is a small farm in Mölltorp, about ten miles east of Lakenäs and Noloset in Ransberg parish. There we find a place called Ö. Hulan (East Hulan). We're uncertain if this is the right place, or if there was another house or farmstead nearby (a West Hulan?). It is certain that Gustaf Adolf came from the area. A further study in the land records at the local court would probably reveal the right answer, combined with a good economic map from the period. Gustaf Adolf's father was not listed as owner of this small farm, just lease holder (see page 78).

Close by is the village of Skäverud, where Gustaf Adolf's fiancée Anna Carlsson came from. However, the village consists of a number of farms and other houses, and we are not certain in what farm or house Anna grew up.

Also in this case we would need more research, if we want to find the right house or farm. A first step would be to talk to the people in the village today. Some of the families are probably descendants of families living in the village in the 1870s. Perhaps there are still people related to Anna still living in the village. Instead of spending days in archives or at the microfilm reader or the computer, it may be quicker and more enjoyable to simply talk to people. This is a typical case where this approach could prove to be fruitful.

Some families have left, but some may have stayed in the village. And there are usually old people and at least a few with interest in local history. Knock on doors. Have a cup of coffee with them. Tell them your story and they will tell you what they know. They'll show you old pictures, deeds, contracts, letters, and other things out of their boxes and drawers. Don't be shy. No one expects an American to be shy anyway!

A good alternative, if you are unsuccessful with your door-knocking, is to turn to the local historical society, *hembygdsföreningen*, or to a local genealogical society, *släktforskarförening*.

Birch trees border the road to the little farm Hulan, possibly the place where the Rapp family lived in 1879.

The farm village Skäverud, where Anna Carlsson's family lived, consists of several farms and cottages. We are not certain in which house her family lived.

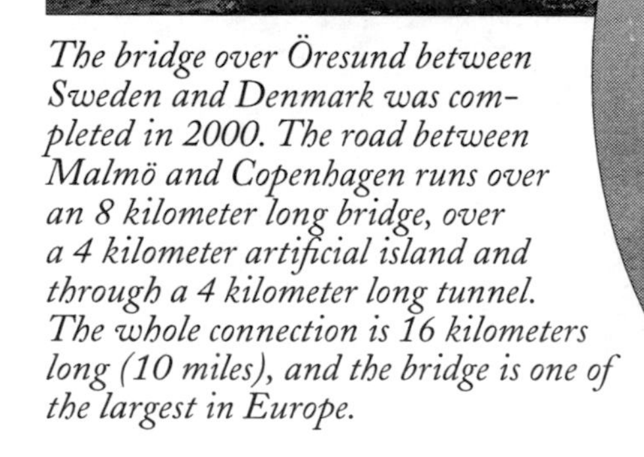

The bridge over Öresund between Sweden and Denmark was completed in 2000. The road between Malmö and Copenhagen runs over an 8 kilometer long bridge, over a 4 kilometer artificial island and through a 4 kilometer long tunnel. The whole connection is 16 kilometers long (10 miles), and the bridge is one of the largest in Europe.

CHAPTER SEVENTEEN

Swedish Provinces

Each of the Swedish provinces, *landskap* in Swedish, has its own specific character and typical physical and cultural features. In this chapter we will describe, briefly, some of these characteristics and list the most important points of interest in each province, places that a tourist should be sure to visit while traveling in each province. We will also list some research facilities, including archives, libraries, and museums.

We start in the south and end in the north (see the map on page 30).

Skåne (Scania)

Skåne in the far south of Sweden is one of the most densely populated provinces. The province was part of Denmark until 1658, and the cathedral city of Lund was one of Denmark's most important cities. Culturally there are still a lot of similarities and connections between Skåne and Denmark.

Skåne has Sweden's best farming conditions. The plain in the south has highly productive and fertile soil, which is used to grow sugar beets, oils seeds, grain, fodder crops, and vegetables. Farming is done both on family farms and on large estates.

The northern part of Skåne has more forest. This area (Göinge) was for centuries a border area between Denmark and Sweden.

To smooth the transition from Danish to Swedish rule a university was founded in Lund in 1668, and this university has become one of Sweden's most important academic centers. The largest town in Skåne is Malmö, located at Öresund, the strait dividing Sweden from Denmark. From Malmö to Copenhagen the new Öresund bridge connects the two countries. Opened in 2000, it is one of Europe's largest and most impressive bridges.

Other main population centers are Helsingborg in the northwest, across from Danish Helsingör (Elsinore), and Kristanstad in the northeast, named after the Danish King Kristian IV, who founded the city in 1622.

Skåne had a rather large emigration in total numbers, even if the emigration rate was lower than in many other parts of the country. Many left rather late, after 1900.

Main Tourist Spots:

- Lund with its impressive Romanesque cathedral, one of Sweden's oldest and most beautiful.
- The many castles built by the nobility of the province. Places like Svaneholm, Trolle-Ljungby, Vittskövle, Glimmingehus, and many others.
- Sofiero, north of Helsingborg, used to be the summer palace of the king, and it has a park famous for its rhododendrons and other flowers.
- The southeast area of Österlen has a beautiful open landscape and a coast with cliffs and sandy beaches where you can find amber after a storm. The small town of Simrishamn is home to many artists. *Ale stenar* is one of many ancient monuments, a circle of stones in the shape of a ship. There is also a house in Backåkra that belonged to Dag Hammarskjöld, the Secretary General of the U.N. between 1953 and 1961. In Kivik, north of Simrishamn, you find vast apple orchards that bloom in May.
- The city of Malmö is a cultural center, with many theaters and art galleries.
- Landskrona, located along Öresund, is dominated by an impressive fortress. You can take a ferry to the island Ven, where the famous astronomer Tycho Brahe had his castle and observatory in the late sixteenth century.

A typical old farm house in Skåne. Both in south Sweden and in Denmark houses are built with visible timber frames.

For Your Research:

Regional Archives in Lund, City Archives in Malmö, Cultural Museum in Lund (*Kulturen*), University Library in Lund. Appeals court (*hovrätt*) for southern Sweden in Malmö. Skåne's Genealogical Society in Staffanstorp has emigrant collections.

Blekinge

Northeast of Skåne along the Baltic coast is Blekinge, one of Sweden's smallest provinces, both in size and population. Just like Skåne, Blekinge also belonged to Denmark until 1658. To take control of the area and gain supremacy over the Baltic Sea the Swedish King Karl XI in 1680 founded the naval station of Karlskrona. It quickly became a major city with churches, wharfs, and different military and naval installations. In 1998 the whole city and its naval port was placed on the UNESCO World Heritage List. (The World Heritage List in 2003 included 754 cultural and natural properties around the world – twelve of these are located in Sweden.)

Blekinge has an archipelago with many small fishing communities. On many of the islands there were also stone quarries. Today Blekinge is an industrial area. Volvo has a large factory in Olofström. North of Olofström in the village of Kyrkhult you find a genealogical research center.

Main Tourist Spots:

- Karlskrona with its naval station and interesting seventeenth and eighteenth century architecture.
- Salmon fishing in the small rivers running into the Baltic. Mörrum is the most famous fishing place.

For Your Research:

Blekinge is part of the district of the Regional Archives in Lund. Kyrkhult Genealogical Research Center. *Blekinge folkrörelsearkiv* in Bräkne-Hoby has emigrant collections.

Halland

Halland used to be a part of Denmark, just like Skåne and Blekinge. Located on the West Coast, it became a Swedish province in 1645. This coastal province is stretched along the west coast south of Gothenburg. The coastline is open with long sandy beaches, and behind them sand dunes. In the summer these beaches are full of swimmers and windsurfers. Inland there is a broad coastal plain with good agricultural land. Halland is well known for its cheese. Further inland the forests take over and the inner part of Halland is hilly. At the turn of the twentieth century much of this area was barren heath. Today it has some of the most productive forests in Sweden. The four rivers (*Lagan, Nissan, Ätran, Viskan*) are famous for their salmon fishing. There are also many excellent golf courses, e.g. at Tylösand.

The emigration from Halland was rather extensive, especially from the poverty-stricken interior of the province.

Halmstad is the largest city and the provincial capital. It has an old castle. Also Varberg in the northern part of Halland has a well-known castle, or fortress, which today is a museum.

Main Tourist Spots:

- The beaches, in the summer, for Sweden's best swimming. Tylösand outside Halmstad and Falkenberg are two of the best.
- Varberg's old fortress and museum.
- Äskhult, old farm village outside Kungsbacka.

For Your Research:

Halland is part of the district of the Regional Archives in Lund. Halland's Genealogical Society in Halmstad.

Småland

The largest of the southern provinces, and, with close to a million inhabitants, also one of the most populous in all of Sweden. In medieval times Småland was a number of smaller provinces (the name Små-land means Small-lands). Because of its size and large population, Småland was divided into three *län* (län, see page 31) in the seventeenth century. Along the Baltic coast is Kalmar län, with its capital Kalmar. In the southern inner part is Kronobergs län, with its capital Växjö. The northern inner part is Jönköpings län, with its capital Jönköping.

Småland has sixteen cities and a myriad of small towns and hundreds of parishes. Much of the inner section of Småland has a relatively high altitude with some points above 1,000 feet. Today the forest totally dominates the landscape. A hundred years ago there were a lot of meadows and pastures and small stony fields. The farmers in Småland had very hard and poor conditions compared to the farmers in Skåne or Halland, and this was a major factor in the emigration of hundreds of thousands of Småland's inhabitants.

In Jönköping the production of matches was long the main industry.

Småland is home to many companies. They are mainly involved in small and middle size manufacturing, and most of them are family businesses. Prefabricated wooden houses are a major product. Furniture is another – the worldwide furniture chain IKEA was founded in Småland and its headquarters are still there, in Älmhult. The area around Nybro, in the southeast part of Småland, is the home of Swedish glass manufacturing – the Kingdom of Crystal. In Jönköping the production of matches was the main industry for a long time. Today there are several big paper and pulp factories in the area.

Main Tourist Spots:

- The city of Växjö with its medieval cathedral and the Emigrant Institute (*Utvandrarnas hus*). A visit to this center for emigrant studies is a must for every Swedish-American visiting Småland. Växjö also has a modern university and a glass museum.
- The glass district (*Glasriket* = the Kingdom of Crystal) around Nybro and Emmaboda, with glass factories like Orrefors, Kosta, Boda, and Johansfors.
- Wilhelm Moberg's home parish and birth place *Algutsboda*, close to Emmaboda. Wilhelm Moberg was a very popular writer who wrote the epic "Unto a Promised Land" about Karl Oskar and Kristina, early Swedish emigrants to the United States.
- Kalmar, the old city on the coast, with its beautiful castle and the baroque cathedral. It is not a seat of a bishop today, but the architecture makes it one of Sweden's most unique churches. The city of Kalmar still has many old wooden houses.
- Stensjö, an old farm village north of Oskarshamn, shows how the farm landscape looked at the time of the big emigration.
- Vimmerby, the birth place of the famous children's book author Astrid Lindgren, who wrote many books, including those about Pippi Longstocking. A theme and play park for children, "the world of Astrid Lindgren" (*Astrid Lindgrens värld*) is located in Vimmerby.
- Eksjö is onc of the best-preserved wooden cities in Sweden. Almost all of the houses in the city center are wooden, mainly from the nineteenth century.
- Jönköping is a modern city with a large exhibition area, Elmia, beautifully located at the southern end of lake Vättern. The city is a center for the free churches in Sweden, congregations independent of the Lutheran church, like Baptist and Pentecostal churches. In earlier years Jönköping's leading industry was the production of matches.
- The small town of Gränna north of Jönköping is worth a visit. The town is renowned for its peppermint candy and its pears.

For Your Research:

All of Småland is part of the district of the Regional Archives in Vadstena. The House of Emigrants (*Emigranternas hus*) in Växjö. *Göta hovrätt* (old appeals court with important historic archives) in Jönköping. *Barkeryds hembygdsförening* near Nässjö has emigrant collections.

Öland

The island of Öland in the Baltic Sea is like a different country. The landscape is mostly flat, dry, and barren. The island stretches some 135 kilometres from the high lighthouse (*Långe Jan* = tall John) on the southern tip to the likewise impressive lighthouse on the northern point (*Långe Erik* = tall Eric). But the narrow island is only a few miles wide from west to east. Strong winds from the sea once powered hundreds of traditional windmills. Today wind is used to produce electricity. The agricultural landscape on southern Öland is on the World Heritage List.

Öland is one of the smallest provinces, with only one small city, Borgholm. Öland also has a lot of historical sites, old churches, and old graves. As the province was very poor at the end of the nineteenth, many left for America, and Öland was the province with the highest emigration rate.

Main Tourist Spots:

- Borgholm with its old castle ruins, and *Solliden*, a large villa in Italian style, the summer residence of the royal family. In the summer you have a good chance of seeing the king and queen in the area.
- The southern point, with lighthouse and bird sanctuary.
- Eketorp – Iron Age fortress, reconstructed as a living museum.

For Your Research:

Öland is part of the district of the Regional Archives in Vadstena.

Gotland

Gotland is larger than Öland, but just like Öland it is an island of limestone and sandstone, very different from the Swedish mainland, with its granite rocks. The island belonged to Denmark until 1645.

The film director Ingmar Bergman filmed some of his movies on Gotland, and he has a home in the northern part of the province – on the separate island of Fårö.

Gotland was in medieval times a center for Baltic trade and the city of Visby was a Hanseatic city. The whole island is a major tourist attraction.

Main Tourist Spots:

- Visby still has a complete medieval wall with towers, and twelve medieval church ruins, beside the beautiful medieval cathedral. The medieval city is placed on the World Heritage List and one of Sweden's most well-known tourist attractions.
- Medieval country churches. On Gotland there are 94 parishes, all of them dating back to the medieval time period. Almost all of the medieval churches are still in use. Many of them have impressive towers.

The lighthouse located at the southern tip of Öland. Millions of migratory birds pass here in the spring and in the fall.

Surrounded by a wall, the old city of Visby is filled with monuments from the Middle Ages; among them a dozen church ruins.

- Rauk fields along the coast. Strange cliff formations.
- Bunge on northern Gotland. Impressive open-air museum with old farm houses.

For Your Research:

Regional Archives in Visby, historic museum (*Gotlands fornsal*).

A rauk is a formation of limestone found mainly on the shores of Gotland. A few can be found on Öland.

Bohuslän

Located on the west coast north of Gothenburg, this province was once a part of Norway, but came under Swedish rule in 1658. The coast is rugged and rocky, with an archipelago, and the weather is often windy. Bohuslän has always been the most important fishing district in Sweden. Fishers from this province have traveled far into the North Sea and the North Atlantic Ocean. Fishing communities along the coast are the typical features of Bohuslän. In the summer these picturesque communities are invaded by tens of thousands of tourists who come to swim and sunbathe on the cliffs, to sail and fish. The largest city is Uddevalla.

Main Tourist Spots:

- The fishing communities along the whole coast.
- The small island city of Marstrand in the south has an old fortress, and was once the first place in Sweden where Jewish merchants were allowed to live.

This old postcard shows the fishing harbors of Käringön, before the seasonal invasion of tourists.

- Kungälv on the river Göta älv was a border fortress protecting the province against the Swedes.
- The rock-carvings at Tanum in northern Bohuslän. They are from the Bronze Age and are placed on the World Heritage List.

For Your Research:

Bohuslän is part of the district of the Regional Archives in Gothenburg.

Västergötland

Västergötland is one of Sweden's most important provinces, with a large size and population. Many emigrants came from this province; in fact, the people highlighted in the case study are from Västergötland.

The area around Skara and Falköping in the middle of the province was very early a cultural focal point. The area is full of archaeological finds, from the Stone Age, the Bronze Age and the Iron Age. The first Swedish king to be baptized as a Christian was king Olof, and the ceremony took place at Husaby in 1060. The cathedral of Skara is believed to be the oldest bishop's seat in Sweden (the old cathedral of Lund was at that time in Denmark).

Main Tourist Spots:

- Göteborg (Gothenburg). The area around the river Göta älv was the only place where Sweden had access to the sea on the West Coast before 1645. Göteborg was founded in 1632, but there had been other towns and ports before that. Gothenburg today is a bustling port city, with half a million inhabitants. The city is home to Volvo (cars), SKF (bearings), Hasselblad (cameras), and many other major international companies. Earlier the city had many big wharves and was home to a large number of shipping companies. Although Sweden never was a colonial power, it had one of the world's largest merchant fleets. Gothenburg has a large university, an advanced technical university (*Chalmers*), and many museums, among them a good maritime museum.

  Famous people from Göteborg include Ingemar Johansson, the only Swedish world champion professional boxer.

  Gothenburg formed a *län* together with Bohuslän to the north, before all the western *län* merged into one large *län* a few years ago.

- Skara. This cathedral city is rather small, dominated by the two spires of the old cathedral.
- Läckö. Castle and museum on the shore of lake Värnern, close to Lidköping, a town with famous porcelain factory (*Rörstrand*).
- Mariestad to the north is the old capital of the Skaraborg's län. The church was once, for a short period, a cathedral.

- Karlsborg on the shore of lake Vättern is a huge fortress built in the nineteenth century. It was meant to house the royal family, the government, and the central bank in case of war.
- Borås in the southern part of Västergötland, is the center of Sweden's garment industry and also for the mail order business. You can find a lot of stores with inexpensive clothing, factory outlets, etc.
- Trollhättan is located at a large waterfall, where Sweden's first large hydropower station was built. Once a year the water is allowed to flow freely through the waterfall. The Saab car factory is located in Trollhättan.
- Vänersborg was earlier the capital of Älvsborg's län. The city lies near where the river, Göta älv, flows out of lake Vänern, Sweden's largest lake.

For Your Research:

Regional Archives, maritime museum, and emigration center in Göteborg. University library in Göteborg and good province library and museum in Skara. Riksföreningen Sverigekontakt in Göteborg, the city library in Borås, and the library in Skara (*Stifts- och landsbiblioteket)* have emigrant collections.

Läckö slott (castle), located on the southern shore of lake Vänern.

Dalsland

One of the smallest provinces, Dalsland is located between lake Vänern and the Norwegian border. The area was for the most part poor farmland and the emigration rate was very high. There is only one small city, Åmål. Along lake Vänern is a plain with rich farmland. The rest of the province is hilly and forested. Dalsland is sometimes described as "a miniature Sweden" with all types of landscapes and natural features.

The aqueduct in Håverud, a waterway on a bridge, was a wonder of engineering when it was built in 1868. It is still a remarkable sight.

Main Tourist Spot:

- The remarkable aqueduct at Håverud, where the boats on the canal pass over the wild river, but under the road and the railroad.

For Your Research:

Dalsland is part of the district of the Regional Archives in Gothenburg. In Mellerud there is a museum with an emigrant center.

Östergötland

Between lake Vättern and the Baltic Sea, this is also, just like Västergötland, a province with a longstanding history. The middle part of Östergötland is rich farmland. To the north and to the south the forest dominates.

Östergötland's most famous historic personality was Saint Birgitta. She was a noble lady who had holy

Vadstena castle is one of several royal castles built during the reigns of king Gustav Vasa and his sons Erik, Johan, and Karl in the sixteenth century.

visions and a calling from God. She went to Rome and she founded a monastery at Vadstena and a new order of nuns, the Birgitta-sisters, in 1370. The order is still in existence.

Main Tourist Spots:

- Vadstena. The monastery church is one of Sweden's most interesting churches. It is possible to stay at the monastery as a guest. The castle in Vadstena was built by King Gustaf Vasa. Today it houses the Regional Archives.
- Omberg and Alvastra. The mountain Omberg south of Vadstena is surrounded by many historical places and old churches. Alvastra is a monastery ruin. At Rök you can see one of the most famous runestones.
- Göta Kanal passes through the city of Motala. This canal built in the early nineteenth century connects the Baltic Sea with Sweden's largest lakes, Vättern and Vänern, and makes it possible to go by boat on an inland route from the East Coast to Gothenburg (*Göteborg*). The trip by canal boat, from Stock-

Ljungsbro. Parti av Göta Kanal.
Foto och ensamrätt: E. B. Bratt.

The boat trip along Göta Kanal is a peaceful way to see the country. The canal was opened through Västergötland in 1822 and through Östergötland in 1832. It has 58 locks.

holm to Gothenburg, takes about five days, and is a wonderful way of seeing Sweden. You sleep on the boat and take your meals in the dining room of the boat.

- Linköping is the largest city, and it is located in the middle of Östergötland. It is the capital of the province and features a cathedral and a university. The old town museum, *Gamla Linköping*, is a good example of how a Swedish town looked before the industrial era.
- Norrköping is a large industrial city, formerly the main center for Sweden's textile industry. One of the old factories has been turned into a museum of labor (*Arbetets museum*). The zoo at Kolmården, north of Norrköping, is Sweden's largest.

For Your Research:

Regional Archives in the castle in Vadstena. In Linköping: Kulturarvet i Östergötland, with emigrant collections. In Kisa, at Café Colombia, a museum for one of the earliest Swedish emigrants to the United States – Peter Cassel, founder of New Sweden in Iowa.

Södermanland

This province is close to Stockholm, and includes its southern suburbs. The area is full of estates and beautiful manors. The nobility wanted to be close to Stockholm, but they also wanted to have a place in the countryside. Therefore they often built houses in the provinces closest to Stockholm (Södermanland, Uppland, and Västmanland).

The name Södermanland refers to the location south (*söder*) of the lake Mälaren.

The province has been called "the smiling Södermanland," or "a garden of Eden," because of its sweet landscape full of lakes, meadows, and oak woods, almost like a park.

Relatively few people emigrated from this part of Sweden; it was more natural to go to nearby Stockholm to seek work and income.

Main Tourist Spots:

- Nyköping is the capital of the area, with an old castle.
- Eskilstuna is the largest city, "Sweden's Sheffield," center for iron and steel manufacturing. The old blacksmith shops (*Rademachersmedjorna*) are today a museum.
- Strängnäs is the medieval cathedral city. The cathedral is large with a high brick tower.
- Mariefred is a small town with a big castle, *Gripsholm*, and a narrow-gauge steam railroad.
- Julita, in the western part of the province, has a quaint open-air museum with old farm buildings. The manor house is one of many that are shown to the public.

Gripsholm Castle, 35 miles west of Stockholm, is one of the most well-preserved castles from the sixteenth century. It has a large collection of portraits and an old court theatre.

For Your Research:

Södermanland is part of the district of the Regional Archives in Uppsala.

Stockholm

The city of Stockholm is located on the border between two provinces, Södermanland and Uppland. Often it is seen as a "province" of its own.

The city was founded around 1250 by Birger Jarl, Sweden's leader at that time. It quickly became the most important city in the country. The city is located near where the lake Mälaren flows into the Baltic Sea; Mälaren's elevation is only a couple of feet above sea level. The castle of Stockholm had a very strategic location, from a military standpoint, and the city and its merchants controlled the trade on the lake and the inland beyond it.

The old city was built on three small islands. But since the medieval times the city has expanded onto more islands, peninsulas and the mainland to the north and to the south. The waterways and many bridges over the waters are characteristic features of Stockholm. The city is considered to be one of the world's most beautiful capitals.

Stockholm today has a population of a million and a half, including suburbs. The city has an excellent system of public transport, with subway, trains, and buses. There is no reason to rent a car if you stay within the city; a car can even be a problem, as finding parking is often difficult.

Main Tourist Spots:

- The Old Town. One of Europe's best-preserved old cities.
- The Royal Palace, built in the eighteenth century in Italian renaissance style, after the old castle burned down in 1697. Changing of the guards every day at noon.
- The open-air museum Skansen, with farm houses and other old houses from all parts of Sweden, and with all the indigenous Scandinavian animals.
- The Wasa Museum, showing the war ship Wasa, which sank on her maiden voyage in 1628 and was recovered from the muddy bottom of the sea in central Stockholm in 1961.
- The City Hall built in the 1920s. This is where the Nobel prize banquet takes place every year on 10 December. The prize ceremony takes place in the concert hall (*Konserthuset*). The Nobel Museum is located in the Old Town.
- The Strindberg museum. The playwright August Strindberg is Sweden's internationally most well-known writer.

Stockholm is often called "the city on water," built on twenty-four islands and peninsulas connected by bridges. To the left is the City Hall (Stadshuset).

The Royal Palace in Stockholm with the cathedral (Storkyrkan) *to the left.*

- The Carl Milles studio and museum on Lidingö (*Millesgården*) is an open-air museum of sculptures. Carl Milles lived in the early twentieth century, for a long period in the United States, where many of his sculptures can be seen.
- The forest cemetery (*Skogskyrkogården*), founded in 1920, is a widespread cemetery that is also on the World Heritage List, because of its architecture and landscaping. The grave of Greta Garbo can be found here. Both she, and the other great Swedish film star, Ingrid Bergman, were born and grew up in Stockholm.
- Drottningholm. Royal palace west of Stockholm with a famous theatre from the eighteenth century. The palace grounds are on the World Heritage List. The Royal family lives in this castle.
- Museums like the Historical Museum, the Nordic Museum (ethnology, folk art), the National Art Museum, the Museum of Maritime History, the Medieval Museum, etc.
- The Stockholm archipelago, along the coast of both Södermanland and Uppland, consists of some 24,000 islands. Although most of them are uninhabited, there are tens of thousands of summer cottages and a lot of permanent residences. Many Stockholmers have a summer house in the archipelago, and many families have sailboats or motorboats. Ferries and boats connect the islands, much like buses on land. Many of these boats land in Stockholm. Be sure to take a boat ride into the archipelago if you have the time and opportunity.

For Your Research:

National Archives (*Riksarkivet*), the Military Archives (*Krigsarkivet*), and Stockholm City Archives, which is the Regional Archives of the Stockholm län. The archive at the Nordic Museum. The Swedish Genealogical Society. The Royal Library (*Kungliga biblioteket*), which houses all books ever printed in Sweden.

Uppland

The province north of lake Mälaren (Upp-land means the upper land). This is the old province of the Swedes, and considered to be the cradle of the Swedish culture and state. The first towns and "capitals" of Sweden were located in Uppland. Birka on Björkö, an island in lake Mälaren, was an important Viking town, and the site is on the World Heritage List. Sigtuna, a bit further to the north, came next. In this small town you can still find early medieval churches and the ruins of an early cathedral.

Uppsala was a Viking cult center, where the Nordic gods were worshipped. The Christians decided to build their cathedral at the same spot. Uppsala is still the residence of Sweden's archbishop. In 1477 Sweden's first university was founded in Uppsala, and it

Uppsala cathedral is Scandinavia's largest, and is also the Archbishop's church. It is a gothic church built of brick. The double towers are each 118.7 meters high (395.7 feet), which is exactly the same as the length of the cathedral.

is still the most prestigious of the Swedish universities. When Stockholm was founded in the thirteenth century it gradually took over a leading position in the kingdom from Uppsala. But both Stockhom and Uppsala had large royal castles. The coronations of Swedish kings and queens took place in Uppsala until 1719.

Uppland has a number of very old and beautiful medieval churches. Many of them, like Härkeberga, Litslena, Tensta and others, are decorated with wonderful mural paintings. The province also boasts many elegant palaces and manors built by the nobility.

The three big mounds at Old Uppsala (Gamla Uppsala) are king's graves from the Viking period.

Northern Uppland has a number of old iron works, called *bruk* in Swedish, with names like Löfsta, Forsmark, Karlholm, Österby, Gimo, and Harg. These early factories were laid out and built as "ideal communities." The workers were imported from Vallonia (today's Belgium) in the seventeenth century to develop Sweden's fast-growing iron manufacturing. You can still find the French sounding names inherited from these Vallonians.

Main Tourist Spots:

- Birka, the archaeological site of the Viking town can be reached by boat from Stockholm in the summer.
- Sigtuna, on the shore of lake Mälaren, is the oldest town. Today a small city full of historic landmarks, like the old court house, the church, and the church ruins.
- Skokloster, close to Sigtuna, is one of Sweden's best-preserved seventeenth century palaces with large collections of furniture, paintings, and weapons.
- Old Uppsala, north of Uppsala, with Viking graves and old church.
- Uppsala is the capital of Uppland, and Sweden's fourth largest city. The cathedral, the university, and the castle are all located in the city center west of the little river. In addition to the regular university Uppsala also houses Sweden's agricultural university. Outside Uppsala, at Hammarby, you will find the home of Carl Linnéaus, the most well-known Swedish scientist. Linnéaus was a botanist who invented the system of classification of species.
- Vaxholm, Norrtälje, Öregrund, and Östhammar are all small towns along the Baltic coast.

For Your Research:

Regional Archives in Uppsala. University Library (*Carolina Rediviva*).

Västmanland

To the west of lake Mälaren you find Västmanland. Västerås is the capital and has one of the three large medieval cathedrals around lake Mälaren (the others being Uppsala and Strängnäs). All these large churches are built in red brick made from the glacial clay deposited in this region. This soil is particularly good for growing wheat.

The area along lake Mälaren is fertile flatland similar to Uppland, with old medieval parishes and large manors and palaces built by rich nobility. To the north and west the province is more hilly and forested.

The area is full of old mines. The whole mining region, Bergslagen, stretches through adjoining areas of Värmland, Dalarna, and other provinces. This whole area had special legislation, with tax exemptions for the miners, special courts, and regulations to promote mining and iron industry. Many of the communities are today modern industrial towns. Some of the old mines and iron works have been preserved as museums.

Main Tourist Spots:

- Ängelsberg in northern Västmanland is one of the most interesting and best preserved of these old iron works. It is on the World Heritage List.
- Västerås is the largest city and provincial capital. The cathedral is the main tourist spot. Västerås is a leading industrial city. "Sweden's General Electric," Asea, today ABB, was founded here, and is still a leading employer.
- Sala is Sweden's old silver mine. The mine for centuries gave the Swedish crown large incomes. Today it is only a museum.
- Köping at lake Mälaren was once the home to Anders Celsius, a chemist, the inventor of the centigrade thermometer, and discoverer of chlorine and many other substances.
- Arboga is one of Sweden's oldest cities and the place where the Swedish parliament met for the first time, in 1432.

For Your Research:

Västmanland is part of the district of the Regional Archives in Uppsala.

Närke

Närke is a small province in the middle part of southern Sweden, located between two of the large lakes – Vättern to the south and Hjälmaren to the east.

The main city of the province, Örebro, has an old castle, where the king often stayed, and where he many times called the parliament to session.

One such session took place in 1810, when the parliament elected the present king's forefather, Jean Baptist Bernadotte, as Swedish crown prince. Bernadotte was a general in Napoleon's army, and the Swedes hoped that he would be able to regain Finland from the Russians. They had captured this old part of the Swedish kingdom in the war of 1809. But instead of taking up war with the Russians, the new "French king" decided on a policy of peace and neutrality. Sweden and Norway formed a union in 1814; Norway had until then been a part of Denmark. The peaceful policy of king Karl XIV Johan (his adopted Swedish name) was followed by his heirs and the policy of neutrality has been a guideline of Swedish foreign policy ever since. It has helped Sweden to stay out of many wars and conflicts, such as World War I and World War II.

Half a century ago Örebro was known as the center of Swedish shoe manufacturing. While this industry has moved to low wage countries, the city has a fast-growing new university. Närke has a very good central location. Many of the main roads and railroads pass through the province.

Main Tourist Spots:

- Örebro, with the castle and Wadköping, an open-air museum showing characteristic old town environments.

For Your Research:

Närke is part of the district of the Regional Archives in Uppsala. *Örebro stadsarkiv* (City Archives) has an emigrant collection.

Värmland

The western province of Värmland, close to Norway, is the province of storytellers and writers. The Nobel prize winner and female novelist Selma Lagerlöf

Rafting on Klarälven is a wonderful way to experience the river. You can chose between a three- or a six-day trip, and the tent on the raft is included.

lived here; her manor Mårbacka remains open to the public as a museum. One of Selma Lagerlöf's most famous books is about Nils Holgersson, a boy who was bewitched and traveled flying on the back of a goose all over Sweden. It is an enchanting story and a geography lesson about Sweden. Other famous writers from Värmland are Gustaf Fröding and Göran Thunström. People of this province are in general considered to be good and humorous storytellers. But don't trust every word to be true!

Värmland is a relatively large province located north of lake Vänern. The northern part has deep forests. The large, winding Klarälven river runs through the province. There are also several beautiful lakes.

Värmland had a very large emigration. Much effort has been made to register and research this big migration. The center for this work is the Kinship Center in Karlstad (*Emigrantregistret*).

Main Tourist Spots:

- *Mårbacka* near Sunne, the home of Nobel prize laureate Selma Lagerlöf.
- Karlstad is the province capital and the largest city of Värmland. The city has a cathedral and a modern university. If you want good Swedish coffee, you can either get Löfberg's, made in Karlstad, or Gevalia, made in Gävle (see Gästrikland).
- Outside the small town of Arvika there is a music center run by the opera singer Håkan Hagegård.
- Filipstad is the hometown of John Eriksson, an industrious inventor, famous among other things for the construction of the battleship Monitor, used in the North American Civil War. It is also the hometown of Wasabread, the largest *knäckebröd* (= hard bread) factory.
- Ekshärad is a small town by the Klarälven where you will find one of Sweden's most remarkable graveyards. Instead of stones the graves have elaborate wrought iron crosses as markers.

For Your Research:

Regional Archives for Värmland in Karlstad and the Swedish American Center in Karlstad.

Dalarna (Dalecarlia)

This province in middle Sweden is in many ways a symbol of Swedish folk culture and romantic folk art and folklore. Folk costumes have been in common use into our time. There are fiddlers and folk dancers in almost every village, and every summer large folk music festivals and gatherings take place. The area around lake Siljan with its large parishes (such as Mora, Orsa, Rättvik, and Leksand) is also an important tourist region. The villages feature wooden houses all painted in red. The paint comes from the copper mine in Falun. It is an inexpensive paint considered to preserve the timber of the houses.

In the western part of Dalarna you find Sweden's southernmost mountains.

Emigration was large from Dalarna. In Leksand there is a well-equipped research center for genealogists.

Main Tourist Spots:

- Falun is the capital of the province. The copper mine of Falun for a long period was one of the best sources of income for the Swedish king and government, and helped to pay for the many wars that Sweden took part in. The mining area of the Great Copper Mountain in Falun is one of Sweden's twelve properties on the World Heritage List.
- Borlänge has a larger population than Falun, but is a much more modern industrial city. Its most famous son is Jussi Björling, the famous opera tenor, and there is a small Jussi Björling museum in Borlänge.
- Mora is the largest town by lake Siljan. It is the host of a yearly cross country ski event – *Vasaloppet* – organized in memory of king Gustaf Vasa, who

Lake Siljan, in the middle of Dalarna, is surrounded by large parishes and a rich folk culture. To go to church, people traditionally took the long rowboats from the villages around the lake.

A painted wooden Dalecarlia horse (dalahäst) *is a famous symbol for Dalarna.*

lived in the sixteenth century and who is considered to be the founder of the modern national state of Sweden. Gustaf Vasa liberated Sweden from the occupying Danes in 1523. But before he managed to summon an army of peasants, from Dalarna, he almost gave up and fled on skis to Norway. A group of men from Mora chased after him on skis and convinced him to return and start the uprising. It is in memory of this ski run that 12,000 or more Swedes every year run the 92 kilometers long *Vasaloppet* from Sälen to Mora.

Carl Larsson's home is in Sundborn, located north of Falun. Carl Larsson added a new room to the house for each child. He and his wife Karin had many children, and the house is by far the most famous of all Swedish artist's homes.

In Mora you also find the studio and museum of Anders Zorn, a painter who also spent much time in the United States.

- *Dalhalla* – situated north of Rättvik. This is a fantastic outdoor opera and concert venue, built in a former limestone quarry.
- *Sundborn* – the home of Carl Larsson. This renowned painter made wonderful watercolors of his home and family around 1900. These pictures are a showcase of Swedish furniture, architecture, and style, combining traditional features and art nouveau.

For Your Research:

Dalarna is part of the district of the Regional Archives in Uppsala. Genealogical Research Center in Leksand.

Gästrikland

Gästrikland is a small province on the border between southern and northern Sweden. From Gästrikland and to the north, the climate is colder, and the vast evergreen forests dominate the land.

Northern Sweden, or Norrland, is more sparsely populated than southern Sweden. Large rivers cross the country, from the mountain range to the west down to the Gulf of Bothnia. Most people live in the river valleys, and there is often a city where the river falls into the sea. The southernmost of these rivers, Dalälven, is considered to be the limit between southern and northern Sweden. It is also the border between Uppland and Gästrikland. The saying is that north of Dalälven there are no oak trees and there is no nobility, and no manors. As the saying implies, there is both a natural and a cultural difference between southern and northern Sweden.

Main Tourist Spots:

- Gävle, the provincial capital where most of the people live, is well-known for its Gevalia coffee, which is also exported to the United States. One of the emigrants from Gävle was the young anarchist, union man and singer Joe Hill, short for Joseph Hillstrom. He emigrated from Sweden in 1902. He was executed in Salt Lake City in 1915, on questionable grounds, and for many became a hero and martyr. Many of his protest songs are still sung, and there is an interesting museum in Gävle, telling and illustrating his story.
- Sandviken west of Gävle has a large steel industry, Sandvik, that produces high quality products for the world market.

For Your Research:

Gästrikland is part of the district of the Regional Archives in Härnösand. The Central Archives in Gävle (*Centralarkivet*) has an emigrant collection.

Hälsingland

Like Dalarna, the province of Hälsingland is also a center of traditional Swedish peasant culture. The area is full of beautiful traditional farms with large wooden farmhouses. Inside many of these one can still find wonderful wall paintings. The area is famous for its linen industry. Flax was grown on the farms and the women would make wonderful woven textiles out of the linen. The large farmhouses and the rich textiles are evidence of the riches brought to the area when the farmers started cutting and exporting timber a couple of hundred years ago.

Main Tourist Spots:

- Delsbo with a big folk music meeting in the summer (*Delsbo spelmansstämma*).
- Järvsö and other villages along the Ljusnan river, with wooden farms and beautiful farmhouses.
- Hudiksvall, on the coast. One of the oldest cities in northern Sweden.

For Your Research:

Hälsingland is part of the district of the Regional Archives in Härnösand. House of Migrants in Alfta has an emigrant collection.

Medelpad

Like all the other provinces along the northern coast this province is crossed by large and swift rivers, that run out into the Baltic. These rivers produce numerous waterfalls that power hydro-electrical stations. The two rivers in Medelpad are called Ljungan and Indalsälven. *Älv* is a Swedish word for a large river. In Medelpad you will find the geographical center of Sweden.

Main Tourist Spot:

- Sundsvall, Medelpad's only city. This city is a center of the Swedish forest industry. Around Sundsvall

Many hydroelectric power stations were built in the rivers during the twentieth century, and today close to half of Sweden's electricity is generated this way.

Åreskutan in Jämtland is one of Sweden's most well-known mountains. On its southern side are some of Sweden's steepest and best downhill ski slopes.

there are several large sawmills and paper and pulp factories.

For Your Research:

Medelpad is part of the district of the Regional Archives in Härnösand.

Härjedalen

This mountainous province is Sweden's least populated, with only around 11,000 inhabitants. The area belonged to Norway until 1645. To the east there are large forests and bog lands. The mountains in the west are relatively high, and home to bears and musk oxes. The bear is a symbol for the province.

The farmers in the villages used to take all their cattle to summer farms (chalets) up in the mountains. The women of the village would stay there through the summer, along with the animals, and make cheese and butter from the milk. Up in the mountains in Härjedalen, Jämtland, and Dalarna, you can still see some of these old summer farms, and they are often open to the tourists (the Swedish word is *fäbod* or *säter*). You will also, as in all the Swedish mountains, find reindeer herded by the Samic people.

For Your Research:

Härjedalen is part of the district of the Regional Archives in Östersund.

Jämtland

Around the lake Storsjön (the Great Lake) is an area that was densely inhabited by farmers in early medieval times. The area belonged to Norway until the mid-seventeenth century (1645). Even today there are strong ties to the Trondheim area across the Norwegian border. The area around Storsjön is the center of the province Jämtland. The outer regions of the province are vast expanses of forests and mountain ranges. The actress Ann Margret was born in one of the mountain villages of northern Jämtland.

The capital city and only city of the province is Östersund. The mountain area has several good ski resorts. The most famous is Åre, a downhill resort that hosts World Cup events every year. Together with Östersund, Åre has several times applied to be host of the winter Olympics, but so far without success. Besides skiing in the winter there is hiking and mountaineering in the summer. The mountains of Jämtland have excellent hotels and lodges for hikers.

Main Tourist Spots:

- Östersund. Located on the shores of lake Storsjön. The open-air museum Jamtli shows the traditional culture of the province.
- Frösön – island in lake Storsjön, with the home (*Sommarhagen*) of composer Wilhelm Peterson-Berger, and a medieval church.
- Åre, skiresort in a narrow valley surrounded by high mountains.

For Your Research:

Regional Archives in Östersund.

The snow is much appreciated, because it lightens up the winter darkness. Most Swedes enjoy winter sports like skiing and skating.

Ångermanland

The province Ångermanland has a steep coastline with fjords, deep bays, and towering islands. The High Coast (*Höga kusten*) is on the World Heritage List. The small fishing communities along this coast are known for their "sour herring," a kind of fermented fish considered by some to be a delicacy, by others to be repulsive for its very characteristic smell. The big river, Ångermanälven, has several large tributaries, and along the rivers there are many beautiful spots.

Main Tourist Spots:

- At Nämforsen along the river you can look at stone carvings from the Stone Age. The biggest waterfalls are gone, sadly enough, as they have been stopped by dams with hydropower stations.
- Härnösand is the provincial capital. The city has a beautiful classic white cathedral, built in the eighteenth century.
- The largest suspension bridge in Northern Europe, *Höga kusten-bron*, crossing the fjord south of Kramfors.

For Your Research:

SVAR in Ramsele is the location of the microfilm division of Sweden's National Archives. An excellent research center is open to the public. Regional Archives in Härnösand.

Västerbotten

The term Västerbotten is used only for the coast region around Umeå and Skellefteå. It used to be the name of the province running all the way up to the Finnish border. Västerbotten means West of Botten(viken), the latter being the big northern bay of the Baltic, the Bay of Bothnia, between Sweden and Finland. Österbotten is the large province on the eastern (Finnish) side of the bay. Today the northern part of the Swedish coast is called Norrbotten (North of Botten). Sometimes the term Västerbotten is used about the whole area up to the Norwegian border, Västerbottens län. The inner part is the southern part of the province Lappland.

Västerbotten has two cities, Umeå and Skellefteå. Umeå is the largest city in all of Norrland, Northern Sweden. The city has grown quickly since the university was founded in the 1960s. Today it is a highly qualified and diversified school, with large departments in medical science and silviculture (forestry science). Umeå is known as the city of birches, as many of the main streets in the city center are lined with white-stemmed birches.

Skellefteå is also a growing city, but more geared towards small-scale industry. The country parish (*Skellefteå landsförsamling*) once was the most populous and vast-reaching of all Swedish countryside parishes. It can therefore be a challenge for a genealogist to find his or her way in the extensive records with all the different villages, farms, and families.

The cheese from Västerbotten (*Västerbottensost*) is a favorite with many Swedes.

For Your Research:

Västerbotten is part of the district of the Regional Archives in Härnösand. The University Library in Umeå. Research Center in Jörn, connected to the demographic database at the university in Umeå.

Norrbotten

This province once was the northern part of Västerbotten. It consists of the coast along the northern part of Bottenviken (the Bay of Bothnia), the lower part of the river valleys of Pite älv, Lule älv, Kalix älv, and Torne älv, and quite a large area along the Finnish border. This area, the Torne river valley, is populated by Finnish speaking people, using their own local version of the Finnish language.

Farming is surprisingly good in this river valley. The soil is fertile and the summers can be quite warm. Because of the midnight sun and the longer summer days the growth rate of the plants is tremendous during the few weeks of summer. The quality of the products is very high. Strawberries, black currants, and other berries and vegetables of the valley are very tasty and have high vitamin content.

Main Tourist Spots:

- Luleå is the largest city and the capital of Norrbottens län. Luleå has Sweden's youngest diocese and cathedral, dating from 1915. It also has a new technical university. There is also a large steel plant.
- Gammelstad, the old parish center of Luleå, a few miles inland, has an old town of small wooden cottages that were used by people from the outer villages in the vast parish when they came to the church at the main holidays and for markets.

  You can find such "church towns" around many of the churches in northern Sweden. Many of the inhabitants in the vast parishes live far from their churches. In the early days, before car travel, they had to stay overnight when they went to church. Gammelstad is on the World Heritage List.
- Storforsen, in the river Pite älv, is one of the few remaining large waterfalls in northern Sweden.
- Haparanda on the Finnish border is a small city, but also a part of a city region where the Finnish city of Tornio is the main center.

For Your Research:

Norrbotten is part of the district of the Regional Archives in Härnösand.

Lappland

Lappland (Lapland) is the largest of Sweden's provinces. It is also the most sparsely populated, with large areas of mountains, bog land, and vast forests. Lappland as an ethnic region stretches through northern Sweden, northern Finland, adjoining parts of Norway, and even into Russia. The Laps, or the Samic people, are some 60,000 persons. A minority of these are herding nomads, who follow their reindeer herds from the lowland forests in the winter to the mountain regions in the summer. Today reindeer herding is a modern business, where equipment like mobile phones, scooters, all-terrain vehicles, and helicopters have made work more efficient. It is, however, in many ways still an adventurous and hard trade.

The northern mountain region is a large wilderness, perfect for hiking. The trails are well marked. In some areas you will find cabins to stay in. In other areas you have to carry your tent along.

Many of the old traditions surrounding the Samic culture and reindeer herding are still maintained. Handicrafts where reindeer horn, reindeer furs and other materials are used, and traditional clothing, samic music and rituals, and the Samic language are some of the features of this culture. Today most Samic people are not reindeer owners. And most people in Lappland are not Samic.

Lappland is crisscrossed by a large number of rivers, with their sources in the mountains to the west along the border to Norway; the border usually follows the water divide. Many of the rivers are being used for hydropower, but some of the northernmost have been spared.

Lappland is also home to some of Sweden's and Europe's richest mines. The iron mines in Kiruna and Gällivare/Malmberget were opened at the end of the nineteenth century and soon fast growing mining communities were established. The mines are still producing. Besides the mine, Kiruna today is a center for space research and development. Northern Lappland is also used by many car companies to test their cars in winter climate and on snowy and icy roads.

The mountain range is not particularly high, but still much loved by tourists for hiking, mountaineering, climbing, and fishing. The wilderness has a number of large national parks.

Lappland only has two cities: Lycksele in the south and Kiruna in the north. Both are young cities.

Main Tourist Spots:

- The mountains. The most famous hiking trail is the King's trail (*Kungsleden*) that runs about 400 kilometers along the mountain range, starting at Abisko in the north, where you can go either by car or by train. In five to seven days you reach Sweden's highest mountain, Kebnekajse. You can stay in lodges along the trail. The northern part of the mountain range is also called Laponia, and is listed on the World Heritage List.
- The Inland Railroad. If you want to explore the forestland below the mountain range you can take the Inland Train (*Inlandsbanan*). This route was finished in the 1930s and today runs from Mora in Dalarna in the south all the way up to Gällivare.
- The mine in Kiruna. You can go deep underground into this huge iron mine.
- Outside Kiruna is Jukkasjärvi, an old village and a modern tourist center. In the winter you can stay in the ice hotel (*Ishotellet*), a hotel completely built of ice. Rafting on the swift river is a popular summer activity.
- Jokkmokk with National Samic Museum, named Ájtte, and some of the largest hydropower stations.
- The midnight sun can be experienced in June and July in the northern part of Lappland, north of the Arctic Circle, which runs close to Gällivare. It is a very special feeling to be up the whole night and never see the sun set.

For Your Research:

Lappland is part of the district of the Regional Archives in Härnösand.

Two Special Signs

The tetragram or the Saint Hans' cross is today used as a symbol for a tourist sight or monument. It is also the symbol of the Historic Museum in Stockholm and the National Heritage Board in Sweden.

The tetragram is an old symbol found on old jewelery and runic stones in Scandinavia, but also on objects in other parts of the world. Its function has been to protect against evil. So, look out for this "pretzel" along the road.

Moose is a common animal in most parts of Sweden, except on the island of Gotland. The moose hunt in the fall is a big event, and tens of thousands of moose are shot every year. The meat is delicious. There is a good reason for the warning signs: a collision with a moose can lead to a serious accident.

CHAPTER EIGHTEEN

Dictionary

Swedish Words Common in the Church Books

A

afvittring	assignment (of an inheritance)
afliden, avliden	deceased
agnatus (latin)	relationship through male line
agricola (latin)	farmer
allmoge	peasantry, country people
amma	wet nurse
arbetare	worker, laborer
arbetskarl	laborer, journeyman
arf, arv	inheritance, patrimony
arkiv	office of records, archives
arfvinge, arvinge	heir
arfskifte, arvskifte	distribution of an inheritance
attest	certificate, testimony, attestation

B

barn	child, children
barnbarn	grandchild, grandchildren
barndop	christening
barnhus	orphanage
barnmorska	midwife
barnsäng	childbed, lying in
befallningshafvande	commander, chief
befallningsman	bailiff, headman
bergmästare	mine master or foreman
bergsfogde	bailiff of mines
bergslag	region abounding in mines; mountain district
bergsman	miner
besittningsrätt	right of possession
besökare	visitor; customs official
betyg	certificate
bevis	proof, testimony; certificate, attest; confirmation; voucher
bevistat (läs)förhör	present at household examination (clerical survey)
boddräng	servant in shop
bodgosse	shopkeeper's assistant, shopboy
bokförare	bookkeeper, clerk
bonddräng	farm hand
bonde	farmer, peasant
broder	brother
bror	brother
brud	bride
brudgum	bridegroom

brukare	user, employer; farmer, tenant
bruksegare	factory manager; factory inspector
bänklängd	pew lists
bär barnet	carried the child at christening
bödel	executioner, hangman
böndag	fast day
böta	(to) pay a fine

C (see also under K)

cantor	organist, choir director
cognatus (latin)	related
conjugata (latin)	married
copulatus (latin)	married, marriage
copulerad	married
crono	pertaining to the crown
crono hem	crown owned home

D

dagsverkare	day laborer
danneman	gentleman, farmer
datum	date
de fattigas andel	the poor's share
den döptes namn	the baptized's name
den yngre	the younger
den äldre	the older
dies (latin)	day
difteri	diphtheria
direktör	general manager, vice president
disponent	(acting) manager
distrikt	district
dito	ditto
diverse	diverse, various, sundry
doktor	doctor
dombok	book of judgments
domkyrka	cathedral
domprost	pastor in a cathedral parish
domsaga	jurisdictional district
dop	baptism
dopattest	certificate of baptism
doplängd	record of baptism
dopvittne	sponsor at a baptism
dotter	daughter
dragon	light cavalryman, dragoon
drunknad	drowned
dräng	farmhand, bachelor, young man
död	dead
död- och begravnings-bok, -böcker	death and burial book, books
dödsdag	day of death
dödslängd	record of death
dödsorsak	cause of death

E

efterlefvande	surviving
efternamn	surname
egare, ägare	owner
embetsman, ämbetsman	official (public or government)
emeritus	emeritus
emigrera	(to) emigrate
enka, änka	widow
enkefru, änkefru	widow (lady)
enkeman, änkeman	widower
enkling, änkling	widower
enskild	private, individual

F

fabrik	factory, mill
fadder	sponsor, godfather, godmother, witness at christening
fader	father
fallsjuka	epilepsy
familj	family
far	father
farbror	father's brother, uncle
farfar	father's father, grandfather
farmor	father's mother, grandmother
fastedag	day of fasting
fattig	poor
fattigdom	poverty, want
fattighjon	pauper
fattighus	poorhouse
fattigkassa	fund for the relief of the poor
filia (latin)	daughter
filius (latin)	son
finsk	Finnish
fiskare	fisherman
fjärdingsman	petty (parish) constable
flicka	girl
fogde	county-steward, bailiff
folio	page
folkräkning	census
folkskola	common (elementary) school
forskare	inquirer, researcher, scientist
fosterbarn	foster child or foster children
frater (latin)	brother
fregdebetyg	certificate of character
frejd	character
frelse, frälse	free, noble (person); free from tax
frelsegård	tax-exempt farm
frelsehemman	tax-exempt farm
friherre	baron
frikyrka	free church
fru	mistress, madam, Mrs, wife
fruntimmer	female creature, used to describe an unmarried girl who has mothered a child
fullmäktig	attorney

fältpräst, feltprest	field preacher, army chaplain
fältskär, feltskär	barber surgeon
fängelse, fengelse	prison
föda	(to) give birth to
födelse	birth
födelsebok	birth book
födelseort	place of birth
förfader	forefather
förhörsbok	examination book
förlofvning	betrothal, engagement
förmyndare	guardian
församling	parish,congregation
församling och socken	congregation and parish
församlingsbok	parish record book
förstår	understand
försvarlig	justifiable, irreproachable
försvarslös	person without guardian or legal protection, vagrant
förteckning	list, catalog, index
förvaltare	administrator, steward
föräldrar	parents

G

gammal	old
garfvare, garvare	tanner
gelbgjutare	brassfounder, brazier
genealog	genealogist
gesäll	apprentice
gift	married; poison
giftermål	marriage ceremony
giftoman	bride's sponsor; guardian, he who has the right to give a young woman in marriage
giftorätt	a wife's share of the estate of her husband
gjutare	foundry worker
glasblåsare	glassblower
gods	goods; property
godsegare, godsägare	estate owner, landed proprietor
gosse	boy
graf, grav	grave, sepulchre
granne	neighbor
grefve, greve	count
grekiskkatolsk	Eastern Orthodox
grofsmed, grovsmed	blacksmith
grosshandlare	wholesale merchant
grufarbetare, gruvarbetare	miner
grufdräng, gruvdräng	mine worker
gruffogde, gruvfogde	overseer of a mine, mine captain
gruffolk, gruvfolk	miners
guddotter	goddaughter
gudfader	godfather
gudmoder	godmother
gudstjenst, gudstjänst	religious service
guldsmed	goldsmith
gumma	old woman

gård	farm, estate; yard, court; house
gårdfarihandlare	peddler, hawker of goods and wares
gårdsbrukare	farm worker
gårdsdräng	hostler, farm servant
gårdsegare, gårdsägare	owner of farm
gårdsfolk	farm servants
gårdskarl	farmhand
gäld	debt
gästgifvare	innkeeper
göra dagsverke	to day work (on a farm)

H

hammarskatt	tax paid for forged iron
hamnfogde	water bailiff, overseer of harbor
handelsbetjent	merchant's clerk, shopman
handelsbiträde	clerk in a shop
handelsbokhållare	merchant's clerk, bookkeeper
handelsidkare	trader
hattmakare	hatmaker
hembygd	native place
hemmansbrukare	farmer
hemmansegare	farm owner
herr	Mr., lord
herrgård	manorial estate
hinderslös	free, unhindered (to travel/marry)
hjelpkarl	charman
hjonelag	matrimony
hofrätt, hovrätt	circuit court of appeal
hofslagare, hovslagare	farrier
hosta	(to) cough; cough
hufvudarvinge	chief heir
husbonde	small farmer; head of household
husdräng	man servant
husegare, husägare	proprietor of a house
husförhör	household exemination
husförhörslängd	household exemination (clerical)
husman	cottager, crofter, tenant
huspiga	housemaid
hustru	wife
hyresgäst	lodger
hytta	smeltery, foundry
håll och stygn	pneumonia
hälftenbrukare	farmer who pays half the profit of the land let to him
häradsfogde	bailiff of a district
häradshöfding	justice of a district
häradsrätt	district court
häradsskrifvare	clerk of a district

I

ibidem (latin)	the same place, the same as, same
inflyttad	moved in from another place
infra (latin)	below

inhyses	lodger
inhyseshjon	a person living gratis at somebody's house; a cottager
in loco (latin)	in this place
in- och utflyttning	in and out moving
inskrifning	entering a person's name, enrollment
inteckning	mortgage; recording of a mortgage
intyg	testimony, witness, certificate, evidence
invandra	to immigrate
inventarieförteckning	inventory
item (latin)	even so, futhermore

J

jordbrukare	farmer
jordebok	public register of land
jordegare, jordägare	landed proprietor, landlord
jordfästning	bury, burial

K (SEE ALSO UNDER C)

kapellförsamling	chapelry, small chapel, dependant branch of a parish
kapten	captain
katekes	catechism
katekismilängd	communion record
katolsk	Catholic
kavalleriinspektör	Inspector General of the Cavalry
kirurg	surgeon
klensmed	locksmith
kofferdi	merchant service
kofferdiskepp	trading vessel
kolorist	colorist, one who deals in colors
kommissarie	commissary, commissioner
kommissioner	commissioner, agent
kommun	parish; commune; to receive the Lord's supper
konfirmationsböcker	confirmation books
konfirmerad	confirmed
konkurs	bankruptcy
kontorist	clerk
kontrahent	contracting party
kontrollör	controller
koppor	smallpox
kristen	Christian
krog	alehouse, public tavern
krono	belonging to the crown (government)
kronobetjent	constaple
kronofogde	district bailiff; attorney
kronohemman	farm owned by the crown
kronojord	land belonging to the crown
kronotionde	tithe due to the crown
kronotorpare	crofter living on land belonging to the goverment
kronoutskylder	government taxes
krögare	alehouse or tavern keeper
kusin	cousin
kvinna	woman

kvinnolinje	female line
kvinnsfaddrar	female sponsors at christening
kyrka	church
kyrkobok	church book, parish register
kyrkoby	village in which the parish church is located
kyrkogång	introduction into church after childbirth
kyrkoherde	parish minister, parson
kyrkoräkenskaper	church accounts
kyrkotagning	churching (introdution of mother into congreation after childbirth)
kyrkovaktare	church officer or caretaker
kyrkvärd	church warden
kyrkoår	church year
köping	small town; market town
köpman	merchant

L

lada	barn
ladugård	cowhouse, cowshed; barn; farm buildings; dairy farm
ladugårdspiga	milk maid
lagfart	legal confirmation of possession; probate
lagfartsprotokoll	probate accounts
lagkarl	lawyer
laglig	legal, lawful
lagman	district judge
lagsaga	district jurisdiction
land	country
landsarkiv	provincial archive
landsförsamling	rural parish of a city
landshöfding	governor of a province
landskansli	provincial chancery office, office of the Clerk of the Peace
landskanslist	servant (clerk) in the provincial chancery office
landskap	province
landskontorist	lower civil servant worker
landtbruksgods	(large) (landed) estate; country seat
landtbrukare, lantbrukare	husbandman, gentleman farmer (well to do)
landtmäteri, lantmäteri	land surveying
lasarett	hospital
legohjon	hired servant
liten	little, small
literat	man of letters
lungsot	consumption, tuberculosis
lysning	bann
lysnings- och vigselböcker	banns and marriage books
låntagare	borrower
låssmed	locksmith
läkare	doctor
länsbokhållare	county accountant's clerk
länsfängelse	county jail
länsherre	liege lord
länsman	sergeant in a district; liegeman, vassal
länsrätt	feudal right
läser och förstår	reads and understands
läser utantill	knows by heart

läsning innantill	reading in the book
läst	last
lätteligen	easily
löf, löv	leaf
lördag	Saturday
lösa arbetare	day laborers

M

madam	Mrs., married woman
magister	master of arts or science
mamsell	miss, young woman
mantal	assessed unit of land; taxation of farm
manufakturarbetare	factory worker
marknad	market, fair
meritlista	(list of) qualifications
middag	noon, noonday, midday
minderårig	underage
ministerialbok	parish register
minuthandlare	retailer
morbror	mother's brother, uncle
morfar	mother's father, grandfather
mormor	mother's mother, grandmother
musikant	musician
myndig	of age, attain majority
måg	son-in-law
mässling	measles
mästare	master, expert
mönsterrulla	muster roll
mönsterskrifvare	roll clerck at regiment

N

namn	name
nattvard	supper (communion)
natus (latin)	born
necessitate baptisatus (latin)	compulsory baptism
nedan	below, beneath
nemdeman, nämndeman	juryman
nepos (latin)	nephew, grandchild, descendant
nerffeber, nervfeber	typhoid fever
nybyggare	settler
nådehjon	almsman, one who lives on charity
nöddop	emergency or private baptism

O

obefintlig	non-existent, not to be found
obefintlighetslängd	list (roll) of absconded parishioners
odalman	freeholder (one who has tenure on property for life), yeoman; farmer who actually owns the land that he farms
odaterad	not dated
odöpt	not baptized
officer	(military commissioned) officer

ofrälse	not noble; the commons (land)
ofvan	above
ofvanföre	above, farther up
ofvanstående	the above (foregoing)
oförmåga	inability, impotency
ogift	unmarried
okänd	unknown
olycka	accident, misfortune
omgift	married again
omyndig	minor, underage
ort	country, region, place, soil
ostindiefarare	East-Indiaman; man from East India
oäkta dotter	illegitimate daughter

P

pastor	reverend, parish minister
pastorat	parish
patron	patron, protector, master
personakt	personal record
piga	maid, spinster, single girl
pingst	Pentecost, Whitsunday
polis	police
polisbetjent	policeman, constable
prost	dean of a cathedral, or rural dean
prosteri	deanery
protokollsekreterare	one who takes the minutes
provinsialläkare	medical officer to county council
präst	minister
prästgård	parsonage
prästman	clergyman

Q

quae, qui, quod (latin)	who, which

R

regementsräkenskaper	regimental accounts
renata (latin)	christened, baptized
reservofficer	officer (in) the reserve
riddare	nobleman, knight
riddarhuset	house of nobility
riksarkivet	national or state archives
riksdag	diet, national parliament
riksdagsman	member of parliament
rote [pronounced root-eh]	a pair, small group; part of a territory; district of a parish or city; ward
rotebonde	farmer who is bound to contribute to a foot soldier's or a sailor's maintenance
rotehjon	pauper within a "rote" (district)
rotehållare	farmer who is bound to furnish a foot soldier's os sailor's equipment
rotemästare	chief of file, quartermaster
roterings- och utskrifnings-längderna	list of grouped potential soldiers and conscripts
rulla	record, list

rusthåll	lands (farms) required to equip a soldier
rusthållare	owner of a farm (land) which is bound to funish supplies for a cavalryman
ryttare	cavalryman, horseman
räkenskaper	records of accounts
räntmästare	treasurer
rödsot	dysentery

S

sammanviga	(to) join in marriage
sepulta (latin)	buried
sergeant	sergeant
sidostyng	pleurisy
silfversmed	silver smith
sistnämnd	last, last mentioned
sjukdom	sickness
sjökapten	sea captain
sjömanshus	general register and record office of shipping and sailors
skadad	injured, badly hurt
skatt	tax
skattebonde	a farmer who pays rent to the crown or a nobleman
skattmästare	treasurer
skattskrifning	tax list
skeppsmönsterrullor	navy muster rolls
skiljobref	bill of divorce
skilsmässa	divorce; seperation
skjutsbonde	postillion, driver
skomakare	shoemaker
skrifva, skriva	(to) write
skräddare	tailor
slaktare	butcher
släkt	family, kindred, relation, tribe
släktbok	lineage book
släktforskning	genealogy
släkting	relative
släktskap	relationship, kinship, affinity
smed	smith, blacksmith
smittkoppor	smallpox
småprotokoll	guardian accounts
snickare	carpenter, joiner
socken	parish
sockenstuga	house where church-wardens and parishioners hold meetings
sockenstämma	parish meeting
sockenstämmoprotokoll	minutes of parish meetings
soldat	soldier
soldattorp	soldier's croft
sponsores (latin)	witnesses
stad	city, town
stadsarkiv	city archive
stadsbetjent	policeman, townsman
stadsfullmäktig	town counsellor
stadsförsamling	city parish
stamfader	progenitor, ancestor, the first ancestor

stammoder	the first mother
statare	cotter, farm laborer
sterbhus	house or family of a deceased person
stjuffader, styvfader, styvfar	step-father
stjufmoder, styvmoder, styvmor	step-mother
stor	big, large
studiosus (latin)	student
styf-, styv-	step- (as in stepson)
sub (latin)	under
supra (latin)	above

T

testes (latin)	witnesses or sponsors at baptism
tjenare, tjänare	servant
tjenarinna, tjänarinna	female servant, maid
tjenstefolk, tjänstefolk	servants
tjänsteman	civil servant
torpare	crofter, cottager, peasant
trolofvad	betrothed; engaged

U

undantagsman	previous farm owner receiving his livinghood/support from the person to whom the farm now belongs (usually related, as in father and son)
undantagsrättighet	the right of exemption or special privilege
uppbud	proclamation
uppbördsman	receiver of taxes, revenue collector
utdrag	extract
utflyttad	moved
utflyttning	removal; migration; emigration

V

vaccinera	(to) vaccinate
vattusot	dropsy
vecka	week
vigd	married
vigselbok	marriage book
vitsord	witness, authority, testimonial
vittnesmål	deposition, evidence
volontär	volunteer; army cadet, candidate for a lietenant's commission; unsalaried clerk (in a bank)
välfrejdad	of good reputation
värnplikt	compulsory military service

Y

yngre	younger
yrke	profession, occupation, trade

Å

åbo	inhabitant, tenant, a farmer who does not own the land, but has the right of possession and habitation

år	year
årlig	annual, yearly

Ä

ägare	owner, landowner
äkta	legitimate, genuine
äktenskap	marriage, wedlock, matrimony
äktenskapslysning	marriage banns
äldre	older, elder
änka	widow
änkeman, änkling	widower
ättling	descendant

Ö

ö	island
öfverste, överste	colonel

For a more extensive list see *Swedish Genealogical Dictionary* by Phyllis J. Pladsen and Joseph C. Huber, available through the Family History Library.

ABBREVIATIONS

ABBR.	TERM	DEFINITION
A		
a	anno (latin)	year
a.a.	ad acta (latin)	to the record
abs.	absens (latin)	absent
abs.	absolvera	(to) absolve
a.d.	anno domini (latin)	in the year of the Lord
adm.	admitterad	confirmed
afg.	afgång	decease, depart to, departure
afl.	afliden	(to) expire, die
afsk.	afskedade	discharged, resigned
a.n.	ante nuptius (latin)	illegitimate, birth before marriage
anm.	anmärkning	remark, annotation
arb.	arbetare	worker, laborer
arb.bet.	arbetsbetyg	work permit
arrend.	arrendator	tenant farmer, leaseholder
afskr.	afskrift	transcript
B		
b.	bonde	farmer, peasant
backst.	backstugesittare	owner of a small cottage and a small piece of land
bar.	barn	child, children
B.B.	bär barnet	carried the child at christening
beg., begr.	begraven	buried
bg., blg.	bergslag	region abounding in mines; mountain district
bl.a.	bland annat	among other things
bond.	bonde	farmer, peasant
br.	brukare	user, employer; farmer, tenant
C		
c:a, ca.	cirka	about, approximately
caut.	cautionister	witness
cop., copul.	copulerad	married
cr.	crono	pertaining to the crown (government), crown owned
cr.h.	crono hem	crown owned home
D		
D.	dotter	daughter
d.	den	the
d.b.	denna bok	this book (current clerical survey)
d.h.	dess hustru	his wife
D.M.	danneman	gentleman, farmer
Dmca.,Dnca.	Dominica (latin)	Sunday
D:o	dito	ditto
Dr.	doktor	doctor
dr.	dotter	daughter

ABBR.	TERM	DEFINITION
dr.,drg	dräng	farmhand, bachelor
Drag.	dragon	light cavalryman, dragoon
dtr.	dotter	daughter
d.v.s.	det vill säga	that is, i.e.
d.y.	den yngre	the younger

E

eg.	egare	owner
e.Kr.	efter Kristi födelse	A.D.
e.m.	eftermiddag	afternoon, P.M.
enk.	enka	widow
enkl.	enkeman	widower

F

f.	fadder	sponsor, godfather godmother, witness at christening
f.	fader, dotter (filia), son (filius)	father, daugther, son
fad.	fader	father
fadd.	fadder	sponsor, godfather, godmother, witness at christening
fam.	familj	family
fast.	fastighet	real estate
f.d.	före detta	formerly
f.Kr.	före Kristi födelse	B.C.
f.m.	förmiddag	morning, forenoon, A.M.
forts.	fortsättning	continuation
frånv.	frånvarande	absent
förs.	församling	parish, congregation
försv.	försvarslös	person without guardian or legal protection, vagrant
fört.	förteckning	list, catalog, index

G

g.	gift	married
gam.	gamla	old
G.B.	gamla bok	old book (previous clerical survey)
gd.	gård	farm, estate, yard, court; house
gdm.	gudmoder	godmother
ges.	gesäll	apprentice
gl.	gammal	old
g.m.	gift med	married to
grat.	gratialist	pensioner
grufarb.	grufarbetare	miner
grufveg.	grufvegare	mine owner

H

H.	herr	Mr., lord, squire, master
H., h.	hustru	wife
h.a.	hujus anno (latin)	same year
hd.	härad	civil district, county
h.eg.	hemmansegare	farm owner

ABBR.	TERM	DEFINITION
H:r	herr	Mr., lord
hsm., husm.	husman	cottager, crofter, tenant
härst.	härstädes	here, at a given location

I

ib., ibid.	ibidem (latin)	the same place, the same as, same
id.	idem (latin)	the same
idm.	idim (latin)	same
i.l.	in loco (latin)	in this place
inh.	inhyses	lodger

J

jbr.,jordbr.	jordbrukare	farmer
jfr.	jungfru	Miss, maiden, virgin

K

k.f.	kvinnsfaddrar	female sponsors at christening
khde	kyrkoherde	parish minister, parson
K.Maj:t	Kunglig Majestät	the King
kr.	kronor	crown (Swedish currency)
Kongl.Maj:t	Kunglig Majestät	the King
Kungl.Maj:t	Kunglig Majestät	the King
kv.	kvinna	woman
kyrkov.	kyrkovaktare	church officer or caretaker

L

l., l:a	lilla	little
landsförslg	landsförsamling	rural parish of a city
lfs.	landsförsamling	rural parish of a city
lärl.	lärling	apprentice

M

m.	man	man, male, husband
m.	mater (latin)	mother
m.fl.	med flera	and several others
m.m.	med mera	and my others
mod., modr.	moder	mother
mort.	mortua (latin)	deceased
mtl.	mantal	assessed unit of land, taxation of farm
mån.	månad	month
mäst.	mäster, mästare	master expert, the boss

N

n.	natus (latin)	born
n.	nomine (latin)	name
N:a, n.	norra	north

ABBR.	TERM	DEFINITION
Nat.	natur	natural (in reference to having had smallpox)
nat.	nata (latin)	born
N.B.	nya bok	new book
nb	nota bene (latin)	note well
NN	nomen nescio (latin)	name not known
nom.	nomine (latin)	name
n:r	nummer	number
nup.	nuptiae (latin)	wedding

O

o.	och	and
og.	ogift	unmarried
osv.	och så vidare	and so forth
oä.	oäkta	illegitimate child

P

p., pag.	pagina (latin)	page
p.	pater (latin)	father
p., pig.	piga	maid, spinster, single girl

Q

q.	qvinna	woman
Qvf	qvinnfaddrar	female sponsors at christening
Qv.mil.	qvadratmil	square mile

R

r., rytt.	ryttare	cavalryman, horseman
reg.	regemente	regiment
ren.	renata (latin)	christened, baptized
Rdr	riksdaler	"dollar" (old Swedish currency)

S

s.	son	son
s., sn	socken	parish
s.	söndag	Sunday
S, s, sö	södra	south, southern
sal.	salig	deceased, blessed
sep.	sepultus (latin)	buried
s.k.	så kallad	so called
skplg.	skeppslag	district along the coast
skräd.	skräddare	tailor
sn	socken	parish
sold.	soldat	soldier
spons.	sponsorer	witnesses
S:t	sankt	saint
St.	stora	large, big (name for the large part of a place)
stud.	student	student

ABBR.	TERM	DEFINITION
susc.	susceptrix (latin)	godmother
sv:f	svärfar	father-in-law
sv:m	svärmor	mother-in-law
syst.	syster	sister

T

ABBR.	TERM	DEFINITION
t.	testes (latin)	witnesses or sponsors at baptism
tax.	taxera	(to) assess, tax
test.	testes (latin)	witnesses or sponsors at baptism
t.ex.	till exempel	for example
tg.	tingslag	judicial district, (assize) division
t.o.m.	till och med	including
torp., tp.	torpare	crofter, cottager, peasant
trol.	trolofvad	betrothed, engaged
ty.	tysk	German

U

ABBR.	TERM	DEFINITION
u.	under	under; at; during, while; wonder, miracle
undt.	undantagsman	previous farm owner receiving his livelihood/support from the person to whom the farm now belongs (usually related, as in father and son)
ung.	ungefär	about, approximately

V

ABBR.	TERM	DEFINITION
v., vacc.	vaccinera	(to) vaccinate
V:a, v:a, v	västra	west, western
välb.	välboren	honorable

Å

ABBR.	TERM	DEFINITION
Åb.	åborätt	tenant right, hereditary lease

Ä

ABBR.	TERM	DEFINITION
ä.	änka	widow
äkt.	äktenskap	marriage, wedlock, matrimony
änk.	änka	widow
änkl.	änkling	widower

Ö

ABBR.	TERM	DEFINITION
Ö:a, ö	östra	east, eastern

Carl and his younger brother Gustaf pictured around 1867.
Note how the boys are dressed – in clothes that are too big so they would last for many years of growth.

CHAPTER NINETEEN

Appendices

Church Records Destroyed – Usually by Fire

In the following parishes the church records have been destroyed – in most cases by fire. There are no records before the year given in the list. The year is usually the year of a fire at the vicarage or the church where the records were kept. In some cases single books or records may have been saved. The parishes are listed according to the Regional Archives where the records are kept.

Gothenburg Regional Archives

Angered (1891)
Askim (1898)
Backa (1874)
Fotskäl (1857)
Frösve (1861)
Götene (1807)
Horn (1861)
Kareby (1815)
Kattunga (1857)
Kungälv (1796)
Kville (1904)
Ledsjö (1807)
Romelanda (1815)
Rödbo (1796)
Röra (1870)
Stala (1870)
Surteby (1857)
Svenneby (1904)
Säter (1861)
Säve (1874)
Tegneby (1870)
Tossene (1898)
Tostared (1857)
Vättlösa (1807)
Ytterby (1796)

Härnösand Regional Archives

Borgsjö (1844)
Karesuando (1814)
Nätra (1809)
Ockelbo (1904)
Sundsvall (1803, 1888)

Karlstad Regional Archives

—

Lund Regional Archives

Andrarum (1875)
Asigc (1765)
Ask (1820)
Björka (1783)
Bårslöv (1838)
Båstad (1870)
Dagsås (1875)
Eljaröd (1875)
Fjärestad (1838)
Getinge (1868)
Gualöv (1825)
Gudmuntorp (1796)
Hammarlunda (1815)
Hjärsås (1895)
Hov (1870)
Hurva (1796)
Häglinge (1809)
Högseröd (1889)
Höör (1792)
Knislinge (1895)
Konga (1820)
Långaröd (1792)
Munkarp (1792)
Rävinge (1868)
S:t Olof (1800)
Södra Rörum (1809)
Trolle Ljungby (1825)
Vedby (1712, 1781)
Årstad (1765)
Östra Herrestad (1806)
Östra Ingelstad (1806)

Stockholm Regional (City) Archives

Blidö (1795)
Skå (1795)

Uppsala Regional Archives

Kattnäs (1795)
Nykyrka (1795)
Skagershult (1893)

Vadstena Regional Archives

Bosebo (1856)
Horn (1851)
Hycklinge (1851)
Mjölby (1771)
Sörby (1771)
Tånnö (1869)
Våxtorp (1869)
Värnamo (1869)
Västra Harg (1797)

Visby Regional Archives

Bunge (1870)
Fleringe (1870)
Gerum (1784)
Levide (1800)
Rute (1870)
Sjonhem (1790)

Östersund Regional Archives

Ragunda (1849)
Sveg (1870)
Älvros (1870)

Genealogical Societies in Sweden

Stockholms län

Genealogiska Föreningen	Anderstorpsvägen 16, SE-171 54 SOLNA
Astra-Zenecas Släktforskarförening	Kvarnbergsgatan 12, B410, SE-151 85 SÖDERTÄLJE
Botvidsbygdens Släktforskarförening	c/o Jo Carina Wolff Storskiftesvägen 118, SE-145 60 NORSBORG
DIS-Öst	Anderstorpsvägen 16, SE-171 54 SOLNA
Föreningen för Smedsläktforskning	Anderstorpsvägen 16, SE-171 54 SOLNA
Föreningen G-gruppen Genealogi över Östersjön	Anderstorpsvägen 16, SE-171 54 SOLNA
IBM-klubbens Släktforskningssektion	c/o Gunnar Bergstedt Stagneliusvägen 23, 1 tr, SE-112 59 STOCKHOLM
Judiska Släktforskarföreningen i Sverige	c/o Maynard Gerber Box 7427, SE-103 91 STOCKHOLM
Norrtälje Släktforskarförening	Box 280, SE-761 23 NORRTÄLJE
Sollentuna Släktforskare	c/o Kerstin Myrehed Vidfares väg 7, SE-192 77 SOLLENTUNA
StorStockholms Genealogiska Förening	Anderstorpsvägen 16, SE-171 54 SOLNA
Svenska Genealogiska Samfundet	c/o Thorsell Hästskovägen 45, SE-177 39 JÄRFÄLLA
Svenska Heraldiska Sällskapet	c/o Marcus Karlsson Gillbosträket 17, SE-192 68 SOLLENTUNA
Sällskapet Vallonättlingar	Anderstorpsvägen 16, SE-171 54 SOLNA
Södertälje Släktforskarförening	c/o Ann-Beate Barke Saltsjögatan 3, SE-151 71 STOCKHOLM
Södra Roslagens Släktforskarförening	c/o Carl-Göran Backgård Guckuskovägen 12, SE-184 35 ÅKERSBERGA

Uppsala län

Björklingebygdens Släktforskarförening	c/o Brundin Hambovägen 3, SE-743 64 BJÖRKLINGE
Enecopia Släktforskareförening	c/o Ann-Kristin von Knorring Plommongatan 13, SE-745 63 ENKÖPING
Föreningen Släktforskare i Uppland	Sköldmövägen 15, SE-754 40 UPPSALA

Södermanlands län

Eskilstuna-Strängnäs Släktforskarförening	Dambergsgatan 1, SE-633 41 ESKILSTUNA
Katrineholm-Flen-Vingåkers Släktforskarförening	c/o Åke Spets Åsgatan 30 A, SE-641 34 KATRINEHOLM
Nyköping-Oxelösunds Släktforskarförening	c/o Håkan Linderyd Ringvägen 22, SE-611 35 NYKÖPING

Östergötlands län

DIS-Filbyter	Gamla Linköping, SE-582 46 LINKÖPING
Släktforskarna i Norrköping	c/o Owe Norberg

	Allmänningsgatan 17, SE-602 12 NORRKÖPING
Västra Husby Genealogiska Förening	c/o Roland Staffans Lotshållarvägen 5, SE-605 96 NORRKÖPING
Östgöta Genealogiska Förening	c/o Gunnar Nilzon Kvinnebyvägen 77, SE-589 33 LINKÖPING

Jönköpings län

DIS-Småland	c/o Ingvar Kärrdahl Bäckvägen 18, SE-330 15 BOR
Eksjöbygdens Släktforskarförening	c/o Elisabeth Leek Norra Notåsa, SE-573 73 SUNDHULTSBRUNN
Habobygdens Släktforskarförening	Box 177, SE-566 23 HABO
Jönköpingsbygdens Genealogiska Förening	Lillgatan 20, SE-554 51 JÖNKÖPING
Njudungs Släktforskarförening	c/o Tore Sandh Lyckås Edshult, SE-575 93 EKSJÖ
Nässjöbygdens Genealogiska Förening	c/o Sven Bengtsson Hultarp Södergård, SE-571 93 NÄSSJÖ
Släktforskarföreningen ANE Värnamo	c/o Gunilla Kärrdahl Bäckvägen 18, SE-330 15 BOR
Tranås/Ydre Släktforskarförening	c/o Sven-Olof Friman Nya Timmerövägen 26, SE-590 13 BOXHOLM
Waggeryds Släkt- och Bygdeforskare	c/o Lennart Levén Långsjön, SE-567 92 VAGGERYD
Westbo-Mo Forskarförening	Ölmestad museum, SE-330 21 REFTELE

Kronobergs län

Kronobergs Genealogiska Förening	Box 151, SE-342 22 ALVESTA
SIE - Slektforskare i Elmhult	Södra Esplanaden 11, SE-343 32 ÄLMHULT

Kalmar län

Kalmar Läns Genealogiska Förening	c/o Gullan Olsson Magistratsgatan 12 B, SE-392 35 KALMAR
Person- och Lokalhistoriskt Forskarcentrum	Box 23, SE-572 21 OSKARSHAMN
Släktföreningen Sabelskjöld	SE-570 91 KRISTDALA
Tjusts Släktforskarförening	c/o Stadsbiblioteket Box 342, SE-593 24 VÄSTERVIK
Vimmerby-Hultsfreds Släktforskarförening	c/o Arne Johansson Södra Storgatan 29 D, SE-590 80 SÖDRA VI

Gotlands län

Gotlands Genealogiska Förening	c/o Kerstin Jonmyren Vintervägen 15, SE-611 36 NYKÖPING

Blekinge län

Blekinge Släktforskarförening	c/o Per Frödholm Villa Klockliden 10, SE-374 53 ASARUM

Skåne län

Bjäre Släktring	c/o Bjarne Larsson Svartbrödragatan 9, SE-266 35 KLIPPAN
Bromölla Släktforskarförening	Kyrkvägen 19, 295 35 BROMÖLLA
Dalbybygdens Släkt- och folklivsforskareförening	c/o Inger Björklund Veberöd 271, SE-240 14 VEBERÖD
DIS-Syd	Arkivcentrum Syd, Porfyrvägen 16, SE-224 78 LUND
Göinge Släkt- och Hembygdsforskarförening	c/o Åke Persson Pl 5171, SE-281 91 HÄSSLEHOLM
Helsingborgs Släktforskare- och Bygdeförening	c/o Kerstin Svensson Västra Stationsgatan 5, lgh 12, SE-257 34 RYDEBÄCK
Kristianstadsbygdens Släktforskarförening	c/o Britt-Marie Jönsson Orienteringsgatan 4, SE-291 66 KRISTIANSTAD
Kullabygdens Släktforskare	Linnégatan 15, SE-263 31 HÖGANÄS
Kävlingebygdens Släkt- och Folklivsforskare	c/o Bo Arvidson Högs Skolväg 22, SE-244 93 KÄVLINGE
Landskronabygdens Släktforskare	c/o Gun-Britt Åkesson Saxtorpsvägen 222, SE-261 94 ANNELÖV
Lomma-Burlövs Släkt- och Folklivsforskare	c/o Cay Mathiasson Karstorpsvägen 28, SE-234 42 LOMMA
Lunds Släktforskarförening	c/o Kerstin Olsson Docentgatan 6, SE-223 63 LUND
Malmö Släktforskarförening	c/o Margareta Kroon Kulladalsgatan 22 B, SE-215 64 MALMÖ
Mellanskånes Släkt- och Hembygdsforskarförening	c/o Ann-Mari Persson Lyckhöjdsgatan 3 C, SE-242 34 HÖRBY
Skånes Genealogiska Förbund	c/o Arkivcentrum Syd Porfyrvägen 20, SE-224 78 LUND
Staffanstorps Släktforskarförening	c/o Inger Persson Tegnérs väg 1, SE-245 32 STAFFANSTORP
Svalövsbygdens Släkt- och Folklivsforskarförening	c/o Stig Pettersson Myren 1782 Fridhem, SE-268 90 SVALÖV
Söderslätts Släkt- och Hembygdsforskarförening	c/o Britt-Mari Ridell Gränsgatan 36 A, SE-231 38 TRELLEBORG
Västerlens ForskarFörening	c/o Ann-Christin Andersson Fasanvägen 4, SE-231 78 SMYGEHAMN
Ystadsbygdens Släkt- & Bygdeforskarförening	c/o Gertrud Andersson Kristians väg 3, SE-270 35 BLENTARP
Åsbo Släkt- och Folklivsforskare	Box 191, SE-264 22 KLIPPAN
Ängelholms Släkt- och Folklivsforskarförening	c/o Torbjörn Stjerndahl Astrakantorget 6, SE-262 65 ÄNGELHOLM
Österlens Släkt- och Folklivsforskarförening	c/o Greta Jönsson Ingelstorp 10, SE-270 21 GLEMMINGEBRO

Hallands län

Hallands Släktforskarförening	Ryttarevägen 4, SE-302 60 HALMSTAD
Knäreds Forskarring & Hembygdsförening	Västraltsvägen 4, SE-310 20 KNÄRED
Södra Hallands Släktforskningsring	c/o Gun Bergenfelz

Kristianstadsvägen 55, SE-312 32 LAHOLM

Västra Götalands län

Ale Släktforskare	c/o Kjell Mattsson Göteborgsvägen 97B, SE-445 57 SURTE
Alingsås Släktforskarförening	c/o Hans Fredriksson Alevägen 8, SE-44139 ALINGSÅS
Borås Släktforskare	Alvestagatan 31, SE-504 33 BORÅS
Carlsborgs Släktforskarförening	c/o Ulla Hansson Valla Torpelund, SE-545 93 TÖREBODA
DIS-Väst	c/o Anita Gartz Strandgatan 12, SE-465 31 NOSSEBRO
Falbygdens Släktforskarförening	Pia Wallengren Ocelgatan 5, SE-521 30 FALKÖPING
Färgelanda Släktforskarförening	c/o Leif Karlsson Ljungvägen 1, SE-458 31 FÄRGELANDA
Föreningen Släktdata	c/o Inger Drottz Kransen 2A, SE-416 72 GÖTEBORG
Göteborgsregionens Släktforskare	Erik Dahlbergsgatan 36 B, SE-411 26 GÖTEBORG
Götene Släktforskareförening	c/o Dagny Lindgren Gärdhult Hangelösa, SE-533 92 LUNDSBRUNN
Hjo-Tibro Släktforskarförening	c/o Anders Brissman Västra Långgatan 93 B, SE-543 33 TIBRO
Inlands Släktforskare	c/o Jan Augustsson Stenåldersgatan 63, SE-442 54 YTTERBY
Kinds Forskarklubb	c/o Ingrid Eriksson Röllekevägen 7, SE-512 52 SVENLJUNGA
Kville Härads Personhistoriska Förening	c/o Tore Johansson Tallvägen 5, SE-457 72 GREBBESTAD
Lidköpingsbygdens Släktforskare	c/o Bibbi Larsson Karlagatan 26 B, SE-531 32 LIDKÖPING
Mariestadsbygdens Släktforskareförening	Drottninggatan 12 – 14, SE-542 34 MARIESTAD
Marks Härads Släktforskarförening	c/o Lennart Ryhd Kungslid 14, SE-511 31 ÖRBY
Orusts Släktforskare	c/o Bertil Bengtsson Kastetvägen 4, SE-472 97 VAREKIL
Skara Släktforskarförening	c/o Bengt Bengtsson Valhallagatan 17A, SE-532 34 SKARA
Skövde Släktforskarförening	c/o Christina Helmby Carlsrovägen 3A, SE-541 52 SKÖVDE
Släktforskare på Dahl	c/o Bertil Landegren Lövåsvägen 30 C, SE-464 50 DALS ROSTOCK
Sotenäs Personhistoriska Förening	c/o Marelius Dalstigen 17, SE-451 34 UDDEVALLA
Strömstads Släktforskare	c/o Kjell Samuelsson Saltö Kyrkoväg 25, SE-452 96 STRÖMSTAD
Sundals Släktforskare	c/o Gunnar Karlsson

	Ryr, SE-460 65 BRÅLANDA
Sällskapet Strömstierna	c/o Kerstin Jungebro Västra Kronbergsgatan 10, SE-453 33 LYSEKIL
Tidaholms Genealogiska Förening	c/o Kjell Henrysson Enebacksvägen 30, SE-522 34 TIDAHOLM
Tjörns Släktforskare	c/o Göran Hermanson Alen 6497, SE-471 72 HJÄLTEBY
Trollhättebygdens Släktforskare	c/o Sven Åhlander Hedeängsvägen 33, SE-461 44 TROLLHÄTTAN
Töreboda Släktforskarförening	c/o Irene Fredriksson Ängshaga 6059, SE-545 91 TÖREBODA
Uddevalla Släktforskare	c/o Berit Berntsson Kaselyckan 10, SE-451 63 UDDEVALLA
Ulricehamnsbygdens forskarklubb	c/o Anna-Lena Hultman Hössna Bregärdet 101, SE-523 97 ULRICEHAMN
VGN Släktforskare	c/o Ann-Britt Dahlström Kungsgatan 2, SE-467 40 GRÄSTORP
Vänersborgs Släktforskare	c/o Gunnel Jende Kyrkogatan 35A, SE-462 30 VÄNERSBORG
Västgöta Genealogiska Förening	c/o Nils-Olof Olofsson Lars väg 7 B, SE-515 35 VISKAFORS
Åmåls Släktforskare	c/o Bo Öberg Kasenbergsvägen 16, SE-662 91 ÅMÅL
Öckerööarnas Släktforskarförening	Box 34, SE-430 93 HÄLSÖ

Värmlands län

Nordvärmlands Släktforskarförening	c/o Gösta Löfqvist Lövåsvägen 4, SE-685 32 TORSBY
Värmlands Släktforskarförening	c/o Bengt Nordstrand Herrgårdsgatan 12, SE-652 24 KARLSTAD

Örebro län

Askersunds Släktforskarklubb	c/o Gunnel Cunei Loggatan 5, SE-696 32 ASKERSUND
Finnerödja-Laxå Släktforskarklubb	c/o Thomas Persson Nyborgs hage 4, SE-695 93 FINNERÖDJA
Hallsbergs Släktforskarklubb	c/o Birgitta Edholm Västra Storgatan 7B, SE-694 30 HALLSBERG
Hällefors Släktforskarklubb	Klockarevägen 20B, SE-712 33 HÄLLEFORS
Karlskoga-Degerfors Släktforskareklubb	c/o Hilding Helgeson Skolgatan 49, SE-691 41 KARLSKOGA
Kumla Släktforskarklubb	c/o Jan Klingberg Mästaregatan 1, SE-692 33 KUMLA
Linde Bergslags Släktforskarförening	c/o Ingalill Eriksson Norevägen 10, SE-711 32 LINDESBERG
Nora Släktforskarklubb	c/o Britt-Marie Lundell Trädgårdsgatan 14 H, SE-713 32 NORA

Örebro Släktforskare	Fabriksgatan 8, SE-702 10 ÖREBRO

Västmanlands län

DIS-Bergslagen	Ekevägen 2B, SE-723 41 Västerås
Sala-Heby Släktforskare	c/o Sven-Erik Grahn Humlevägen 7 Kumla Kyrkby, SE-733 93 Sala
Släkt- och Bygdeforskarföreningen Engelbrekt Norberg	Hebbegatan 6A, SE-738 30 Norberg
Sällskapet Släktforskarne Fagesta	c/o Ulla Göthe Markörgatan 6B, SE-723 38 Västerås
Västerås Släktforskarklubb	c/o Sven Olby Ragnaröksgatan 12, SE-723 55 Västerås
Västra Mälardalens Släktforskare	c/o Åke Dahlqvist Gulsparvsvägen 3, SE-731 42 Köping

Dalarnas län

Dalarnas Släktforskarförbund	c/o Elisabeth Hernström Stadsbiblioteket, SE-791 83 FALUN
Falubygdens Släktforskarförening	c/o Elisabeth Hernström Stadsbiblioteket, SE-791 83 FALUN
Folkare Släktforsklarförening	c/o Studieförbundet Vuxenskolan Box 1, SE-774 21 AVESTA
Föreningen Dalfolk	c/o Släktforskarnas hus Insjövägen 52, SE-793 33 LEKSAND
Föreningen Släkt och Bygd i Borlänge	Parkgatan 9, SE-784 32 BORLÄNGE
Gagnef Släktforskarförening	c/o Madeleine Nygårdh Nisses Backe 4, SE-780 40 MOCKFJÄRD
Ovansiljans Släktforskare	c/o Jojje Lintrup Norebergsvägen10 A, SE-792 50 MORA
Västerbergslagens Släktforskare	Engelbrektsgatan 19, SE-771 30 LUDVIKA

Gävleborgs län

Dellenbygdens Släktforskarförening	c/o Sussie Sundberg Bondevägen 7, SE-820 60 DELSBO
Forskarföreningen ALIR	c/o Rigmor Strandberg Lerviksberget 1B, SE-820 22 SANDARNE
Forskarföreningen Släkt och Bygd	c/o Odengatan 17 SE-821 43 BOLLNÄS
Gästriklands Genealogiska Förening	Tordönsgatan 2B nb, SE-802 77 GÄVLE
Hudiksvallsbygdens Släktforskarförening	c/o Ingela Fahlberg Kilarne Njutångers Boda 13, SE-825 93 NJUTÅNGER
Nordanstigs Bygd- och Släktband forskarförening	c/o Harriet Frandén Nordanbrovägen 2B, SE-820 78 HASSELA
Ockelbo Släktforskarförening	c/o Wij Säteri i Ockelbo AB Herrgårdsvägen 2, SE-816 26 OCKELBO
Sällskapet Släktforskarna (Sandviken)	Folkbiblioteket, SE-811 80 SANDVIKEN
Västra Hälsinglands Forskarförening	c/o Söderin

Box 58, SE-827 22 LJUSDAL

Västernorrlands län

DIS-Mitt
c/o Anna Söderström
Björneborgsgatan 66, SE-854 62 SUNDSVALL

Hembygds- och Släktforskare Nolaskogs
Box 91, SE-891 22 ÖRNSKÖLDSVIK

Härnösands Släktforskare
c/o Peter Sjölund
Ulvviksvägen 9, SE-870 10 ÄLANDSBRO

Midälva Genealogiska Förening
c/o Karl-Ingvar Ångström
Hemmansvägen 87, SE-871 53 HÄRNÖSAND

Sollefteå Släktforskare
c/o Elsa Hörling
Hallstagatan 8, SE-881 30 SOLLEFTEÅ

Ådalens Släktforskarförening
c/o Gunilla Bergwall
Nyadal 162B, SE-872 94 SANDÖVERKEN

Jämtlands län

Härjedalens Släktforskarklubb
c/o Elisabeth Hedh
Nilsvallen 125, SE-842 93 SVEG

Jämtlands Lokalhistoriker och Släktforskare
c/o Kerstin Ellert
Näcksta 1412, SE-830 23 HACKÅS

Västerbottens län

Bygdeå-Nysätra Släktforskarförening
c/o Vivianne Bäckström
Brännstan 153, SE-915 93 ROBERTSFORS

Lappmarkens släkt- och bygdeforskare
c/o Roland Tidström
Nästansjö 80, SE-912 92 VILHELMINA

Lyckselebygdens Släktforskarförening
Hällforsvägen 3, SE-921 35 LYCKSELE

Norsjöbygdens Släktforskarförening
c/o Ruth Eriksson
Bränntjärnliden 11, SE-935 91 NORSJÖ

Skelleftebygdens Släktforskare
Nordanå, SE-931 33 SKELLEFTEÅ

Södra Västerbottens Släktforskare
c/o Josefin Mikaelsson
Dunkersgatan 8, SE-905 27 UMEÅ

Norrbottens län

Arvidsjaurs Släktforskarförening
c/o Gun Nilsson
Sandbacksgatan 16, SE-933 33 ARVIDSJAUR

Boden-Överluleå Forskarförening
Idrottsgatan 2D, SE-961 64 BODEN

DIS-Nord
c/o Anna Lövgren
Box 61, SE-962 22 JOKKMOKK

Gellivare Släkt- och Bygdeforskare
Hantverkargatan 5, SE-982 31 GÄLLIVARE

Kalixbygdens Forskarförening
c/o Bengt-Göran Nilsson
Sänkvägen 16, SE-952 36 KALIX

Kiruna Forskarförening
Finngatan 4, SE-981 31 KIRUNA

Matarengi Forskarförening
Box 18, SE-957 21 ÖVERTORNEÅ

Notes:
1-DIS stands for *Föreningen för Datorhjälp i Släktforskningen*, an organization for computer supported genealogy.
2-For a complete list of current addresses, see www.genealogi.se

Websites, etc

Selected Scandinavian and American Sites

Swedish sites

www.genealogi.se	Federation of Swedish Genealogical Societies: Find your Swedish Roots *(Rötter)*
www.statensarkiv.se	SVAR, Swedish Archives, ordering of microfilm, Ramsele Research Center
www.ra.se	The National Archives in Stockholm, and the regional archives in Sweden
www.utvandrarnashus.se	The Swedish Emigrant Institute, Växjö
www.swedenamerica.se	Swedish American Center in Karlstad (Immigrants from Värmland)
www.goteborgs-emigranten.com	Göteborgs-Emigranten
www.genhouse-sweden.com	The House of Genealogy, Leksand
www.foark.umu.se/folk	The Demographic Database. Sweden's Population 1890. Jörn Research Center
www.lantmateriet.com	The Archives of Landsurveying
www.kyrktorget.com	Addresses of Swedish Parishes
www.dis.se	DIS Computer Genealogy Society. DISBYT helps you in finding Swedish Ancestors
www.slaktdata.org	Föreningen Släktdata. Parish Files for Genealogical Research
www.genealogi.net	The Genealogical Society of Sweden
www.genline.com	Genline. Swedish Church Records on the Internet
www.genealogi.se/gravsten	Records of Old Tombstone Inscriptions in Sweden
www.kyrktorget.com	The Parishes of Sweden. Addresses, phone-numbers
www.nad.ra.se	Database of Swedish Archives. Ordering of microfilm
www.vallon.se	Society The Descendents of the Walloons
www.svar.ra.se	Databases of probates, seamen, pictures, letters etc
www.arkion.se	Databases of Swedish Census 1870–1900, released prisoners, pictures etc
www.svenskhistoria.nu	Swedish history
www.eniro.se	The Swedish Phone Book
www.gulasidorna.eniro.se	The Swedish Phone Book
www.microscan.net	Skåne, Halland and Blekinge. Scanned Church Books, Census etc
www.sjofartsmuseum.goteborg.se	The Maritime Museum of Gothenburg. Information about ships
www.sjohistoriska.nu	The Maritime Museum of Stockholm. Information about ships

www.sverigekontakt.se	Riksföreningen Sverigekontakt Swecon. Society for Swedish Culture Abroad. Information about emigration
http://per.clemensson.net	Per Clemensson. Ordering of swedish genealogical books
www.ssa.stockholm.se	Stockholm City Archives

Other Scandinavian Sites

www.genealogia.fi	The Federation of Finish Genealogical Societies
www.emiarch.dk	The Danish Emigration Archives
www.uib.no/ahkr	The Norwegian Emigration Archives

American Sites

www.americanswedishinst.org	American Swedish Institute, and Swedish American Council, Minneapolis
www.ancestry.com	Databases of Census 1860–1930, Passenger Lists of New York 1851–1891, etc
www.collectionscanada.gc.ca	Archives in Canada
www.augustana.edu/swenson	Swenson Swedish Immigration Research Center, and Swedish American Genealogist, Augustana College, Rock Island
www.cyndislist.com	Cyndi's list of genealogical sites
www.ellisislandrecords.com	Database of Manifests 1892–1924
www.familysearch.org	The Church of Jesus Christ of Latter-day Saints. Family History Library
www.familytreeresearch.com	Family Tree, site with links to genealogical sources
www.fgs.org	Federation of Genealogical Societies, Austin
www.genealogy.com	Genealogical information
www.greatoceanliners.net	Information about ships
www.mapquest.com	Information about American Maps
www.archives.gov/research	National Archives USA
www.ngsgenealogy.org	National Genealogical Society, Arlington
www.rootsweb.ancestry.com	Social security death index
www.samac.org/index1	Swedish-American Museum Center, Chicago
www.sfhs.eget.net	Swedish Fin Historical Society, Seattle
www.swedishamericanhist.org/index	Swedish-American Historical Society/Library
www.vasaorder.com	The Vasa Order of America
www.vitalrec.com	Vital Records of the U.S.

Bibliography

Philip J Anderson and Dag Blanck, *Swedish-American Life in Chicago.* Uppsala 1991.

Michael J Anuta, *Ships of Our Ancestors.* Genealogical Publishing 1983.

Angus Baxter, *In Search of your European Roots.* Baltimore 1988.

Sten Carlsson, *Swedes in North America 1638–1988.* Stockholm 1988.

Per Clemensson, "Emigration Research V. Step by Step" (in *Swedish American Genealogist* 1991:2).

Carl-Erik Johansson, *Cradled in Sweden.* Utah 1995.

Nils William Olsson, *Swedish Voters in Chicago 1888.* SAG Publications 1999.

Nils William Olsson, *Tracing your Swedish Ancestry.* Uppsala 1987.

Nils William Olsson and Erik Wikén, *Swedish Passenger Arrivals in the United States 1820–1850.* Stockholm 1995.

Nils William Olsson and Erik Wikén, *Passanger Ships Arriving in New York Harbor 1820–1850.* Utah 1991.

Loretto Dennis Szucs & Matthew Wright, *Finding Answers in U.S. Census Records.* Ancestry 2001.

Loretto Dennis Szucs & Sandra Hargreaves Luebking, *The Source – A Guidebook of American Genealogy.* Ancestry 1996.

Swedish American Genealogist

The Swedish-American Historical Quarterly 1982 –

The Swedish Pioneer Historical Quarterly 1950–1981.

Alan H Winquist, *Swedish American Landmarks – Where to go and what to see.* 1995.

Illustrations in the Book

Documents

Copies of documents in different archives have been made available by these archives and institutions. In most cases we have relied on the Regional Archives in Gothenburg, where records from the parishes of our example case are located. These documents are available according to the Swedish law.

Maps and Charts

The maps on pages 143, 154, and 155 are printed with permission from *Lantmäteriet,* the Swedish Land Survey.

Other maps were produced by the authors, with layout by Susanne Linde (pages 27, 68–69), and NYMEDIA Stig Lindberg (pages 29, 30, 31, 33, 64, 153).

Charts were produced by the authors and NYMEDIA Stig Lindberg (pages 42, 44, 52), and Susanne Linde (page 22–23).

Photos

Most new photos were taken by the authors, Kjell Andersson and Per Clemensson, with some exceptions:

Pages 9, 10, 65: Allen Grover, Portland, Connecticut
Pages 12–13: Henry Melin, Chicago, Illinois
Page 28: A. Loeffler, courtesy of the Library of Congress
Page 96: John Gary Brown, Lawrence, Kansas
Pages 152, 156, 157 (two photos), 158 (three photos), 173, 182: Seth Lund, Genline, Stockholm.

The photos from the different research centers, pages 51–53, were graciously made available by the different research centers. The photos from Ramsele were taken by Bjärne Engholm, Backe.

The pictures in the chapter 17 about Swedish provinces have in most cases been furnished by the local tourist boards. Most of the tourist information centers around Sweden have photos available free of charge on their web sites.

Page 171: Inge Rylander
Page 178: Sverigeflotten (www.sverigeflotten.se)
Page 179: Carl & Carin Larssons släktforening, Carl Larsson-gården, Sundborn
Page 183: Håkan Landström (www.laponia.se)

The old photos are either the property of Per Clemensson or of NYMEDIA Nina Soneson (family pictures), or postcards owned by Per Clemensson.

Drawings

There are also illustrations out of old books:

The "vignettes" early in this book and on page 75, 216, and 222 are from the book *Emigranterna* by Isolé, 1917.

In chapter 17, about Swedish provinces, there are drawings from a couple of books from the end of the nineteenth century:

Pictures from *Ur Fosterländska minnen, tillegnade svenskarna i Amerika,* Chicago 1894.
Pages: 167, 169, 170, 172, 176, 181.

Pictures from *Genom Sveriges bygder* by Herman Hofberg, 1896.
Pages: 165, 171, 176, 179.

Index

CPSIA information can be obtained at www.ICGtesting.com
Printed in the USA
LVOW031606200412

278506LV00001B/5/P